the GUINNESS *book*

of

BRITISH

PLACE NAMES

To Tony and Philip,

with love and thanks

The forest of Skund was indeed enchanted, which was nothing unusual on the Disc, and was also the only forest in the whole universe to be called – in the local language – Your Finger You Fool, which was the literal meaning of the word Skund.
The reason for this is regrettably all too common. When the first explorers from the warm lands around the Circle Sea travelled into the chilly hinterland they filled in the blank spaces on their maps by grabbing the nearest native, pointing at some distant landmark, speaking very clearly in a loud voice, and writing down whatever the bemused man told them. Thus were immortalised in generations of atlases such geographical oddities as Just A Mountain, I Don't Know, What? and, of course, Your Finger You Fool.

Terry Pratchett, *The Light Fantastic*
Copyright © 1986 Terry Pratchett
Published by Colin Smyth Ltd.

Even as a rough stone on the sea-shore becomes rounded in time by the action of the water, so does a name become worn and contracted by being passed from mouth to mouth by successive races and generations of races.

J.J. Kneen, *The Place-Names of the Isle of Man*

the *GUINNESS* book
of
BRITISH
PLACE NAMES

FRED McDONALD *and* JULIA CRESSWELL

GUINNESS PUBLISHING

Contents

Foreword

Every author of a book on place names must draw on the work of previous writers and researchers in the field. The authors of this book are no different, and we have drawn heavily on the works listed in the back of the book under Further Reading, particularly the works of Professor Kenneth Cameron and Margaret Gelling. We have also had a lot of help and advice from a number of people, although needless to say any mistakes in this book are our own. We have been lucky enough to live in an area where the libraries are still properly funded, and are very grateful to the Oxfordshire County Libraries, which have been a great help in providing the books we have needed.

We would also like to say a special thanks to the following: John McNeill Dodgson, whose teaching was the inspiration behind the book; Mary and Bob Burns, Dianna Reynolds, Jim Mulvenn, John Grey and Martin Marix Evans, who helped with the research; Trish Stableford for provisional proof-reading, encouragement and moral support; Mark Collard for his invaluable advice on matters archaeological; Vivienne Reid-Brown for permission to use her MA dissertation on the place names of Kent; Christopher Davis for a small but important bit of research and Pamela Davis for the birthday card quoted on page 12; the people at Guinness for their patience and help and Alex Goldberg who did the picture research. Thanks also to Constance Fishwick, the best of grandmothers, for all her help looking after Alexander, without which this book would never have been finished, and to Alexander Cresswell who was more patient than a 3-year-old could be expected to be, and above all to Tony Davis and Philip Cresswell for all their help and support.

Abbreviations

Ant: Antrim
Arm: Armagh
Beds: Bedfordshire
Berks: Berkshire
Bord: Borders
Bucks: Buckinghamshire
c.: *circa*, about
Cambs: Cambridgeshire
Cent: Central
Ches: Cheshire
Clev: Cleveland
Corn: Cornwall
Cumb: Cumbria
D&G: Dumfries & Galloway
Derbs: Derbyshire
Don: Donegal
Dors: Dorset
Dur: Durham
ESx: East Sussex
Fer: Fermanagh
G: Gaelic
Gal: Galway
GLon: Greater London
Glos: Gloucestershire
GMan: Greater Manchester
Grmp: Grampian
Gwyn: Gwynedd
H&W: Hereford and Worcester
Hants: Hampshire

Herts: Hertfordshire
High: Highland
Humb: Humberside
I: Irish
IoM: Isle of Man
IoS: Isles of Scilly
IoW: Isle of Wight
Kild: Kildare
Lancs: Lancashire
LD: Londonderry
Lei: Leinster
Leics: Leicestershire
Lincs: Lincolnshire
Long: Longford
Loth: Lothian
ME: Middle English
Mers: Merseyside
MidGlam: Mid Glamorgan
Mon: Monaghan
Nflk: Norfolk
Nmbd: Northumberland
Northants: Northamptonshire
Notts: Nottinghamshire
NYorks: North Yorkshire
ODan: Old Danish
OE: Old English
OF: Old French
Off: Offaly
ON: Old Norse
ONor: Old Norwegian
Orkn: Orkney
Oxon: Oxfordshire
Ros: Roscommon

Sflk: Suffolk
SGlam: South Glamorgan
Shet: Shetland
Shrops: Shropshire
Som: Somerset
Staffs: Staffordshire
Strath: Strathclyde
Sur: Surrey
SYorks: South Yorkshire
T&W: Tyne and Wear
Tays: Tayside
Tip: Tipperary
Ty: Tyrone
W: Welsh
Warks: Warwickshire
Wat: Waterford
Wex: Wexford
WGlam: West Glamorgan
Worcs: Worcestershire
Wick: Wicklow
Wilts: Wiltshire
WIs: Western Isles
WM: Westmeath
WMid: West Midlands
WSx: West Sussex
WYorks: West Yorkshire

An * before a word indicates
that it is a reconstructed form,
rather than one found in old
records.

Pronunciation Guide

Sometimes we have to distinguish between the way a word is written, and the way it is pronounced. In the following pages the pronunciation of a word is indicated by the use of //.

a	as in	cat	owə	power	n		nun
ah		cart, father	oy	boy	ng		sing
aw		law	u	cut	p		pip
ay		say	uh	bird	r		rose
e		said, bed	ə	another	s		sun
ee		see, me	b	bed	sh		should
eə		their, there	ch	chap	t		tiger
i		pick	d	dog	th		thing
ie		might	dh	this	v		view
ieə		higher, fire	f	fish	w		wash
iə		here	g	guy	y		you
o		lots	h	house	z		zoo
oh		hope	j	jug	zh		pleasure
oo		put	k	kid			
ooh		boot	kh	loch			
ooə		cure	l	live			
ow		how	m	mouse			

Introduction

We all name places every day. Sometimes the 'names' we use are very simple; we refer to the church, the shop, the school, etc. when we and the person we are talking to know which one we mean. But in most cases we need to make it clear. We may actually use the official name, but we are more likely to make up our own name, choosing one that describes the place or shows why it is important to us – the Catholic church, the fish shop, my son's school. A single place may be given several such 'names'. A house may be known officially as The Laurels or 28 Bridge Road, but it may also be known as the cottage, Number 28, the house on the corner, the vicarage, where the Rottweiler lives, Granny's, or simply home. It all depends on who is referring to it and what, for them, distinguishes this house from all others. Each is a kind of mental snapshot of the house, taken from a different angle and showing its most important feature as far as the 'photographer' was concerned.

Our ancestors were no different, and most official place names began in this way. Most consist of two parts, or elements. One element indicates what the place is – a village, a field, a hill etc. – and is often called the generic element. The other, the descriptive element, reveals what is special about it – where it is, who it belongs to, what it looks like, what is produced there, etc. These two- (or occasionally three-) part names are called compound names. Names with only one element (the church, Granny's, etc.) are called simplex names.

Elements, particularly generic elements, are like building blocks; each with its own form and meaning but put together in various combinations and connected in different ways. One of the aims of this book is to introduce as many elements as possible and to describe what they usually mean. A word of warning – the first of many. Names change over the years, and it would be unwise to guess their meanings from their present forms. The earliest possible version must be studied. Similarly it cannot be assumed that an element always means the same thing in different names. There is only one rule in place-name study that has no exception, and that is that there is an exception to every rule! However good a guess is, it can only be a guess.

The British people, and the English language, have been formed from successive waves of immigrants – Celts, Romans, Anglo-Saxons, Vikings, Normans and many other smaller ethnic groups – and each has brought its own set of building blocks. This means that a name can reveal not only what the place was like and what was important about it to the person that named it, but who named it and when. This brings us to another problem. Most names of towns and villages are very old, many more than a thousand years, and most existed by about 1500. The elements are in languages, such as Latin, Old English, Norse, Norman French and the various forms of Celtic, that we no longer speak. The 'snapshots' are crumpled and faded, and may be indecipherable even to the experts in historical linguistics who specialize in the study of old names.

Although many place-name elements are fairly standard and a guess at a name is always possible, working out the origins and meanings of old place names is really a job for the specialist. Non-specialists can find out more about later names. There is more documentary evidence of later names, the documents are easier to obtain and written in more modern language. The amateur can make a real contribution to the study of local history.

The same only different

A selection of names beginning with **Min-** illustrates one of the problems of studying early place names. It reveals why it is necessary to get expert opinions from dictionaries and textbooks (this is not to say that the experts are always right, but they are more likely to be).

In **Minety**, Wiltshire, **Minstead**, Hampshire, and **Minterne Magna**, Dorset, **Min-** comes from Old English *minte*, and the name indicates that mint grew or was grown there. In **Minting**, Lincolnshire, the origin is an Old English personal name *Mynta*, and in **Minton**, Shropshire, it is Welsh *mynydd* 'mountain', in this case the Long Mynd. **Minsmere** in Suffolk is from Scandinavian *mynni* meaning the mouth of a river, while **Miningsby** in Lincolnshire is from a Scandinavian personal name. **Minskip** in North Yorkshire is different again. It comes from Old English *gemaenscipe* meaning a community or piece of land which was communally owned. So in eight similar names we have six different meanings for the same syllable, from three different languages.

Even identical names can have different meanings, often only revealed by looking at earlier spellings. The very common name **Milton** usually means 'middle farm or estate', from Old English *middel*. But an *n* in an early form of the name indicates the meaning 'farm or village with a mill' from Old English *myln*. **Middleton** also means 'middle farm or estate', except in the case of **Middleton on the Hill** (H&W), where the early spelling *Miceltune* shows that it comes from Old English *micel* meaning large. In the case of **Middleton Priors** in Shropshire, where the earliest spelling is *Mittilton*, even the experts are not sure what it means.

How place names change and why they stay the same

The earliest form of a place name in a dictionary or other document is hardly recognizable today. **Burslem** in Staffordshire, for example, was *Borewardeslyme* in the 13th century, and **Thelwall** in Cheshire was *þelœl* in 923. Both names contain words that have long gone out of use, and Thelwall was written with letters that have not survived. (Burslem was the estate in the old Celtic district of *Lyme* which belonged to a man named *Burgweard* or to the *burh weard*, the guardian of the fort. Thelwall comes from two Old English words, *thel* meaning a plank, probably in this case a plank bridge, and *wael* meaning a spring.)

Names change because language changes. Old words are dropped and new ones coined, and pronunciation changes, often causing a change in spelling. The idea of having only one spelling per word is in any case quite new. Shakespeare spelled his name in several different ways and no one thought any the worse of him.

A name can also change because its features or circumstances change. A new building may provide a new landmark that gives rise to a new name. A place changes hands and is renamed, sometimes in a new language. Often the old name has been lost, but sometimes it survives in a slightly different form. Many place names beginning with **Church** or **Kirk** came about when a settlement built a church and this fact was added to the existing name. **Castle Bolton** (N Yorks) had a castle added to the village and to the name in the 14th century. **Bolton** comes from Old English *bothl-tun*, which means a settlement with a special building. It would be interesting to know what special building was there before the castle.

One effect of a change in language is that the original meaning of a name is lost. Once this happens then the name becomes just a series of syllables, with nothing to stabilize it. It can change simply because there is no reason not to. Those who had never heard of *Burgweard* or the *burh weard* saw no need to say all those meaningless syllables clearly. People started running them into each other and they disappeared. Once they were lost in speech they were soon lost in writing, as people wrote down what they heard. A simple example is the

---

Old, Middle and Modern English

Place names in the British Isles come from several different languages. Old English was the Germanic language spoken by the Anglo-Saxons. It was the chief language of England from about the year 700 to 1150. Middle English was spoken in England from about 1150 to about 1500. It was a kind of slowly changing *Franglais* of Old English, Norse (the language of the Vikings) and Norman French, with some Latin terms. Eventually it developed into Modern English, the still-evolving language that we speak now.

---

part of Ireland which was the *tir* or territory of a tribe called the Ulaid. Say the name *Ulaidztir* quickly a few times and you soon end up with **Ulster**.

A name that has lost its meaning can change for any number of reasons, sometimes simply because people don't like the sound of it. As these changes take place the original meaning becomes more and more obscure. However, the loss of meaning may actually help to preserve the name from other forms of change. The words which formed it may alter in meaning or spelling, or go out of use altogether, but these changes will probably not occur in the name because people no longer recognize the words. The syllables of *Borewardeslyme* were run together, but *burh weard*'s estate did not become 'fort guardian's estate' because the word Burslem no longer meant that. It meant simply 'this place'.

Once a name has become established, especially once it has been recorded in writing, it can easily last for hundreds or thousands of years. It preserves the language that the people who named it spoke and the features that were important to them. It is this durability of names that makes them so interesting and so valuable to the historian.

What does the name tell you once you know what it means?

If you look up **Burslem** (see p. 10) in a place-names dictionary you will find that it comes from an Old English personal name or from two Old English words, plus the Celtic name of the district, which probably refers to elm trees. So you know that it was named by the Anglo-Saxons before the Norman Conquest, who had sufficient contact with the local Britons to have taken the name of the district from them, although they may not have understood what it meant. If *Burgweard* was a personal name the trail stops there. We are unlikely to find out any more about him unless he is mentioned in some other document. If the name refers to the guardian of a fort, we can then ask where the fort was, who built it, who were they defending themselves against, and what happened to it. Other names raise other questions. Names like **Melton**, **Middleton** and **Milton** usually mean 'middle farm or estate', which begs the question – where were the others?

Place names often have a significance beyond their meaning, especially if they are considered together with the surrounding names or with other facts which are already known. A name meaning 'wheat field' is perhaps not very interesting in itself. But if it is surrounded by names meaning 'vegetable patch', 'sheep meadow', 'clover field', 'dairy farm' etc. then we may be looking at some sort of economic unit of interdependent settlements. A name meaning 'the northern wood' to the north of one meaning 'the southern farm' may give us one dimension of an estate. If it lies to the south

of the southern farm it suggests the boundary between one land unit and another.

Recently there has been a suggestion that 'black' in an Anglo-Saxon place name points to a site previously occupied by the Romans. Many field names on sites known to be Roman contain 'black', and the theory is that the dark earth which gave rise to these names was a sign of an earlier, abandoned settlement. There is a danger of jumping on the bandwagon and assuming that any 'black' name was a Roman site (in at least one case the dark soil comes from a former sewage works). But important discoveries have been made by painstakingly plotting names against known archaeological sites.

Another word of warning – it is always dangerous to rely too much on place-name evidence by itself, or to read too much into it (something we are sometimes guilty of ourselves). Places can be renamed, and the ethnic group who named the place were not necessarily the first ones to settle there. A place name may have existed for many years before it was first recorded in writing. There are instances where a name meaning 'secondary settlement' is recorded before the name of the main settlement. Written records of early place names are scarce, documents have perished or exist in the form of later copies which are only as accurate as the scribes who made them.

Place names are a form of linguistic archaeology, laid down in layers by successive peoples and languages, often burying or distorting what has gone before. They cannot give all the answers, but they provide many clues and, perhaps the most important thing, they can make us ask questions. In this book we aim to reveal the sort of information hidden in place names and how to get at it. We also aim to warn the reader of some of the problems, and to show how place names can be used to shed light on the history of any part of the country.

Folk etymology

When we embarked on this book 'Auntie Fred' received a birthday card from her niece which gave the following 'derivations' for two place names in Kent. Tonbridge meant bridge which can take loads of one ton, and Tunbridge (s)Wells is where the posh people of Tonbridge went to get away from the traffic across the bridge.

These are good examples of 'folk etymology', where a derivation is based on what the name looks as though it ought to mean, sometimes with a little story made up to reinforce it. Visitors to **Helston** in Cornwall are sometimes shown the 'hell stone' that the devil dropped there, miraculously without doing any damage. No one actually believes this, of course, but other derivations are more plausible. Blackheath in London and Tombland in Norwich are both often said to be burial pits for victims of the Black Death. This is easily disproved (both names were recorded long before the Black Death in the mid-14th century) but serves as a warning not to take the obvious explanation on trust.

In fact **Tonbridge** means the 'tun bridge', or bridge belonging to the estate or manor, and **Tunbridge Wells** refers to the wells (in this case medicinal springs) near Tonbridge. Tonbridge was spelt with a 'u' at the time the wells were discovered, and reverted to its earlier 'o' spelling later, probably to help distinguish it from its neighbour. **Helston** is an estate on an old court or hall, **Blackheath** is a heathland with dark soil, and **Tombland** comes from Danish toom land 'open space'.

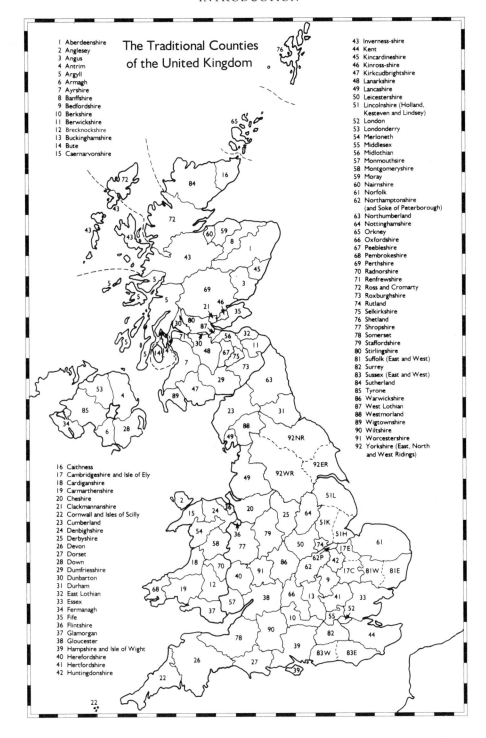

The Traditional Counties
of the United Kingdom

1 Aberdeenshire
2 Anglesey
3 Angus
4 Antrim
5 Argyll
6 Armagh
7 Ayrshire
8 Banffshire
9 Bedfordshire
10 Berkshire
11 Berwickshire
12 Brecknockshire
13 Buckinghamshire
14 Bute
15 Caernarvonshire

16 Caithness
17 Cambridgeshire and Isle of Ely
18 Cardiganshire
19 Carmarthenshire
20 Cheshire
21 Clackmannanshire
22 Cornwall and Isles of Scilly
23 Cumberland
24 Denbighshire
25 Derbyshire
26 Devon
27 Dorset
28 Down
29 Dumfriesshire
30 Dunbarton
31 Durham
32 East Lothian
33 Essex
34 Fermanagh
35 Fife
36 Flintshire
37 Glamorgan
38 Gloucester
39 Hampshire and Isle of Wight
40 Herefordshire
41 Hertfordshire
42 Huntingdonshire

43 Inverness-shire
44 Kent
45 Kincardineshire
46 Kinross-shire
47 Kirkcudbrightshire
48 Lanarkshire
49 Lancashire
50 Leicestershire
51 Lincolnshire (Holland,
   Kesteven and Lindsey)
52 London
53 Londonderry
54 Merloneth
55 Middlesex
56 Midlothian
57 Monmouthsire
58 Montgomeryshire
59 Moray
60 Nairnshire
61 Norfolk
62 Northamptonshire
   (and Soke of Peterborough)
63 Northumberland
64 Nottinghamshire
65 Orkney
66 Oxfordshire
67 Peebleshire
68 Pembrokeshire
69 Perthshire
70 Radnorshire
71 Renfrewshire
72 Ross and Cromarty
73 Roxburghshire
74 Rutland
75 Selkirkshire
76 Shetland
77 Shropshire
78 Somerset
79 Staffordshire
80 Stirlingshire
81 Suffolk (East and West)
82 Surrey
83 Sussex (East and West)
84 Sutherland
85 Tyrone
86 Warwickshire
87 West Lothian
88 Westmorland
89 Wigtownshire
90 Wiltshire
91 Worcestershire
92 Yorkshire (East, North
   and West Ridings)

The Earliest Names

N inety-nine per cent of the human story of Britain is prehistory, dating from before the coming of the Romans and the introduction of the written word. Even the simplest of societies needed some means of describing how to get from place to place, and the very earliest of Stone-Age settlers must have used some form of place names. However, we can only study old names once they have been written down and so the history of place

names is linked to the history of writing. Sometimes careful detective work combined with quite a lot of guessing can show us a glimpse of the lost past, but most of the very earliest names are lost forever, replaced, or changed beyond recognition by later inhabitants. Even for as great a prehistoric monument as Stonehenge we use a name that is not recorded before the 12th century. It means 'stone gallows', presumably because the arrangements of the stones reminded people of the gibbets used to hang people on – a sorry fate for a monument which had taken so much effort to build, and must have meant so much to the society that created it.

Sound changes

No one knows exactly why certain sounds change at certain times, but we do know that the changes follow rules, and that the steps that have occurred as different languages evolved can be reconstructed. The sounds of a language are always shifting, but so gradually that the speakers rarely notice. If you watch an old film on television you will notice that the way the actors sound is not quite what you would expect today. Their syllables are often more clipped, and many sounds seem to be made further back in the throat. More noticeable are the differences that have developed between the English of England and that of Australia, South Africa and America in not much more than 200 years. This is sound change at work.

The same process on a larger scale is what has turned, over thousands of years, the language of a single prehistoric tribe into the family of languages we now call Indo-European. This family includes: Sanskrit and various other languages of India; Persian; Greek; Latin and its comparatively modern offshoots Italian, Spanish, French, Portuguese etc.; the related Celtic languages; the Baltic Lithuanian and Lett; and the Germanic group of languages spoken in Scandinavia, Germany, Holland and elsewhere. There are only a few European languages such as Basque and Finnish which do not belong to this group.

Although they may differ in detail, all these Indo-European languages share a basic structure in their grammar and a common core vocabulary which has evolved from an original root form. The sound changes that have made them seem so different have followed set rules, and are always to a sound made in a neighbouring part of the mouth. If you try saying the sounds represented by the letters 'd', 't', 'th', 's', 'z', one after the other you will find that it takes only a slight movement of the tongue and a few minor changes in the shape of the mouth to move from one sound to another. A slight error or sloppiness in how you make a sound can easily produce the neighbouring sound or something close to it. We are used to hearing this sort of error in children's speech. When we do it ourselves we normally hear our mistake and, using the feedback from our ears, correct the error. However, for unknown reasons at different times and places certain 'errors' become acceptable or fashionable and gradually build up into distinct sound-changes. This sort of process can be seen today when an irritated parent asks their child 'How can you understand that noise?' of a song lyric that is crystal clear to the younger person.

It was realized in the last century that Indo-European languages were related and it became possible to work out the so-called 'laws' of sound changes. It became clear that if Latin 'd' regularly appears as 't' in English, and Latin 't' becomes 'th' and Latin 'p' becomes 'f' then the Latin word **ped**em, which gives us the word 'pedestrian', could develop into the English 'foot'. Similarly the Latin **dent**em, the source of our 'dental', could become 'tooth'. By working out the order in which these sound changes occurred and noting where a place name has been affected by them it can be possible to tell both the approximate date of a place name, and sometimes to deduce the original form. This is one of the reasons it is essential to work with the earliest possible form of a name.

Of course nothing to do with humans is entirely predictable, and there are all sorts of factors that lead to names that do not obey these 'laws'. These include the process called 'analogy', when an unusual name or name element is pronounced as if it were a more common one. In 'folk etymology' a name that almost sounds like a familiar word takes on the form of the familiar word. Moreover the Norman invasion (see pp. 82–93) illustrates what can happen when invaders meet place names in a foreign language.

Of the earliest names that have come down to us, the vast majority are British, a Celtic language spoken by the peoples conquered by Rome. Celtic speakers are thought to have arrived in these islands some 2500 years ago. The earliest inhabitants of Britain were speakers of some unknown non-Indo-European language (see box). There are a number of names – particularly of rivers and some of the Northern and Western Isles – that cannot be explained in terms of any known languages, and since no expert likes to admit defeat, these names are often ascribed to some lost ancient language. Attempts to identify the language have ranged from proto-Basque, proto-Berber, something labelled Eurafrican, Phoenician, even a language related to that of tribes living round the North Pole (seen by some as the descendants of the peoples who lived in Europe in the Ice Age). However, as we have no records all this must remain theory, and cannot be proved one way or another.

A much more convincing argument can be made for the existence of a language sometimes called Old European, traces of which can be found in the river names throughout Western Europe. It would be a Bronze Age language and an ancestor of both the Germanic languages that give us the majority of our place names, and Celtic. Since the later Celtic settlers in these islands would have recognized some of the elements of this language, it is argued that they would have had no difficulty absorbing the names into their own language. If this theoretical language does lie behind many modern ones, it would be part of the great Indo-European family of languages, and thus it is possible to guess at the root meanings behind the names.

The best evidence for the existence of 'Old European' is found in river names. One of the biggest groups of possible Old European river names is that which include rivers called **Allan** and similar forms. The name is certainly old, for the Roman form *Alauna* or *Alaunus* is used in ten different places in the records of Roman Britain. Seven of these are settlement names, most of which have gone out of use, although **Alcester** (Warks) on the river **Alne**, shows the survival of one of them. The other three are rivers, and it is assumed that the settlements also took their names from the rivers they stood on. There is, for instance, a Roman fort at Maryport (Cumb) on the river **Ellen**, and another at Ardoch (Tays) on the **Allan Water**, both of

The true name of Stonehenge (see previous page) is just one of the mysteries surrounding the monument on Salisbury Plain. In one myth it is called the Giant's Ring, but the name we use, meaning 'stone gallows', only dates from the 12th century. (POPPERFOTO)

which have been confidently identified as one of the places called *Alauna*. The **Aln** (Nmbd) is also recorded in Roman sources.

Other rivers probably from the same root are the **Ale Water** (Borders), **Ayle Burn** (Nmbd), the **Allen** which joins the Tyne, the **Alwin** or **Alwyn** flowing into the Coquet (Nmbd), the **Alaw**, **Alyn**, **Alan** and **Nant Alun** (from which the personal name Alun comes) in Wales, the Somerset **Alham**, the **Yealm** in Devon and **Allow** in Cornwall (a name no longer used, but from which **Porthallow** gets its name). In Europe we find the **Alma** and **Almo** in Italy, the **Lom** (earlier the *Almus*) in Bulgaria, the Lithuanian **Alme**, two more Almes as well as the **Aller** and **Elz** in Germany, the Norwegian **Ala** and the **Aumance** in France. Unfortunately, while it cannot be denied that these names are all related and so must be very old, their meaning has been much debated, and various conflicting theories put forward. One theory, attractive because some of the evidence is based on the French fish name *alose* (the English shad), claims that it means 'the shining' or 'brilliant one'. Another theory suggests that the name means 'Holy' or 'mighty'. A more prosaic view is that the name comes from *ala-*, 'water', from an Indo-European root meaning 'to flow'.

The following is a list of some other rivers, with the possible meaning of the name and the European rivers that share the name. If the similarities seem rather distant this is because the comparison is based on the oldest recorded forms of the names, rather than today's.

The **Ayr**, flowing into the Clyde, the **Oare Water** (Som), the **Orwell** (Sflk), the **Arrow** (H&W) and the **Erme** (Devon) gain their name from *ara-* meaning 'water-course' from the verb 'to move'. In Europe there are the **Ahr**, **Ahre** and **Erms** in Germany, the **Aar** in the Netherlands and the **Ara** in Spain.

The **Black** and the **White Cart**, which flow into the Clyde (Glasgow's **Cathcart**, 'fort on the River Cart', comes from the same name), the six Scottish rivers called **Carron**, the **Carrant** flowing into the Avon (Glos), the **Carey** (Devon), **Cary** (Som) and two Welsh rivers called **Ceri**, come from an Indo-European root *kar* (meaning 'hard' or 'stony') des-cribing the river beds. In Europe we find the **Chéran**, **Charente**, **Charentonne** and **Cher** in France, the **Chiers** in Luxemburg and the **Horund** in Norway, which share the same root.

Loch **Ness** (Roman *Nassa*) and **Deerness** (Dur) mean 'wet'. In Europe we find several ancient Greek rivers from the same root, and the **Nette** in Germany.

The **Ure**, a tributary of the Ouse (NYorks), comes from a root *is-/*eis* meaning 'to move fast or violently'. In Europe there are the **Isar** and **Iser** in Germany, and the **Isère** and **Isarn** in France. The Roman name for the Ure was probably *Isura*, for the Roman name of Aldborough near Boroughbridge, which lies near the Ure, was *Isurium Brigantum*, the capital of the Brigantes tribe.

For the Thames see box on p. 24.

Why are so many rivers wet?

An extraordinary number of early river names seem to mean 'wet' or 'flowing water'. Bearing in mind that almost all place names start off as a description, here are various theories to explain it.

a) Our ancestors were amazingly unimaginative, and could think of nothing better. As with all theories it is impossible to prove this theory one way or another, but there is no good reason why this should be the case.

b) The name was originally longer, and only part of it has come down to us. What has survived would be the equivalent of our River Thames losing its distinctive half and just being known as 'the River'. It could be argued that this does not sound very likely – common sense would suggest keeping the distinctive part – and we could also question why it seems to have happened in so many cases.

c) We do not understand the finer shades of meaning in the names, which were much subtler than we can appreciate. The modern equivalent would be the way in which Inuit are said to have many different words for 'snow' to describe what they can see but we can't, but only to have one word for 'tree' where we have all the species names.

d) We know from the discovery of the offerings made by Bronze and Iron Age inhabitants that they worshipped at water sites. Our custom of throwing money into fountains for luck is said to be a survival of this. There is a theory that maintains that many river names were felt to be too sacred for everyday use, so the river was just called 'the wet one' instead. This is supported by the survival of some river names such as Severn and Shannon which are thought to be divine. On the other hand their very survival also shows that it *was* possible to use the sacred names of rivers.

e) The surly native theory is a variant of Prattchet's 'your finger you fool' (see p. 4). The idea here is that an invader grabs the nearest local, points to the river and demands to be told its name. The native mutters something about 'the river' and makes a sharp exit before further harm comes to him. The objection to this view is that just the one encounter would have to give the river the new name. The invader would have to tell everyone else the river's 'name' and have no one else reply 'Actually, the native *I* asked said it was the Thames'.

f) A more convincing theory is that in a society where travel was rare and maps non-existent, someone who had made a journey would pass on information about the route in terms such as 'You walk until you reach the foot of the hill you can see over there, turn left when you come to the flowing water (or 'the sparkling water' or whatever), and carry on for half a day . . .'. In this way the description of a river could become fixed by tradition and turn into a name.

The place names of Roman Britain

The Romans

Julius Caesar took a tentative look at Britain in 55 BC and again the following year. After this the Romans traded with the Britons, but the Roman conquest and occupation did not begin until AD 43. The Roman province of Britain was divided into two distinct parts. South of a line from the Mersey to the Humber Roman civilization flourished. Latin became a common language for the various sections of the population and the Celtic leaders who accepted Roman rule were encouraged to take part in Roman society and local government. Towns and cities were founded and trade and industry developed. To the north of this line was a military zone, with troops based at the major fortified towns of York, Chester and Caerleon, which means 'fort of the legions', and at numerous smaller forts. In this area the British were subject to Roman rule, but far less affected by Roman civilization. Hadrian's Wall marked the northern boundary of Roman rule. The Antonine Wall was built further north, between the Forth and the Clyde, but southern Scotland was never subdued. The Romans ruled to the Welsh borders but not Devon and Cornwall, and do not seem to have settled south of Exeter.

Considering that Britain was such a relatively unimportant part of the vast Roman Empire, the records of the place names used by the Romans are surprisingly full. More than 100 writers in Greek or Latin mention places in the British Isles, and inscriptions, such as those on milestones along Roman roads, give us names we would not otherwise know.

Three major works give us the bulk of our useful knowledge. The oldest of these is Ptolemy's *Geography*, written in Greek around AD 145, but containing material from earlier sources. Next comes the *Antonine Itinerary*, dating from about the 3rd century, but also containing earlier material. This is a practical guide, rather like the route map in a modern road atlas which gives the distances between points on a journey, thus helping to verify the places the names refer to. It contains 225 routes throughout the Roman Empire, 15 of which deal with Britain. Linked with this is the *Peutinger Table*, a section of an ancient map of part of the Roman Empire. We do not know for certain the age of the map, which is undoubtedly a copy of a copy, but it probably dates from about the 3rd century. It shows a small part of Roman Britain containing 16 names, all found in the *Itinerary*. Finally we have the *Ravenna Cosmography*, a mishmash of place names put together about AD 700, again using earlier sources.

An extract from the Domesday Book meaning:

In Hoxton the Canons of St. Paul's have 1 hide. Land for 1 plough; it is there now.
   3 villagers hold this land under the Canons.
   Pasture for the livestock.
The value of this land was and is 20s.
   It lay and lies in the lordship of St. Paul's Church.

The Canons hold Hoxton as 3 hides. The land is for 3 ploughs, they are there.
   7 villagers, who hold this land, 16 cottagers.
In total, value 55s; when aquired the same; before 1066, 60s.
   This manor lay and lies in (the land of) St. Paul's Church.

It is important to remember that we do not have originals of any of these documents, and that the versions we have contain errors. These have crept in inevitably as unfamiliar names were copied and re-copied by hand from manuscripts containing the same sort of shorthand seen in the illustration from the Domesday Book (see above).

What sort of a country would the Romans have found? Although it lacked the trappings of civilization the Romans brought with them, it would be a mistake to think of it as totally barbarian. Archaeologists disagree about how much the great hillforts that crown so many of our hills were still used – it probably varied from region to region. Most people would have lived in farming communities, but there were a good number of towns where extensive trading took place, many of them still the sites

18

The magnificent hill fort of Maiden Castle, Dorset – also known as Mai Dun – dates from the Iron Age. It's name probably means 'flat hill' but 'maiden' was sometimes used to refer to a fort whose defences had never been breached. (COWSTOCK PHOTO LIBRARY)

of towns today. The towns were usually the centres of tribal groupings, ruled by an aristocracy with chiefs at their heads. In the southern half of the country at least, the aristocrats could be exceedingly wealthy judging by the riches found in their graves. Much of this wealth would have come from trade with the Continent, which had been going on since at least the Bronze Age. It was Britain's wealth of exports: hides, hunting dogs, slaves, freshwater pearls and particularly metals – lead, gold, silver and above all the scarce tin needed to turn soft copper into bronze – which had first attracted the Romans.

The Romans called their new province *Britannia* after the inhabitants the *Britanni*, although in the earliest Greek sources the name is spelt with a 'p', and the Celtic form of the name was probably **Pritani* or **Priteni*. This form survives in the Welsh name for the country *Prydain*, and in the name of the mysterious Picts of Scotland (see p. 122). When writing about the people of Britain the Romans described them as one race, and this is confirmed by the place-name evidence. Apart from the elusive pre-Celtic names and the few Latin names they introduced, the place names recorded by the Romans are nearly all in the same British language, suggesting that virtually everyone spoke it. Some speakers may indeed have briefly used a dialect influenced by the related

Place names and current archaeology

In 1729 farm workers in Risley Park, Derbyshire found a badly corroded silver tray. It was obviously Roman, and drawings made from it, showing the beautiful decoration and the inscriptions on it, were published. But a few years later all trace of the tray was lost, and for over two hundred years it was only known from the drawings. Then in 1991 a farmer brought a large silver tray to a dealer to sell. The decoration was recognized, but the tray was in too good a condition to be what was found in 1729. However, the British Museum was interested and carried out analysis of the metal and other tests, and concluded that what had happened was that the original tray had been too badly damaged to be restored, so moulds had been made from it, the original Roman silver melted down, and recast from these moulds. The tray has since been bought by the American Friends of the British Museum and given to the nation.

What has all this to do with place names? The importance of the tray, lies not in its size and value, and only partly in its beauty. It also bears an inscription showing that it was a piece of church silver, given by a Bishop Exuperius to the church on the estate of someone with the unlikely name of Bogius. This gift was made in the 4th or 5th century, right at the end of the Roman period. There are two significant place names involved in the research surrounding the tray. One is the name **Silver Hill** which is found on a map of the area where the tray was found which had been published in 1722, seven years before its discovery. Roman silver often came in sets, and the name may indicate that other silver had been found there at an earlier date. Secondly, Bogius' name seems to have been preserved. The Latin Bogius would represent a Celtic name **Boii*, **Boie* or **Bogi*. A mile and a half north of Silver Hill lies **Boyah Grange**. This is recorded in 1200 as **Boyhag** meaning 'Boie's enclosure'. It has been suggested that this could have been the administrative centre of the estate, while traces of 4th-century Roman remains noted some years ago near Silver Hill may even be the remains of the church the tray was given to.

Gaulish language, for Julius Caesar tells us that members of two tribes – the *Belgi* and the *Atrebati* – had emigrated to Britain (probably c. 100–80 BC), and this is confirmed by the old names for **Winchester** (*Venta Belgarum* meaning 'The Market of the Belgi' which developed into Old English *Uintancaestir*, 'Roman town of Venta') and **Silchester** (*Calleva Atrebatum* meaning 'The Atrebate's town in the woods').

The names that have come down to us from Roman sources fall into two groups: those that come from Latin and would have been given to places by the Roman conquerors, and those that were taken over into Latin from existing British names. When dealing with the history of this second group it is important to remember that the form that has survived from ancient texts is the Latin version of the British names, so that the names have already been exposed to alterations to make

them seem more natural to Latin speakers. Moreover, those names which have survived into modern times were mostly taken over by the invading Anglo-Saxons in the form used in British, rather than from the Latin form, so that we are left trying to reconstruct their meaning through a double veil of language change. In addition, it is important to remember that the Latin spelling system was not the same as ours; in particular all letters in a word were pronounced, 'c's were hard and the letter 'v' represented a sound like our 'w', illustrated by the way the names have developed. However, Latin was the language of the Church and the Roman forms of the names could still be preserved in written texts. The Venerable Bede (?673–735), an Anglo-Saxon saint and scholar, used many Roman forms of names in his Latin writings. It is possible that this knowledge influenced the development of some names.

Latin survivals

Only a small proportion of the 460-odd names that are recorded from Roman Britain are fully or partly Latin (and even then we do not know how many were more than official names). They included such places as *Villa Faustini* (now Scole; Nflk) probably named from the family whose magnificent treasure, buried to protect it from Saxon raiders, was dug up in the winter of 1992; but they were usually new settlements and therefore often military foundations. The strategic reasons for military foundations differed from the considerations which led to the growth of civilian towns.

A market town will develop where the geography of the country dictates – where a number of routes meet for instance. This is why so many of our towns are so old, for this basic geography does not change. In the same way more evidence is coming to light to suggest that while their names may change with new owners, units such as our parishes and even farms may go back centuries, some to pre-Roman times. These settlements developed from natural units, their shapes often dictated by the resources they provide, and their boundaries formed by streams and hills that have changed little since these islands were settled.

Military foundations, on the other hand, tend to be placed wherever the countryside can be most effectively dominated, any lack of convenience being compensated for by the hard work of the soldiers. Many Roman forts were short-lived, abandoned once their purpose was fulfilled. Others were more permanent, and settlements would grow up round them to supply the soldiers' needs. Sometimes these would grow into sizeable settlements, and the authorities would officially found a city there.

The cities tended to be established a little way from the camp, for the same disciplinary reasons that make the authorities today prefer barracks to be out of town – thus in the case of York the official town was the other side of the river from the fort. Romans tended to use the local place names, even when they founded new towns such as London which we know is a Celtic name but, embarrassingly for the place-name experts, we do not know its meaning. The old view that it comes from a personal name *Londinos* is no longer generally accepted.

Only two fully Latin names have survived down to the present day: Catterick (NYorks) and Speen on the northern outskirts of Newbury (Berks). **Catterick** is recorded in Latin as *Cataractonium* and this has long been identified as coming from the word *cataracta* meaning 'waterfall' or 'rapids'. Catterick does not, of course, come directly from the Latin even though it looks as if it might have done, but has been through Old Welsh and Old English to reach its modern English form. In early Welsh Catterick appears as *Catraeth*. As a general rule place names lose syllables with age, and this has obviously been the case here. The Anglo-Saxons took over the name as *Cetreht*, and it is from this name that the modern Catterick has developed.

Speen can be identified with the Roman place name *Spinis*, 'at the thorn-bushes'. In the *Antonine Itinerary* this lies on the Roman route from Caerleon via Bath to Silchester, then a major town. It has been firmly identified with **Woodspeen**, where, although the actual site of the Roman road-station has not been identified, traces of Roman occupation are known. Woodspeen lies just north-west of modern Speen, on the River Lambourne and would have been where the river was crossed. On the Ordnance Survey map part of the nearby B4000 is marked as Roman Road (The Ermin Way). Although this is only a short stretch, on either side the dead straight line of a Roman road is continued as a footpath, and if a ruler is placed on this path to extend its line, it passes directly through Woodspeen.

The Romans would have built a station to guard the crossing which was probably a new settlement, since it bore a Latin and not a native name. The Latin name would have survived the departure of the Romans, becoming something like **Spin* in everyday British speech. This would normally have developed into a modern place name, **Spine*. So why is it Speen

> ## Improving your image
>
> The influence of Latin on British place names is not confined to the distant past. The ancient records give us a name *Morikambe*, 'curve of the sea', which *might* have applied to the area we now call **Morecambe** Bay but could well have been elsewhere. Wherever it was, the name died out, and Morecambe and its bay were called Poulton (Old English 'settlement by the pool') until the 18th century. In 1771 a Manchester antiquarian, the Rev. John Whitaker, published a book which suggested that it might be the ancient *Morikambe*. The fledgling resort quickly adopted the more attractive name. A similar situation occurred in Ireland, where the tourist area south of Wicklow was given the name the **Vale of Avoca**, based on the name *Oboka* which appears in Ptolemy's *Geography*. It is believed to have referred to the river Avonmore which flows through the Vale of Avoca.

instead? When the Anglo-Saxons arrived the name **Spin* would have meant nothing to them. However, they did have a word **spene*, meaning 'place where wood-chippings are left' or 'place where shingles are made'. Since the Roman name suggests the site was a wooded one, this probably seemed an appropriate name, and folk etymology worked to change a strange-sounding name into something familiar.

Lincoln belongs in part with these names, for it comes from the first syllable of each half of its Roman names *Lindum Colonia*, 'The Roman colonia [an officially founded town succeeding a legionary fortress] at Lindum', a Celtic name for 'the pools' referring to Brayford Mere and the marshes and pools of the Witham. The Lincolnshire district of **Lindsey** means 'the people who live in the Lindum area' + the Old English ending meaning 'island', while the Island of **Lindisfarne** means 'the island of the travellers from Lindsey'. Similarly, **Colchester** has long been interpreted as 'Roman town on the River Colne', but some people now think that the first part of the name owes something to the Roman name *Colonia Camulodunum*.

The island of Britain and its divisions

Most of the names which have survived from Roman times are of towns or rivers, but we do have the names of some Scottish islands and major divisions of the country. Britain we have already dealt with. The unromanized area north

of the Forth-Clyde line was called **Caledonia**, and the term was occasionally used of the whole of the north of the island. The name comes from the *Caledonii*, a tribe who lived in the Great Glen and who had given themselves a name meaning 'the hard men' or 'the tough men'.

The Romans did not have a specific name for Wales, much of which they did not control, and **Ireland**, called *Hibernia* and inhabited by the *Hierni*, was right outside their sphere of influence. The Greek name for Ireland was *Ierne*, but the Romans had been influenced by their word *hibernus*, 'wintry', and had altered its form. The Greek was obviously closer to the true form, for the Old Irish name for the island was *Ériu*, and it is from this that the modern name **Eire** comes.

A good number of the names of the other islands off the Province of Britannia have come down to us. In Scotland the Island of **Bute** was *Botis* (modern Gaelic **Bod**), probably meaning 'the dwellings'. The Inner **Hebrides** were called by the Romans *Ebudae* or *Hebudes*. This appears in the form *Ebudes* in the work of the 3rd-century writer Solinus. In ancient manuscripts it can be very difficult to distinguish between groups of letters made up of small vertical strokes – n, m u, r, i, – and this led to *Ebudes* being misread as *Ebrides*, hence our modern form. The name, which appears to be pre-Celtic and is of unknown meaning, was only later applied to the modern larger area. The isle of **Mull** (modern Gaelic **Muile**), appears as *Malaia* probably meaning 'hill (island)'.

There are many names in Europe with a shared root, so the name is probably pre-Celtic. The **Orkneys** get their name from Latin *Orcades*, from Celtic a word with the root meaning 'pig'. There are two possible interpretations here. It could be that a Celtic tribe calling themselves 'the boars', indicating fierceness and strength, lived there, or that the name could come from a related word meaning 'whale' or 'sea-monster', indicating that they are to be found there. **Skye** is found in the Latin form *Scitis*, possibly connected with the mod-ern Gaelic word *sgian*, best known today from the *sgian-dubh*, the knife worn in the stocking in full Highland dress. The name may refer to the deep cuts in the coastline as seen from a small ship.

Further south, **Man** comes from *Manavia* meaning 'high or mountain island'. This meaning is shared with *Mona*, modern Welsh **Môn** or **Anglesey** in English. In the south of the country, the Isle of **Wight** comes from the Latin name *Vectis*, the 'v' having been pronounced as a 'w', the Latin 'ct' being a /kh/ sound, which was later lost. It is of obscure meaning, but may come from a word meaning 'fork in the road', or 'watershed' which could refer to the position of the island dividing the Solent into two branches. The **Scilly Isles** come from *Silina*, of unknown meaning, but it has been suggested that the name could be connected with the goddess *Sulis*, who also gave her name to the Roman name for Bath, *Aquae Sulis*. The Isle of **Thanet**, although now only an honorary island, was separated from the mainland of Kent in Roman times and was known as *Tanatis* or *Tanatus* meaning 'shining'. This may be a water name, for the same root is found in rivers **Tanat** (Shrops), **Tennet** (Tays) and **Tynet** or **Tynot** (Grmp), but it has been suggested there may have been a beacon or lighthouse on the island. The 'h' in the modern names seems, like the 'h' in Thames, to be a modern pseudo-scholarly invention.

Among our county names, **Kent**, in Latin *Cantium*, was known to the Roman world from at least the 1st century BC. Its meaning is debated, but most probably means 'land on the edge' or 'corner land', which would fit its shape and position. Names from the same Indo-European root meaning 'border, edge' are found throughout Western Europe, so the name is probably very old. **Devon** and **Dyfed** come from the old Roman names for their areas, *Dumnonia* and *Demetia*.

Roman rivers

There is an interesting rule-of-thumb when dealing with river names: the larger the river, the older the name is likely to be. There are, of course, more exceptions to this rule than can be counted (this is always the case in place names). The reason for this rule is not difficult to find.

The larger the river, the more need there was for a name. In a primitive society a large flow of water formed a barrier which had to be avoided or crossed, and information on how to do this needed to be passed on, so it needed a name. Streams were known to fewer people, almost all of them local. Locals knew where the streams were and could probably wade across. It was only when rivers and streams were used as boundaries, roads improved, and more importantly when the detailed map makers came along demanding a name for every ditch, that official fixed names came to be given to smaller streams. Because this happened later, the names tended to be later. They were more likely to be derived from names which already existed such as the hills they rise on or the farms near them.

Similarly it was at this stage that a river, which may have had different names in the various areas through which it flowed, was given a single official name along its whole length, although locals may have continued to use a local name. The survival of the old names was also a matter of practical convenience. If a new group of people settled in an area they needed a universally-accepted term by which to refer to the major rivers. It was much easier to take over the already-established local name than to get everyone to agree to a new name. However, the rate of take-over depended on how much contact there was between the two language groups. In addition there was a gradual eroding of old names with time (although modern map-making has probably put a severe brake on this process).

These processes are very clearly shown in the river names of England. If we look at the density of river names that we think come from Celtic names and compare it with the stages of the Anglo-Saxon takeover of the country, we get an interesting match. (See map.) If we take an area east of a line drawn from the Yorkshire Wolds through Salisbury Plain and the New Forest to the Solent we find there are few river names from British, and they belong mostly to rivers which would form major barriers. This is also more or less the area that the Anglo-Saxons first settled in the 5th and early 6th centuries, and where there is least evidence of continuing British culture. Traditionally the eastward spread of the Anglo-Saxons in the south was halted for fifty years around the year 500 by the battle of Mount Badon when King Arthur is supposed to have inflicted a swingeing defeat on the invaders. To the west of this area there is a strip running north to south that was occupied by the Anglo-Saxons in the second half of the 6th century and the first part of the 7th century. Here Celtic river names are not only more frequent, but are used for smaller rivers. Cumbria and Lancashire in the north, Shropshire, parts of Hereford and Worcester and Gloucestershire and all the south west except Cornwall were not occupied until the mid-7th to early 8th centuries and there is far more archaeological evidence of British activity in the area. Even the language lasted longer, for it is thought that a dialect of British was spoken in Cumbria into the 11th century. Not surprisingly, more river names were also passed on, for in this area even small streams may have British names. Finally in Cornwall and Wales the overwhelming majority of river names are Celtic, not surprisingly as English was hardly spoken in these areas until after the Norman Conquest, and Cornish, which died out in the 18th century, and Welsh which flourishes today are both direct descendants of the language spoken by the British during the Roman occupation.

Twenty seven river names have survived from Roman times. Of these the best known is probably the **Avon** which runs through Bristol. This is recorded as the *Abona*, the British

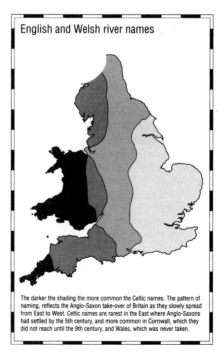

English and Welsh river names

The darker the shading the more common the Celtic names. The pattern of naming, reflects the Anglo-Saxon take-over of Britain as they slowly spread from East to West. Celtic names are rarest in the East where Anglo-Saxons had settled by the 5th century, and more common in Cornwall, which they did not reach until the 9th century, and Wales, which was never taken.

The Thames

The River Thames may be one of our most important rivers, but we do not really know what its name means. There are two views about its meaning. One, which was long the accepted view and still followed by some, is that it means something like 'dark' describing its water. The great Ekwall, in his pioneering *English River Names* pointed out that related river names could be found as far away as India, where a tributary of the Ganges is called the Tamasā from the Sanskrit *tamasá*, 'dark', which matches very well with the Roman names for Thames, *Tamesa* or *Tamesis*, from British **Tamessa*. A name that widely spread would have to be a very old one indeed, and it is a most attractive view. However, modern scholars on the Continent feel that this connection is coincidental, and take the rather duller view that the name comes from an Indo-European root **ta-* or **t$^\theta$* meaning 'to flow'. This view links many river names together, from places as far apart as Scotland and Turkey, so it would still be at least an Old European name. Names closely related to the Thames, according to this theory, include the rivers **Thame**, **Team**, **Teme**, **Tavy**, **Teviot** and **Tawy** in Great Britain, and others in Spain, Italy, Belgium and France. Also related are the **Tone**, **Tain**, **Tean**, the **Taw** and the **Tay**. The **Tyne**, in Latin *Tinea*, has a root meaning 'to flow, melt' so is connected with the Thames names. Rivers from the same root but not found in Roman sources are another **Tyne** in Lothian, **Tyne Brook** (H&W), **Tindale** (Cumb) and more distantly **Till** (Nmbd) and the **Tille** in France.

word for 'river', which has survived in Welsh as *afon* and in Irish as *abhainn* (pronounced 'owen'). Although this is the only river of this name in Roman records, there is another Avon and another Avon Water in Scotland, a second Avon and a Little Avon running into the Bristol Channel and two more Avons and another Avon Water which flow into the English Channel. Ireland has several Avonmores or Owenmores, the -*more* element meaning 'great'.

Many river names have religious associations. The **Annan** (South-west Scotland), Latin *Anava*, means 'rich river'. The Irish goddess of prosperity was called Anu, another form of the word. The **Clyde**, Latin *Clota*, comes from a Celtic word meaning 'to wash', and it has been suggested that Clota is really the name of the river-goddess whose name meant 'the strongly-flowing one' or 'the washer'. The **Dee** is a river name meaning 'the goddess'. There are four rivers called this, although only the two Scottish ones are recorded in Roman times. The Modern Welsh form of the Latin name *Deva* is found in the two rivers in the Lleyn Peninsula called the **Dwyfawr** (Great Dee) and **Dwyfach** (Little Dee) as well as the Welsh name for the Chester Dee, the **Afon Dyfrdwy**.

There are six different places called *Derventio* in the record of Roman Britain, four of them Roman forts named from the rivers on which they stood, the other two now the **Derwent** and probably the **Dart** in Devon. The name

means 'river in the oakwood' and may have some religious significance, since the Celts worshipped in woodland glades. The four River **Derwent**s, the **Darwen** and **Darent**, the two **Darts** and the **Little Dart** probably come from the same word. Most importantly, the **Severn** from *Sabrina* was a divine name. Its meaning is not at all clear, and it may be pre-Indo-European. It is found throughout Western Europe, for example in the Belgian Sambre and the French rivers Sèvre and Sèvres and reappears in Britain in the name of **Savernake Forest**. The old form of the Severn's name remained in use a long time. The legend that the river got its name from a drowned princess may be an echo of a goddess.

Other river names describe the water in them. The **Coquet** (Nmbd) comes from the Roman name *Cocuveda*, 'red appearance', and indeed this river is stained a dark reddish colour by the minerals in it. There are five **Eden**s in Great Britain: those in Fife and Cumbria are recorded as *Ituna*, 'water', in Roman sources. The others are **Eden Water** (Nmbd) the **Eden Burn** (Dur) and the **Afon Eden** (Gwyn). But the River Eden in Kent is a backformation from the town of **Edenbridge**, an Anglo-Saxon name meaning 'Eadhelm's bridge'. The **Exe** (Devon) and **Usk** (Gwent) are recorded as *Isca* also meaning 'water'. Other rivers from the same root are the **North** and **South Esk** (Tays) plus three other northern rivers called the **Esk**, the **Nant Wysk** in Wales, two West Country **Axes** and the **Exe Water** in Cornwall. The **Lossie** (Grmp) comes from *Loxa* 'winding, crooked river' and gives its name to the town of **Lossiemouth**. The **Meon** (Hants), from *Moina*, comes from a Celtic root meaning 'to go' so probably means 'fast-moving river', while the **Naver** (High) comes from *Nabarus*, perhaps 'misty river'. The **Trent** comes from *Trisantona*. There are two main interpretations of the name, 'great wanderer' or 'very liable to flood'. Other rivers from the same word are three other rivers Trent in England, the Welsh **Trannon**, and the **Tarrant** in Dorset.

The **Wear** (T&W) from *Vedra* is sometimes interpreted as coming from a word meaning 'clear', but the sense 'wet' found in Indo-European is now preferred. The second part of the name of the **Traquair** (Borders) is probably from the same root. The **Wharfe** (Ilkley; W Yorks) is from *Verbeia* 'winding river'. Scandinavian settlers seem to have interpreted it as coming from the Norse *hverfr* also meaning 'winding' which led to the form *Weorf* (963), *Werf* (1158) and the modern Wharfe. The **Yare** (Sflk/Nflk) has come a long way from Roman *Gariennus*. It was first shortened to *Yerne*, for the Saxons had no hard 'g' sound at the beginning of words, and then developed into Yare. Its meaning is debated. Finally the **Ystwyth** (Dyfed) comes from the Latin *Stuctia*, from a British word **stuctio* 'bent, curved' which still survives in the modern Welsh word *ystwyth* 'supple'. Although the modern word looks an unlikely descendant of the old, it follows the regular sound changes that took place as British became Welsh. (**Aberystwyth** grew up around the castle built in 1110 on the River Ystwyth, but when, a hundred years later, a second castle was built a mile and a half to the south on the River Rheidol, the new town kept the old one's name, despite the fact that it now stands on a different river.)

The towns of Roman Britain

In other chapters of this book we will be concentrating on different groups of place-name elements, but this is not a practical course with the surviving Roman settlements: there are too few of them with too many different elements. Moreover, only part of the Roman name tends to survive into modern times. Elements such as *dunum* (used for 16 names in Britain and countless names on the Continent), which originally meant 'hill' and then 'hill fort' and was later often transferred to the Roman town that developed in the same area, are often lost. When the Anglo-Saxons adopted the old names they adopted the names as spoken by the British, without their Latin endings. They tended to add an ending such as *-chester*, 'Roman town' (see p. 40), often a replacement for the word *caer*, 'fort', which the British used in front of the name. As time passed the first part of the name was often reduced even more, sometimes to a single syllable. We will go into some detail of how the names changed, to give an idea of how this worked.

The meanings of Roman settlement names fall into the same sort of groups that the majority of names of other periods do. The commonest type of name is what is called topographical, that is it describes the country-side it is in or where it can be found. Another group of names comes from personal names – either of an individual or group of people who live there. Other places are named after the function of the place or the trade that is carried out there. Sometimes, of course, the different types overlap. And there will always be a large group of names which can only be classed as 'we don't know' or 'we're not sure, but possibly . . .'.

If we look at the largest group of names, the topographical, the features referred to can be a large aspect of the landscape as in the case of **Manchester** from *Mamucium* 'breast-like hill', probably a description of the hill on which the original Roman fort stood. (Other places derived from the British word for 'breast' are **Mamhead** (Devon), **Mamble** (H&W), **Mam Tor** (Derbs), **Maumbury Rings** (Dors), and **Mamhilad** (Gwent). Alternatively the feature can be small but significant as in the case of **Dorchester** (Dors) from Roman *Durnovaria*. The first part of this name means 'fist', probably 'stone the size of a fist' judging by the Scottish **Dornock** and **Dornoch**, both meaning 'site covered with fist-sized pebbles'. *Durnovaria* is found as *Dornwaraceaster*, still close to its original

---

Durobrevae to Rochester

The Roman name of **Rochester** was *Durobrevae* which seems impossibly far from modern Rochester. How could it have happened? The argument runs that the Latin name represents a British name something like *Durobriu*, the first syllable of which was not stressed, and therefore was dropped along with the final vowel, leaving **Robri*. It would be quite normal for the invading Anglo-Saxons to hear the 'b' as an 'f' and to identify the name with their word *hrof*, 'a roof', as in Old English words are as likely to begin with 'hr' as 'r'. They turned the name into something like *Hrofesceaster*, 'Hrof's Roman town', the form given by Bede about 730. He wrote in Latin and gave what he knew as the Latin form, *Durobrivis*, but also gave the Anglo-Saxon name, so called he said 'after one of their former chieftains called Hrof'. By 1086 this had been shortened to *Rovecestre*, only a short step from the modern form. The Anglo-Saxon account of the name is easily explained. Many Old English place names do come from the name of the one-time owner, and the Anglo-Saxons liked to find a founding father for a place. We have a similar case in **Portsmouth**, which is thought to come from the Latin *portus* 'a port' + the English 'mouth' as it stands at the mouth of the great harbour named after it. However, it is described in the Anglo-Saxon Chronicle for 501 as being named after an entirely imaginary chieftain called *Porta*.

The Roman ruins at Wroxeter were once described by an Anglo-Saxon poet as one of those 'Splendid cities . . . the work of Giants'. The picture shows the wall of the Roman baths at Wroxeter. (BRITISH TOURIST AUTHORITY)

form, by the 9th century, but had been reduced to *Dorecestre* by the 11th century. (The other Dorchester in Oxfordshire is not recorded until Anglo-Saxon times when it is *Dorcic*. It was a flourishing Roman community, and that this was known is shown by the '-chester' ending. However, it has not been possible to work out what the first part means.)

Carmarthen from *Moridunum*, 'sea-fort', was shortened and had the Welsh *Caer*, 'fort', added. It has a confused history for the Welsh form of the name, Caerfyrddin, can be interpreted as 'Merlin's Fort', which has led to various local legends growing up round the town's name. **Lichfield** (Staffs) bears an old name only indirectly. The name *Letocetum*, 'grey wood', was used in Roman times to describe the nearby town at **Wall** (so-called from its Roman remains), but the main place of settlement seems to have moved later 2½ miles north to Lichfield which by c. 710 had gained an Old English second half to its name and become *Licitfelda* 'the open land in the Grey Wood'.

Reculver (Kent) comes from *Regulbium*, 'great headland'. The form the name takes suggests that it may have been known to the

Anglo-Saxons at a very early date, perhaps before their occupation of Kent either through use by mercenaries employed by the Romans, or else from knowledge gained on the earliest Saxon pirate raids of this shore. **Richborough** (Kent) comes from *Rutupiae*, probably meaning 'muddy shallows'. **Gloucester**, from *Glevum* meaning 'bright place', via early Welsh *Cair Gloiu* + chester, also belongs in this group. It has been suggested that the rather puzzling meaning of **Mancetter** (Warks), from *Manduessedum* 'the horse chariot' + *cetter* from *chester*, may also be topographical.

The final puzzle is **Penkridge** (Staffs) from *Pennocrucium*, a Roman settlement 2½ miles to the south. It appears to mean 'chief mound' or 'tumulus (grave mound) on the hill'. The problem is that there is no hill at the settlement, and no known tumulus. This latter could have been lost through ploughing, but it has also been suggested that the name may refer to some kind of tribal meeting place marked, perhaps, by a small mound; or that the name belonged originally not to a town but to the area. The nearby River Penk gets its name by back-formation, which must have happened after people lost the meaning of Penkridge as the original division of the sense was *pen* 'chief, hill' (still used in Wales) + **croco*, 'mound', not the modern apparent division 'Penk-ridge'.

The Roman name for Dover, *Dubris,* means 'waters, stream', and surprisingly referred not to the sea, but to the river, now called the **Dour**, on which it stands. Dover is quite a common name element. It is found in **Doverdale** (H&W), **Dovercourt** in Essex (the second part possibly the remains of the Roman *cohors* meaning 'court, yard') as well as in **Andover** (Hants) 'ash-tree waters' and **Wendover** (Bucks) 'white waters', although we do not have Roman names for these. It is worth pointing out that **Andoversford** (Glos) does not belong in this group. It is an Old English name, being found in 759 as *Onnan ford,* 'ford of a man called Anna'.

Abergavenny (Welsh **Abergefenni**), means 'town on the mouth of the river Gefenni'. Gefenni, Latin *Gobannium*, means 'river of the blacksmiths' or 'of the Ironworks'. The remains of Roman, possibly earlier, ironworks have been found by the river. More prosaic is **Caerwent** which comes from *Venta Silurum* 'the market of the Silures'. Here the tribe name is lost and the 'venta' kept. Welsh *caer* was put in front and it became first *Caer Guent* then Caerwent with the district of **Gwent** getting its name from the same source.

Places from personal names include **Carlisle** (Cumb) from *Luguvalium*, 'Town of Luguvalos', perhaps meaning 'Strong one dedicated to the god Lug'. This became *Cair Ligualid* in Old Welsh, *Caer Liwelydd* in Welsh which the Anglo-Saxons adopted as *Luel*, hence modern Carlisle. The 's' probably crept in thanks to folk etymology identifying the second element with the French *l'isle* 'the island'. Another possible example is **Wroxeter** from *Viroconium Cornoviorum* which may mean 'Town of **Virico*', a personal name + the tribe name *Cornovii* whose capital it was. The name is thought to have belonged originally to the hill-fort on the Wrekin, then transferred to the Roman fortress. The *Vir* forms seem to have become *Vr-* in British speech and both Wroxeter

---

Eburacum to York

The Latin *Eburacum* seems a very long way from modern **York**, but there is no doubt that the one is descended from the other. The Roman name probably means 'place with lots of yew-trees'. An alternative interpretation is that it means 'Estate of Eburos' (a personal name found in Roman France), but this is less likely, as plant names are rather more common in British names than estate names. In common speech the British form of the name would have been shortened to something like *Evorog*, and this would have been the form met by the Anglo-Saxon conquerors. As in the case of Rochester, they would have found the nearest equivalent in their own language, *eofor*, 'a wild boar' and turned the name into *Eoforwic*, 'boar town'. The process may well have been helped by the fact that Roman York seems to have used the boar as its municipal badge. When York was conquered by the Vikings they adapted the name to their own language and called it first *Evorvik*, then *Jorvik* (the 'J' being pronounced with the same sound as the 'Y' in the modern name). From there it only needs the 'vi' to be swallowed to produce modern 'York'. The old Latin name was never lost, and is still used today in the signature of the Archbishop of York and in the name of the horse race, The Ebor Handicap.

---

and the **Wrekin** developed from this word.

Despite its unknown meaning **Cirencester**, from *Corinium*, is an interesting case of how sounds change. The first part of the name became something like **Corin* in Welsh, and appears as *Caer Ceri* in the Latin of the 8th-century Welshman Nennius. The Anglo-Saxons developed this into *Ciren* + *cester* (i.e. chester). A 12th-century form of the name, *Chirencester*, shows the way in which Old English turns c + e, y or i into 'ch'. This tendency is reflected in the modern name of the river on which the town stands, the **Churn**, which also comes from *Corinium*.

Also of unknown meaning are **Corbridge** (Nmbd) 'the bridge near Corchester' which in turn gets its name from the first part of the Latin *Coriosopitum*. **Binchester** (Dur) is probably from *Vinovia*, again of unknown meaning, but by all the rules of sound changes Binchester should not come from the Latin, which would normally give us a W at the beginning, and another **Winchester*. However it is quite possible that Anglo-Saxon settlers heard the old name and changed **win* or **vin* to *binn* 'manger' by popular etymology, thus giving us the modern name.

The Anglo-Saxons

Anglo-Saxon is a convenient catch-all term for the Germanic tribes and peoples who settled in parts of Britain from the 5th century onwards. In the later years of the Roman occupation Germanic pirates raided southeast England. Traditionally, the first Anglo-Saxon settlers were the followers of Hengest and Horsa, who arrived after the Romans left in the 5th century. The story goes that the British king Vortigern offered land if they would protect his kingdom from other Germanic raiders. But the gamekeepers promptly turned poacher and overran the country with fire and the sword. In fact, archaeological and place-name evidence suggests that some Germanic peoples were living in England before the Romans left.

Germanic pottery dating from the 4th and 5th centuries has been found in graves or used as cremation urns, and distinctive buckles and belt-fittings worn by barbarian soldiers serving with the Roman army have also been found. It seems likely that Germanic troops were stationed in southeast England from the mid-4th century (perhaps even earlier) and that some may have settled here, staying on after their period of service was up.

Magnificent as Ludlow castle on its hill may be it is probably not the 'low' from which Ludlow, 'the mound by a rapid', got its name.
(POPPERFOTO)

Like the Celts the Anglo-Saxons were not a single united people, and there was no single 'invasion'. The Venerable Bede (?673–735), an Anglo-Saxon monk and historian, wrote of three main groups: the Angles, the Saxons and the Jutes. The Angles settled in the Midlands, the north and east of England, and Scotland south of the Forth and Clyde estuaries, the Saxons in south and west England, and the Jutes in Kent and the Isle of Wight. It seems that Bede was more or less right, although he does not mention the Frisians, Swabians or other smaller ethnic groups.

We know a lot less than we would like to about the early years of Anglo-Saxon settlement. We know that they didn't just stream across the country with fire and the sword. The process of colonization took a long time and was probably something like the European colonization of North America – a gradual spreading-out rather than a single determined campaign. For example, they did not reach Devon and Cornwall until some three to four hundred years after Hengest and Horsa's time.

Because we know comparatively little about the Anglo-Saxons, and especially about their early years here, they tend to fall down a crack in history known as the Dark Ages. We forget that they ruled parts of these islands for 600 years – longer than the Romans – and during that time they developed from a collection of quarrelsome, illiterate pagan tribes into one of the great Christian civilizations of Europe. As far as England is concerned, they largely created the landscape as we know it, and they certainly named most of it. The vast majority of English place names are partly or entirely of Anglo-Saxon origin, and even the areas of the 'Celtic fringe' – Wales, Ireland, Scotland and Cornwall – have some Anglo-Saxon names. By the time of the Norman Conquest most of our present towns and villages, and their names, existed in some form.

The Anglo-Saxons spoke various dialects of a language we now call Old English. To us this is like a foreign language, but it is the ancestor of modern English and many words seem familiar: *hus* (house), *stan* (stone), *straet* (street, often denoting a Roman road), *boc* (book, but also used to mean a title deed, as in various places called **Buckland** – the land granted by charter) and *aet* (at) are all similar to modern English. Some words common in place names, such as stream and ford, have come down to us unchanged.

It has been estimated that about 90% of words found in Old English manuscripts still exist in some form. The Scandinavians, who later settled in Britain, spoke dialects of a very similar language, known as Old Norse. Many Norse place-name elements are very like their Old English equivalents, and much of the explanation of place names and naming practices in this chapter could also be said with reference to Scandinavian communities. Where there is a close likeness we have dealt with both languages and communities here, rather than repeat ourselves.

The Anglo-Saxon landscape

In some ways the land the Saxons discovered was the land we know today; hills and valleys don't move around, after all. But in other ways it was quite different, and this is where the names can help us picture the country as it used to be. In general, the names tell us that it was much wetter and much woodier, with far less farmed land and fewer towns and villages. There were more wild animals but fewer species of cultivated plants.

The Anglo-Saxons were largely a peasant, agricultural community, living closer to the land than we do and sensitive to different aspects of it that we might not even notice,

Where we have a few words for hills, valleys and streams, they tended to have a range of words, describing different characteristics of such features. Sometimes we know exactly what an individual word meant, sometimes we can guess or work it out from looking at all the features referred to by a particular word; often we feel that some kind of distinction is being made but we cannot pinpoint exactly what it is. Sometimes an observant person with detailed local knowledge can point the experts in the right direction.

The Old English place-name elements that indicate different kinds of hills and valleys are

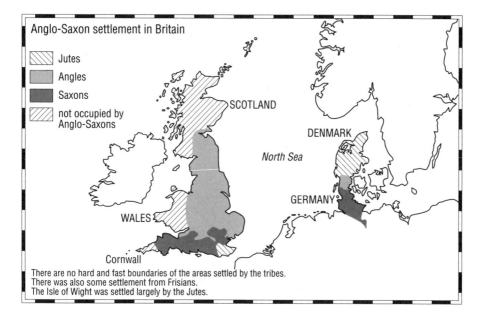

Anglo-Saxon settlement in Britain

- Jutes
- Angles
- Saxons
- not occupied by Anglo-Saxons

SCOTLAND

DENMARK

North Sea

GERMANY

WALES

Cornwall

There are no hard and fast boundaries of the areas settled by the tribes.
There was also some settlement from Frisians.
The Isle of Wight was settled largely by the Jutes.

listed here in their most common modern forms. Those with capital letters appear as the first element, although some can appear as a separate word. It would be wrong to assume that because something has a certain meaning as a first element that it will have the same meaning as a middle or final element; some do, many don't.

Names with the following elements usually refer to a valley:

> *Botham Bottom- -bottom -cleaugh Clof-
> -clough Comp- -coombe Dal(e)- -dale
> Dean- Den- Hol(e)- -hole Slade-
> -slade -slate -sled*

Names containing the following elements usually refer to a hill, mound or slope:

> *Back- Cam(b)- -cett Cleve- Clif-
> -cliff(e) Com- -don Down- Edge-
> -edge -el Head -head Hel-
> Hil(l)- -hill Hoo- Hough- How-
> Hu- Hul- -ide -leth -linch
> -linge -lith -lynch Nas- Naze-
> -ness -over -ow Ridg(e)- Rudge-
> -rudge Tor- -tor*

There are also some elements which may refer to a hill or valley, but which need to be treated with caution because they often have other meanings:

> *-al(e) -all -bach -badge -bage
> Batch- -beach -bech Betch- Comb-
> -combe -dean -den Dun- Haigh-
> Hal(e)- -halgh Hall- -hall -ham
> Hol(e)- Hop(e)- -hop(e) Hurst- -hurst
> -le(y) Oare -oe Old- -op
> Or(e)- -or(e) Over- -over -ridge
> Shel- -side -ton(e) Wal(d)- -wald
> Walt- Wauld- -wold -would*

Once it is known that a name contains one of these elements it is usually possible to identify the hill or valley concerned. What is interesting is the other part of the name which shows what made this one different. It is important to realize, however, that 'hill' is relative and that quite a small bump may give rise to a 'hill' name in a flat landscape. There is a world of difference between the 'cliff' of **Radcliffe Highway**, a few feet above the Thames in East London, and the dramatic gorge spanned by the **Clifton** suspension bridge just outside Bristol.

Hills provided lookout places – essential for communities apt to squabble with neighbouring tribes and later threatened by Danish and Norwegian invaders. *Ward* or *weard*, meaning a watch or lookout, gives rise to **Warden** (Beds), **Wardle** (Ches and GMan), **Warborough** (Oxon) and **Wardlow** (Derbs). **Wardour Old Castle** (Wilts) is near the *ward ora* 'lookout slope', although the castle itself dates only from the 14th century. The element *tot* or *toot*, probably from Old English *totian* 'to peep out', is found in place names mainly from the late Anglo-Saxon and early Norman period, such as **Totternhoe** (Beds), **Great Tosson** (Nmbd), **Tostock** (Sflk), **Toot Baldon** (Oxon) and **Totland** (IoW). However, **Totley** (SYorks), **Totnes** (Devon), **Tottenham** and **Tooting** (GLon), and **Tottenhill** (Nflk) come from Anglo-Saxon personal names. Old English *yppe*, 'a raised lookout place', is found in **Uppingham** (Leics), **Epping** (Essex), and **Ipsden** (Oxon). Names such as **Beacon Hill** are usually late, often 19th century, but the Old English word *beacen* is found in **Bechney** (Essex) and **Beaconsfield** (Bucks). **Warcop** (Cumb) comes from Norse *varthi* 'beacon' and Old English *copp* 'hill'.

Two types of 'hill' names need to be looked at more carefully. The first contains elements which could refer to natural or to man-made hills or mounds (see pp. 39–40). The second type can refer to either a hill or a wood. *Hyrst* (modern 'hurst', also found as **hirst** in place names) means a hillock or a small wood. It is sometimes translated as a 'wooded hill', but the word seems to have both 'hill' and 'wood' senses throughout its history, and either is possible. *Hangra* could mean just a slope, but usually indicates a wooded slope. In any case, there is little sign now of woodland around the notorious **Hanger Lane** gyratory system at the top of Hanger Hill in west London, or at nearby **Pitshanger** (*pyttelshanger* – *pyttel* may be a personal name or may refer to a bird of prey, the kite, which likes woodland or scattered trees but not thick forest). In the case of *weald* or *wald*, found in such names as the **Weald** of Kent, the Yorkshire **Wolds**, the **Cotswolds**,

---

Old English

The grammar of Old English was more like modern German than modern English. Like German it was an inflected language: one that adds an ending (an inflection) to the main part of the word (the stem) to indicate the part that a word plays in a sentence. Each noun belonged to a type or class that had its own range of inflections, according to whether it was singular or plural, its grammatical gender (see below) and the grammatical case it was in, which depended on the part it played in the sentence. A word is said to be in the *nominative case* when it is the subject of the sentence (e.g. *wood* in *the wood is dense*); in the *accusative case* when it is the direct object (we cut down the wood); in the *genitive case* when something belongs to it (the wood's edge, the edge of the wood), and in the *dative case* when it is the indirect object or with certain words which show position or movement in relation to it (the cottage in the wood, we went to the wood). The word for wood in Old English would be *wudu* in the nominative and accusative, *wuda* in the genitive and dative. The plural woods would be *wuda* in the nominative, accusative and genitive and *wudum* in the dative.

Old English also used grammatical genders. This means that each noun is described as being masculine, feminine or neuter. This has very little to do with sex. Although words for men such as *mann* or *cyning* (king) were masculine and most words for women were feminine, words for things could be of any gender. *Stan*, *wudu*, *stream* and *ford* were masculine, *boc* and *straet* were feminine, and *hus* was neuter.

An adjective would have different inflections according to the gender and case of the noun it described and whether it was singular or plural. The word *the* would also change according to the word it referred to.

There is no need to worry too much about all these endings unless studying place names seriously, but it is important to realize that the same word may appear in different guises in different names. In some words the vowel in the stem of the word might change: mouse and the plural mice (*mus* and *mes* in Old English) have survived.

Pronunciation of Old English

Below is an approximate guide to the most important differences between Old English and modern English pronunciation.

Vowels

a = ah as in *father, oompah*

ae = a as in *bad, fat*

e = e as in *bed* or ay as in *make*

u = oo as in *put* or oh as in *note* (**NOT** u as in *hut* – the letter **u** was sometimes also used to represent **v** or **w**)

y = roughly oo as in *put* or ooh as in *boot* – the sound was actually closer to French *tu* or *musée*

Consonants

h at the beginning of a word, before a vowel, was pronounced as in *hot*. Elsewhere it was pronounced rather like German ch (*ich, nicht*), a slightly softer sound than the ch at the end of *loch*.

c before a, o, u and y = k as in *king*; c before e and i = ch as in *cheer*

g before a, o, u and y = g as in *gay*; g before e and i = y as in *yet*

c at the end of a word was usually pronounced ch

g between a and u was pronounced something like the modern w

sc = sh as in *sheep, fish*

cg = j as in *edge*

All consonants were pronounced; in combinations such as **cn** (modern kn as in *knight*), **hw** (modern wh as in *wheat*), and **mb** (*lamb*) both would be heard. This also applies to double consonants: in the personal name Sunna the **nn** would be pronounced as in 'soon now'. There were differences in spelling and pronunciation in northern and eastern areas of England. The most noticeable were: **ea** in the south and west was often just **a** in the north and east; **weald** as opposed to **wald**, **ceaster** as opposed to **caster**. **sc** was pronounced **sk** in the north and east, and **cg** was pronounced **g** (*gay*). This ultimately affected the spelling, e.g. Shipton and Skipton, both from *sceaptun* 'sheep farm', and Felbridge and Felbrigg, both containing *brycg* 'bridge'.

Waldershare (Kent) and **Waldron** (ESx), the apparent ambiguity actually reflects a change in the landscape during the word's lifetime. At one time much of Britain was covered by woodland, although some of this had already disappeared by the time the Saxons arrived. As the original settlers multiplied and more arrived they needed space for their settlements, land to farm, and wood for fuel and building. Gradually woodlands were cleared, the landscape changed, and the meaning of *weald* also changed, from forest to wooded hillside to open upland.

Many pieces of woodland survived, of course. The element **wood** (from *wudu*) usually indicates something in or beside a wood. **Woot(t)on** and **Woodham** are common names meaning a settlement beside a wood; others are **Woodstock** (Oxon) (*stoc* 'place') and **Woodcott** or **-cott** (*cot* 'cottage'). **Woodford** is self-explanatory. **Underwood** means '(the place) by the wood' and **Grendon Underwood** (Oxon) means the 'green hill by the wood'. **Westwood** (Kent) was to the west of the wood. **Sherwood Forest** belonged to the shire ('forest' is a later addition, from Old French). **Woodhall** or **Woodhouse** may indicate a building where some kind of administration relating to the woodland was carried out.

Bearu and *grafa* both mean a grove or small wood; *graefe* means thicket or brushwood. All the names, however, need to be treated with caution. *Bearu* gives rise to various names containing **beer**, **beare** or **barrow**: **Barrow** (Sflk), **Barrowford** (Lancs), **Barrasford** (Nmbd), **Sedgeberrow** (H&W), **Bere Regis** (Dors) and **Beer**, **Rockbeare** and **Sedgebeare** in Devon. Similar names can come from Old English *beorg* meaning a hill, mound or tumulus; particularly tricky if the mound no longer exists (see p. 39). *Graefe* and *grafa* both give rise to names containing **grove**, **grave** or **greave**,

> ## The Old English alphabet
>
> Old and Middle English had some characters that do not exist in modern English. We have used modernized spellings, but these older characters will be found in many place-name books, as well as in old documents.
>
> æ (as diphthong) = 'ash', for which we have used *ae*
> Ð, ð = 'eth' and þ = 'thorn' for which we have used *th*
> p = 'wynn' for which we have used *w*
> ȝ = 'yogh' has different pronunciations according to its position in a word and the sounds surrounding it, but it is usually either *y* or *kh*. We have used whatever spelling best represents the sound in each case.

Holmfirth may look Scandinavian and suggest the meaning of 'the woodland belonging to Holme' but Holme is in fact Old English for 'place at the holly tree'. (IMAGES COLOUR LIBRARY)

Chesil Beach – 'the gravel beach' – has been constantly built up and eroded by tides for thousands of years. Recently built breakwaters further up the coast mean that no new material will be deposited, and in time the name will be all that remains. (IMAGES COLOUR LIBRARY)

but these can also come from Old English *graef* or *grafa*, a pit or trench. Sometimes the other element can give you a clue: the first element of **Orgreave** (W Yorks) and **Orgrave** (Lancs) is *ora* (ore), so these are 'pit' names. **Orgreave** (Staffs) had an early spelling *Ordgrave*, possibly from *ord* 'a point'; if this is so then the name is more likely to refer to the shape of a grove.

Boxgrove (WSx) was a grove of box trees, and **Ramsgreave** (Lancs) a grove where the wild garlic plant ramsons (*hramsa*) grew. **Palgrave** (Sflk) and **Staplegrove** (Som) provided poles (*pal*) and posts (*stapol*). As far as we can tell the 'woodland' names are far more common than the 'pit' names; it would be better to settle for a 'woodland' name unless there are grounds for suspecting otherwise. Usually it is not possible to tell the difference between a 'grove' and a 'thicket' name; the Anglo-Saxons do not seem to have made this distinction consistently.

Holt often occurs with an element meaning a particular kind of tree, and it may be that the word was used particularly for a wood or plantation containing one species: with *ac* 'oak' in **Acol** (Kent), **Occold** (Sflk), and surprisingly in **Knockholt** (Kent). In the latter's case it would have changed from Ochholte to Nocholt, with the 'n' added from the form of 'the' in the phrase 'at the oak holt' *(aet then acholte)* – presumably the 'K' was then added because that's the way we usually spell knock). *Aesc* 'ash' appears in **Aisholt** (Som) and **Esholt** (WYorks), and *boc* 'beech' in **Buckholt** (Hants and ESx). **Holt** also occurs alone in several counties, and with other descriptive elements: **Kensal** (*Kingisholte*) **Green**, London, belonged to the king, and either rams or ramsons were found at **Ramsholt** (Sflk).

Choosing a home

Woodland and water were both important factors in deciding where to settle; both ruled to a great extent by the underlying geology. The nature of the soil was also important. The ideal site for a farm or village was probably a gravelly, well-drained place within easy reach of fertile alluvial clays. When you see a 'gravel' name in the vicinity of 'clay' or 'water-meadow' names (but not too near the river), and probably with some 'woodland' names nearby, the chances are that the site was a good one, probably occupied at an early stage, perhaps by evicting its former inhabitants. *Greot* (gravel) gives rise to various names beginning with **Great-** or **Greet-**, *cisel* (gravel) and *cisen* (gravelly) to some names with the first element **Chis-**. *Claeg* (clay) often appears as **Clay-**, also in **Clee** and **Cleethorpes** (Humb), **Clehonger** (H&W) and **Cockley Cley** and **Cley-next-the-Sea** (Nflk). Chalky soil was not quite so desirable, although it was dry and provided pasture for sheep; *calc* or *cealc* (chalk) give names with the first element **Chal-** and also appears in **Cawkwell** (Lincs), **Calke** (Derbs), **Kelfield** (NYorks) and **Great Kelk** (Humb). **Sand-** in place names usually means what it says; grains of sand or gravel are referred to in the **Isle of Grain** (Kent). Stones (*stan*) are referred to in **Stanfield** (Nflk), **Standerwick** (Som), **Standish** (GMan), and **Stainland** and **Stainley** (WYorks). Sometimes the colour of the soil was commented on; red (*read*) in various names beginning with **Rad-** or **Red-** and in **Rodmell** (ESx); white (*hwite* – presumably chalk or pale sand) in names beginning **Whit-** and in **Wheatfield** (Oxon), although in most instances **wheat** refers to the cereal. With names of buildings, such as **Whitchurch**, the usual inference is that the building was made of stone; the personal name Hwita can also confuse matters. *Fealu* meant a wishy-washy yellowish colour like dried grass and *fealg* or *felg* meant newly ploughed land or land only recently cultivated. Either may account for **Fallowfield** (GMan). **Fallowdon** (Nmbd) and the various **Fawley**s were probably yellowish, whereas there was probably newly cultivated land at **Felpham** (WSx) and possibly **Felliscliffe** (WYorks). Both words have given rise to modern 'fallow'; *fealg* in the sense of land that is left to rest for a season and *fealu* in the colour sense and in 'fallow deer'.

Water – streams and marshes

The existence of wells, watercourses and marshes would have dictated the position of many settlements. An adequate supply of water was essential, but too much could make life very uncomfortable. Some settlers would arrive by water, using rivers and streams as highways, and many settled along the banks. Names of these settlements often incorporate a river or stream name, either an Old English name or an older one learned from the British. In some cases the process worked the other way and the settlement gave its name to the river or stream, in a process known as 'backformation' (see box on p. 65).

Broc (modern 'brook') and *burna* (modern Scots 'burn') both meant stream; *burna* is believed to be older than *broc* and was more widely used. It also covered a wider range of watercourses: in early use it could mean anything from a spring to a river. *Burna* appears as **bo(u)rne** or **burn**, either as the name of a stream or of a place by a stream.

Burnham is usually the village by the stream. **Bourne End** (Bucks) is the river's end, where the river Wye meets the Thames; **Bournemouth** is the mouth of the river. **Sherbo(u)rne** means (the place by) the bright or clear stream (*scir* 'bright, clear, pure') and

Settlement in a river loop

If place names obeyed rules, this medieval town would have a name containing the Old English word *hamm*. The main street might be called Castle Street or Market Street. After the fork, the right-hand road, once Ferry Lane, would now be Bridge Street. The left-hand road might be Cornmarket, Buttermarket, or Horse Fair, leading to The Hythe. The settlement on the other side of the river could be totally unrelated, but could have a name containing the word 'Overy' or 'North'. Equally likely are the names Wick, Berwick, Barton or Thrupp.

Pangbourne (*Pegingaburnan*) (Berks) was the stream of Peaga's folk, the Paegings. **Winterbo(u)rne** referred to a stream which was dry except in winter: it is fairly common as a village name, especially in the West Country, and there are at least two instances of strings of **Winterbourne**s, with some kind of distinguishing word added, along the course of a river. In Wiltshire **Winterbourne Dauntsey**, **Earls**, and **Gunner** lie along the River Bourne. ('Dauntsey' is from Roger Dauntseye, who held the manor in the 13th century; the Earl of Salisbury held Winterbourne Earls; Winterbourne Gunner has no military connections, despite the number of army camps and ranges in this area – it was held by a lady called Gunnora de la Mare in 1250.) The 'winter burns' referred to cannot have been the Bourne; each village had a tiny stream, dry in summer but flowing into the Bourne in the winter months. Winterbo(u)rne in a street name may indicate that such a stream once existed, perhaps now culverted and used as a storm drain.

Brook (Kent and IoW) and **Brooke** (Nflk and Leics) mean 'place by the brook'. More often, **brook** appears as part of a complex name; the water in **Shirebrook** (Derbs) was clear (*scir* – see above), at **Fulbrook** it was dirty or muddy (*ful*, modern 'foul'). **Wambrook** (Som), **Cringlebrook** (Lancs) and **Wrangbrook** (WYorks) mean 'winding brook'.

Fleot(e) is usually translated as 'estuary, inlet' or 'small stream'; it commonly refers to a place where a stream flowed into a river or a river met the sea. In a marshy area it could refer to drainage channels. It appears in **Fleet** (Hants), **Fleetham** (Nmbd) and **Swinefleet** (Humb), and is fairly common in names of rivers and streams. Probably its best-known appearance is in **Fleet Street** in central London which crossed the river **Fleet** just before it joined the Thames near Blackfriars. The Fleet can still be seen at its source on Hampstead Heath, but then flows underground through various pipes and tunnels. The 'bourne in the hollow' which gave its name to **Holborn** is part of the Fleet, now covered by Farringdon Road.

The element **Lake-** or **-lake** is frequently found in names of places where there is no lake to be seen; it comes from *lacu* 'small stream' and appears in **Shiplake** (sheep stream), **Standlake** (stony) (Oxon), **Mortlake** (GLon) (Morta's, or perhaps indicating *mort* 'young salmon'), **Fishlake** (WYorks) and **Lake** (Wilts). **Lakenheath** (*Lakingahethe* in the Domesday Book) means 'the landing place (*hythe*) of the lakings – the people that live by the small streams', **Bablock Hythe** (Oxon) means the hythe on Babba's stream. A related word, *laec(c)*, meaning a muddy stream or bog, appears in the River **Leach** and in **Eastleach** and **Northleach** (Glos), in **Lashbrook** (Oxon and Devon), **Blacklache** (Lincs), and in some names beginning with **Latch-**. Other elements with the basic meaning of a small stream are *rith* or *rithig*; **Meldreth** (Cambs) – *myln ryth* 'mill stream', **Fulready** (Warks) – foul stream, and **Rye** in such names as **Peckham Rye** (GLon). Similar in meaning is *lad*, becoming *lode* in Middle English and appearing in **Load** (Som), **Shiplate** (Som; 'where sheep were washed'). **Well** can sometimes refer to a stream, although it usually means a spring (see below).

The modern word lake comes from Middle English *lac*, from Latin *lacus* 'a basin or tub', via Old French. The Old English word for an enclosed piece of water was *mere*, which could refer to anything from a duckpond to **Windermere** or **Grasmere** in the Lake District. Occasionally, as in **Almer** (Dors) (eel pool) and **Westmoor** (Staffs), *mere* is used for a place where a river widens. But more common words for a pool in the course of a waterway, or where two streams meet, were *pyll*, *pull* or *pol*, giving rise to such names as **Pulham** and **Bradpole** (Dors), **Poulton** (Glos), **Polstead** (Sflk) and **Welshpool** (Powys). In some cases the pool is no longer evident, for example because of improved drainage or a change in the water table. Near the coast these elements can refer to a creek, as in **Pilton** (Devon and Som) and **Liverpool** (pool or creek with thick, dirty water – 'creek with water that looks like liver', as the offal and the name are both from Old English *lifer*). It may occasionally refer to a harbour, as in **Poole** (Dors). Old English *sae* (modern 'sea') often means 'lake', although it can also have its modern meaning; it depends where the place is. **Skipsea** (NYorks) means lake for ships (Norse *skip* 'ship'), **Seahouses** (Nmbd) the houses by the sea.

Aewell and *aewelm* both mean 'source of a river'. They appear in **Ewell** (Kent and Sur), **Ewelme** (Oxon) and **Ewen** (Glos), in **Alton** (Dors, Hants and Wilts), **Aldon** (Shrops), **Carshalton** (GLon) (*Cresaulton* – where watercress grows) and heavily disguised in **Clyst William** (Devon) (*Clisterwelme* – the source of the River Clyst). The usual word for a spring was *well*, *wiell* or *waella*. The spelling differed according to dialect and gave rise to various names such as **Welford**, **Welham**, **Wilton**, **Willesden** (GLon), and **Walhampton** (Hants), and many names ending in **-well**. **Bakewell** (Derbs) was *Badequella* – Beadeca's spring – in the Domesday Book, and **Holywell** (Clwyd) refers to the sacred spring or well of the 7th-century Saint Winifred. **Well** could also mean a stream, and this seems more likely in the many **Cranwell**s, where cranes or herons were found. A source of water was essential for a settlement, and it is rather surprising that, although there are a huge number of names containing this element, it is quite rare among very early names.

Like woodland names, the names which refer to marshes are often interesting because of where they are; it can come as quite a surprise to find that a familiar patch of brick and concrete was once a swamp. The most obvious ones are those which contain the elements **marsh** (*mersc* or *merisc*) and **fen** (*faenn* or *fenn*): names such as **Marsh**, **Marsham**, **Marston**, **Marshfield**, **Marshwood**, **Saltmarsh(e)**, **Killamarsh** (Derbs; Cynewald's) and **Titchmarsh** (Ticcea's); **Fenton**, **Fencott** or **-cote**, **North & South Fambridge** (Essex) and **Matfen** (Nmbd; Matta's). Less obvious are **Merston**, **Morston** (Nflk), **High & Low Marishes** and **Marske** (NYorks) and, from *fenn*, **Mason** (*Merdisfen* – Maerheard's) and **Mousen** (*Mulefen* – Mul's; Nmbd) and **Pinvin** (H&W; Penda's). **Slough** (Berks) is obviously a marsh name, from *sloh*, which also appears in **Polsloe** (Devon; pool slough) and in **Upper & Lower Slaughter** (Glos). *Soc*, meaning 'sucking', is used for a marsh in **Sockbridge** (Cumb), **Sock Dennis** (Som) and its neighbour, the less-than-inviting **Old Sock**.

Mos or *meos* usually referred to moss, in names such as **Measden** (Herts) and **Muswell Hill** (GLon). In the northwest it came to mean a bog, probably influenced by a Norse word *mosi* which could mean either a bog or a swamp. *Mos* or *mosi* is found in various **Mostons**, **Moss** (SYorks), and **Mosser**, **Mosedale** and **Mozergh** (Cumb), and in the names of bogs, particularly in Lancashire, such as **Pilling Moss** (with Welsh *pwll yn* 'little pool') and

Ham or Hamm?

There is no foolproof way to tell if 'ham' in a place name comes from *ham*, meaning a village, or *hamm*, denoting a piece of land enclosed by some natural feature of the landscape. There are, however, some clues:

1) *ham* never appears alone; places called **Ham** are always from *hamm*. This also applies to names such as **East** and **West Ham** where 'Ham' is a separate word. Names such as **Norham**, **Eastham** etc. however could come from either word.

2) *ham* does not appear as a first element, except when combined with -*stede* in names like **Hampstead** and **Hemel Hempstead**.

3) 10th-century or earlier spellings with o (*hom*, *home*), with mm (*hamm*), or with a final e (*hamme*) usually indicate *hamm*, for example **Cheltenham** (Glos; *Celtanhomme* in 803), **Chippenham** (Wilts; *Cippanhamme* in 900).

4) both are found in the southeast of England. *Ham* is more likely in the north, *hamm* is more likely in the west. The geographic limits of both elements are still being investigated.

5) both are recorded early in the Anglo-Saxon period. *Ham* is believed to have gone out of use during the Anglo-Saxon period, so a name first recorded in the late Anglo-Saxon or early Norman period is more likely to be from *hamm*.

6) *hamm* is related to the landscape, where *ham* is not, so a look at the place would help. Sometimes the landscape will have changed, for example when a river has become a canal, so that the bend which enclosed the *hamm* has gone. If you suspect this might have happened try to find an early map – the earlier the better. A local public reference library or museum will help. Surrounding topographical place names can also be useful.

Rawcliffe Moss ('red cliff', cliff probably referring to the bank of the River Wyre). Moss is still a dialect word for a bog, and a village or district name such as Moss Edge or Moss Side can be 16th century or later, as more land was needed and drainage schemes pushed back the edges of the marsh.

Land that we would regard as unpleasantly wet or soggy was not necessarily a bad thing. It was generally fertile and provided lush grazing for cattle, reeds for thatching and willows for hurdles and baskets. A dry spot to build on was the only necessity, and there are some place-name elements, including some recorded quite early in the Anglo-Saxon period, that mean 'dry ground in a marsh'. *Hyll* could have this meaning, although it usually refers to something closer to modern hill. The word *e(i)g* (*ey* in Norse, both usually pronounced /ee/) means 'island' in such names as **Brightlingsea** and **Canvey** (Essex; which sometimes has the modern 'island' tacked on the end), but in other names it often has the 'dry ground' sense. It appears in such names as **Eye** and **Eyton**, in **Rye** (ESx) (actually from Middle English *atter eg* ('at the island') and in many names ending in -**ey**. It is less obvious in **Pixey Mead** in Oxfordshire (the meadow on Pic's island) and

Hoy in the Orkneys (Norse *Ha ey* 'high island'). *Eg* could also mean an 'island' of good land in the midst of wasteland, as in **Edale** and **Abney** (Derbs). The name **Eaton** is one to beware of, as the first element can be either *eg* or *ea*, a river or stream. If the land has been drained neither island nor stream may be obvious; a look at an old map may help.

A great deal has been written over the years about the Old English word *hamm*. A thorough treatment of it, though probably not the last word, is in Margaret Gelling's book *Place-Names in the Landscape*. To begin with, it is easily confused with *ham*, meaning a settlement or village, and although there are clues it is not always possible to know which one you are dealing with (see box). *Hamm* also appears to have had several meanings, based on the idea of land enclosed or partly surrounded by some natural feature, although some experts would go so far as to say that a *hamm* could be any piece of enclosed land. The most common seems to have been 'land in the bend of a river' and, possibly as a development of this, 'water meadow'; others are 'dry ground in a marsh', 'piece of dry or higher land jutting out into lowland' and 'cultivated land in the midst of wasteland'.

'Land in a river bend' names include **Fulham**, **Twickenham** and **Hampton Court** along the Thames (GLon); **East & West Ham** lie in the corner between the Thames and the Lee, and **Southampton** (Hants) between the Test and the Itchen, whereas **High & Low Ham** (Som) are on a promontory of dry ground jutting out into marshes. In some places later drainage has obscured the nature of the terrain so that it may be difficult to decide what *hamm* meant in a particular case. Older maps may help and nearby place names may give clues: the *hamm* may be surrounded by marsh or wasteland names, or the name of a street may commemorate a culverted river or a long-drained watercourse. Sometimes, of course, you have to admit defeat!

The word *mor* (modern 'moor') is a bit of a puzzle. The Anglo-Saxons applied it, as we do, to barren uplands, but also to low-lying marshes. So the heathland of **Snelsmore** (Berks) and low-lying, boggy **Otmoor** (Oxon) some 20 miles away are both *mor* names, although the terrain is quite different. The presence of frogs at various places called **Frogmore** and at **Podmore** (Staffs) and **Poddimore Milton** (Som) (*pad* or *pod*, Norse *padda* 'frog or toad')

38

indicate that these were marshy rather than dry. Incidentally, the name of the water-bird **moorhen** makes much more sense once you know it could mean 'fen hen', although the word is not recorded until the 14th century. This 'low marsh' sense seems to have been in use earlier and to be more common, but there is evidence that the 'upland' sense did not replace it but co-existed with it for some time before the 'low marsh' sense fell out of use. It may be that the important characteristic of all the *mor* places was wasteland, and this has led some experts to an intriguing speculation. Could it be that the difference between a *mersc* and a *mor* was that a *mersc* was already being cultivated or managed when the Anglo-Saxons arrived, while a *mor* was still waste? This might be something for the archaeologists to explore.

The Saxons' inheritance – traces of earlier folk

The Anglo-Saxons did not walk into virgin territory. They found the remains of Roman and even earlier inhabitants: earthworks such as burial mounds and ancient fortifications, towns, villages, and roads.

The Anglo-Saxons had two words which they used for both natural and man-made hills or mounds, *beorg* (Norse *berg*) and *hlaw*. The first needs treating with extreme care; not only because of the nature of the hill but also because some of the modern forms which come from *beorg* can also come from other Old English words. The main forms are **Barrow**(-), **Bar-**, **Berg-**, **-ber**, **Berrow-**, **-berry**, **-borough** and **-burgh**, and a look at the index will show other possible sources for some of these. **Barrow** remained as a dialect word in the southwest of England for a burial mound, and has been adopted as a technical term by modern archaeologists. *Hlaw* appears as **Law**(-), **Lew**(-) or **Low**(-) in such names as **Lawton** (H&W), **Pike Law** (Lancs), **Lewes** (ESx), **Lowton** (GMan) and **The Lowe** (Shrops), and as the final elements **-law**, **-lew**, **-ley** and **-low**. In particular **-ley** is more often from *leah*, a clearing, as well as having other meanings. Both *beorg* and *hlaw* were used for tumuli, rather than hills, more often in the south than in the north, although there is no strict cut-off point. *Beorg* seems only to have been used for existing barrows or mounds, but *hlaw* was also used to refer to Anglo-Saxon burial mounds: **Taplow** (Bucks) and **Challow** (Oxon) both contain Anglo-Saxon personal names. The picture is further complicated by the fact that tumuli were sometimes erected on hill-top sites, and that they could be destroyed by later building work on the site or simply by centuries of ploughing.

Ludlow (Shrops) is a *hlaw* by a rapid, and there is certainly a hill to justify the name. But there is also some record of a large tumulus, which no longer exists, in the churchyard, and this may have been what the Anglo-Saxons were referring to. *Hlaw* might also refer to a hill which had undergone some 'landscaping'. At **Harlow** (Essex) the slope of the hill has been altered and a surrounding ditch added, presumably by the Romans who built a temple on the hill-top. The Scandinavians also had a word, *haugr*, which was used for either a hill or a tumulus and which can present the same problems of interpretation; **Becconsall** (Lancs) contains a personal name and may refer to a burial mound; **Clitheroe**, also in Lancashire, means 'hill with loose stones' so is more likely to be natural.

Although pagan Anglo-Saxons were buried with weapons, coins and jewels it would not be wise to rush out with a metal detector and spade at every *beorg*, *hlaw* or *haugr*. For one thing, untold damage can be done to an archaeological site by treasure hunters. For another, someone has probably been there before. There are many instances of Broken Barrows and Idle (empty) Barrows up and down the country. According to the Anglo-Saxons, where there is a treasure horde there is a dragon. The hero of the great Old English poem *Beowulf* killed both the 'invincible' monster Grendel and its mother, but met his death at the claws of a dragon guarding a treasure horde. **Drakelow** (Derbs and Worcs) and **Dragley Beck** (Lancs) both mean 'dragon's mound', while **Drake North** (Wilts) is first recorded as *Drakenhorde* 'dragon's treasure'. *Wyrm* could mean any kind of reptile, including a dragon, and dragons must be suspected when it appears with a 'hill' or 'tumulus' element. **Worm Hill** near Durham commemorates the legend of the Lambton Worm: a member of the Lambton family, fishing on a Sunday, dragged up a monster which terrorized the district for years. Worm Hill is an old hill fort and its outline looks distinctly like a coiled 'creature'.

The Old English word *burh* meant a fortified place, and was used to refer to the great prehistoric hill-forts which are still such impressive features of the landscape, to Roman fortifications, and to settlements nearby. The most common modern forms of *burh* are **borough**, **bury**, **brough** and **burgh**, all of which can appear alone or as a final element. Names such as **Burford** (Oxon and Shrops), **Burpham** (WSx), **Bourton**, most instances of **Burton**, **Berry Pomeroy** and **Berrynarbor** in Devon and **Berrington** (Nmbd) also come from *burh*. As usual, however, there are problems. Almost all these elements can come from other Old English words (see the Index for details), and the word *burh* stayed in use right through the Anglo-Saxon period into Middle English, adapting to changing circumstances and referring to different things. The Anglo-Saxons used it to refer to their own fortifications as well as to existing ones, and it was later used to refer to fortified houses, and later still to manor houses and towns, whether fortified or not. So a common name like **Broughton** can be a tun by a hill or barrow (*beorg*), by a brook (*broc*), or by a *burh*, which may be any one of several things (Broughton can also come from an Anglo-Saxon personal name). In such cases local knowledge of the site is invaluable.

When the Anglo-Saxons arrived there were already some linear earthworks and ditches of varying lengths running across tracts of the country. They built others for defensive purposes, to mark a boundary, or for drainage. With the exception of **Offa's Dyke**, believed to have been built by the 8th-century King Offa of Mercia to mark the boundary between Mercia and Wales, the names seldom help to establish the age, as the Anglo-Saxons did not seem to differentiate between those they found and those they built themselves. They tended to associate these earthworks and ditches with the god Woden. **Wansdyke** (*Wodnes dic*), which runs from Andover (Hants) to Portishead

(Avon), is named after him.

Some major earthworks and many odds and ends of man-made ridges and ditches in various parts of the country are called **Grimsditch** or **Grimsdyke**. These contain Woden's nickname Grim – the masked one – from his habit of going around in disguise. **Grimsbury** (Oxon) and **Grimsbury Castle** (Berks) are old hill forts. **Grimes Graves** (Nflk) are also man-made excavations; flint mines worked in neolithic times. **Grave** comes from *graef* or *grafa*, meaning a pit or trench, and probably means nothing more sinister than 'diggings'. However, you cannot assume a pagan connection with a **Grim-** name. Some names are probably too late to consciously refer to Woden, and in Christian times Grim seems to have become associated with the devil, who is credited with (or blamed for) the creation of various Devil's Dykes or Ditches, most of which are ancient earthworks.

In areas of Scandinavian settlement the picture is complicated by the personal name Grim or Grimr: **Grimsby** (Humb), **Grimesthorpe** (WYorks) and the various **Grimston**s are associated with ordinary mortals rather than the god or devil. Some field names containing Grim- probably just show what a grim task it was trying to get a living out of poor soil, although no doubt their owners wished them to the devil more than once. (Goodman in such names as **Goodmans Field**, **Acre**, etc. can refer to the devil, arising out of a reluctance to speak of him – a person struggling with such land had quite enough trouble without the Prince of Darkness appearing.)

Chester and **caster** are probably among the most widely recognized place-name elements, coming from Latin *castra*, a military fort. Although it is well known that these elements refer to a Roman walled town, they can also refer to older fortifications, particularly in the north. For example, no evidence of Roman remains has yet been found at **Casterton** (WMid). The Anglo-Saxons borrowed *castra* as *ceaster* or *caster*, and it can appear alone, as in **Caister** (Nflk), **Caistor** (Lincs), and **Chester** (Ches). Norman pronunciation and spelling produced **-cester** and even **-eter**. Later users sometimes changed these elements to the more familiar **castle**, as in **Castleford** (WYorks) (*Ceaster ford*) and **Bewcastle** (Cumb) (*Bothecastre*, with Norse *buth* 'booth' – meaning temporary huts that may have been built within the shelter of a deserted fort).

Some Anglo-Saxon names incorporate Roman names, which in turn often used British tribal or river names; **Alcester** (Warks) and **Doncaster** (SYorks) are based on the Roman names *Alauna* and *Danum*, derived from the British names for the rivers now called the **Alne** (see p. 16) and the **Don**, which probably meant simply 'river'. **Worcester** and **Leicester** use the name of the local British tribes, the Weogaran and the Ligora; perhaps these people were still in residence when the Anglo-Saxons arrived. In the name **Winchester** (Hants) the tribal name has been lost. The Roman name of Winchester was *Venta Belgarum* 'the market town of the Belgae'. *Venta* was a British word which the Romans used in the names of several tribal centres. The Anglo-Saxons added *ceaster* to *venta*, perhaps thinking that *venta* was the full name. The local British probably just called the place 'the venta', using a distinguishing element only when talking about someone else's *venta*.

Completely new Anglo-Saxon '*c(e)aster*' names were also coined, with no reference to earlier inhabitants – perhaps because the site

had been deserted. **Chesterfield** (Derbs) and **Chesterton** (Cambs) are pure Anglo-Saxon. The Roman name of Chesterton was *Durobrivae*; the earlier name of Chesterfield has been lost. **Ancaster** (Lincs), **Kenchester** (H&W), **Godmanchester** (Cambs) and **Tadcaster** (NYorks) all contain Anglo-Saxon personal names. **Chichester** (WSx) is associated with Cissa, mentioned in the Anglo-Saxon Chronicle as the son of Aelle, the first king of the South Saxons (Cissa's name was later given, with little evidence of any connection, to the much older hill fort of **Cissbury Rings**). **Craster** (Nmbd) (*Craucestr* – crow *ceaster*) and **Hincaster** in Cumbria (*Hennecastre*) were almost certainly deserted, inhabited only by birds. But be warned, not every name that looks as if it comes from *ceaster* does. **Uttoxeter** (Staffs) is first found as *Wotocheshede*, Old English 'heath of a man called ★Wuttuc', **Grantchester** as *Granteseta*, Old English 'settlers on the River Granta' and **Caistron** (Nmbd) comes from *Kerstirn*, 'thornbush by the marsh', made up of a Middle English dialect word for a marsh and the Old Norse *thyrnir*, 'thornbush'.

The British – slaves or neighbours?

As well as the various settlements, the Anglo-Saxons found people. Early settlers probably overlapped with the Romans, and they certainly found the Britons, who had seen the Romans come and go. The Anglo-Saxons adopted a few Latin words into Old English and incorporated them into place names. We do not know when and how they learned them; whether it was during service with the Roman army in Britain or on the Continent or by contact with Latin-speaking Britons. In later years the Anglo-Saxons would have learned their Latin through the church, and most later Latin uses are connected with church matters, but the early settlers were pagans. It has been suggested that the first Germanic settlers were well established before the Romans left and could have adopted Latin words straight from the Romans without any British intermediaries. There is some archaeological evidence to support this, but not enough to be sure.

Experts have argued for years about the

relationship between the Anglo-Saxons and the British. The traditional version of events, according to the Welsh historian Gildas and the Anglo-Saxon Bede, is a grim tale of slaughter and enslavement of the British by the savage and barbarian Anglo-Saxons. We know that many Britons retreated into the hills and marshes of Wales and northern England. Many from the West Country fled to Brittany, and there are many similarities between Cornish and Breton place names (see pp. 105–108).

However, we must not forget that Gildas and Bede were not completely unbiased. Gildas was a Celt, and Bede was possibly emphasizing the barbarity of the pagan invaders to show the civilizing influence of Christianity on their descendants. There is certainly evidence of coexistence by the two communities, although we do not know on what terms. Archaeological evidence suggests a period of peaceful immigration, followed by invasions with accompanying bloodshed, and then a gradual

The coat of arms of Middlesex, 'the kingdom of the Middle Saxons', shows an imaginative reconstruction of the *seax*, the sword that supposedly gave the Saxons their name. The county officially no longer exists, but many people still include it in their address.
(ANN RONAN)

assimilation of the remaining Celts with the eventual loss of their language and culture.

Recent excavations at a cemetery in Oxfordshire have found two sorts of burial custom corresponding to two distinct physical types, suggesting that the two communities shared the settlement but that each followed its own ways and kept itself to itself. Excavations elsewhere have suggested that the two communities did mingle and intermarry and that the Anglo-Saxons and Celts were soon virtually indistinguishable. Scientists are currently experimenting with DNA recognition techniques on samples of ancient skeletons. Archaeologists hope that this will give accurate information about the racial mix in early medieval Britain.

We know from Bede that in the 8th century there were British speakers in some areas, and by this time Latin gave a common language to more educated members of the two communities. But there was some degree of communication much earlier. Some Celtic place names survive even in areas where Anglo-Saxons were dominant from very early on, and there are many others with both Old English and Celtic elements. In particular the Anglo-Saxons seem to have adopted Celtic river names, some of which, as we have seen, contained elements from even earlier times (see p. 16). How well the two communities actually understood each other is another question.

Names like Pendle Hill (see p. 97) suggest that *pen* meant as little to the Anglo-Saxons as Pendle does to us; it was simply a name. The fact that the two communities talked to each other should not surprise us. If the Anglo-Saxons were to have anything to do with their neighbours other than to slaughter them they needed to be able to communicate. Even if their only interest in them was as slaves they needed to be able to order them about. Some scholars have pointed to the fact that very few Celtic words, apart from names, were adopted into Old English and use this as evidence that the two communities did not communicate, or even that the Celts, in general, did not survive. The British experience in India might be a useful parallel. The British traded with, and then ruled, the Indian people for a great many years. The two communities communicated on many levels and for many purposes. But only a very few words were adopted from the Indian languages into English, and generally only when a 'new' word was needed for an unfamiliar object or idea. Perhaps the loss of the Celtic languages under Anglo-Saxon domination, compared with the survival of so much of Old English in Middle and Modern English despite Norman rule, means that the well-known maxim that 'all foreigners should learn to speak English' is even more ingrained than we thought – perhaps the Anglo-Saxons managed by speaking loudly and slowly and waving their arms about!

A group of names that may be significant are those based on Latin *vicus*. This gave rise to Old English *wic*, which basically meant a settlement but which developed a range of specialized meanings (see p. 43). *Vicus* was the source of most instances of the name **Wickham** and **Wickford**, and some examples of **Wycomb**, **Wyk(e)ham** and **Wyckham**. Archaeological evidence shows that many of these places are near Roman settlements, usually small towns or villages, but not major cities. The term *vicus*

Words for towns and villages

The Anglo-Saxons created small settlements rather than move into the existing Romano-British towns. Many of these small settlements later became towns and cities, and some quite large towns have names which indicate their origin in a farm, homestead, or village.

Tun is probably the most common Old English word in place names. It originally meant an enclosed piece of land, then a farm or farmyard, later coming to mean a village or an estate; although it is the ancestor of modern *town* it did not have this meaning in Old English. It usually appears as **-ton**, sometimes as **-don**, when it can be confused with *dun* meaning 'hill'. The suffix **-ton** was still being used to form place names after the Norman Conquest, and occasionally even in modern names: Carterton (Oxon) was founded in 1901 by William Carter, who aimed to establish a self-sufficient village of smallholdings. In modern use, however, it has lost any specific meaning; it is just something you can use to form a place name.

Ham meant a village, probably at first no more than the collection of huts housing an extended family. It is associated with very early settlements and does not seem to have survived into the late Anglo-Saxon period. It appears as the middle or final element **-ham**, which can also represent *hamm* (see box on p. 38 for how to tell them apart). *Ham* is the ancestor of the word 'home'; despite its meaning it is not directly related to 'hamlet', which is from Old French.

Both *tun* and *ham* combine with **-ing** (see p. 46), forming **-ington** and **-ingham**. Ham combines with *stede* to form **ham(p)stead** 'homestead' and with *tun* to form **ham(p)ton** 'home farm', although 'tun in a hamm' (see p. 38) is also possible.

The modern English word 'borough' comes from Old English *burh*, which was used for various kinds of fortified place (see p. 40). It also seems to have been used from the late Anglo-Saxon period onwards to mean a settlement larger than a village. The later meaning, of a town incorporated by royal charter and having a degree of self-government, stems from about the end of the 14th century; 'burgh' is the Scottish equivalent. Place-name elements **borough** and **burgh** need treating with care, as both can have other meanings (see Index).

Wic – a site of special interest

Wic (wick or -wich) has had an interesting life; it means a dwelling, farm or settlement, but usually one of a specific or unusual kind. It comes from Latin *wicus* and was combined with *-ham* in the very early days of Anglo-Saxon immigration to mean a Romano-British settlement.

'Farm' names are usually associated with a particular animal or crop: with sheep in **Shapwick** (Dors and Som) and **Shopwyke** (Som), with bees in **Bewick** (Nmbd). It often refers to a dairy farm, as in **Cowick** (Humb), various **Butterwick**s and **Keswick**s (*cese, ciese* 'cheese'), **Cheswick** (Nmbd) and **Chiswick** (GLon) many places called **Hardwick(e)** (*heorde* 'herd').

In settlements, *wic* is often associated with a particular trade or industry: fish in **Fishwick** (Devon and Lancs) and **Fiskerwick** (Staffs; fishermen's dwelling), charcoal in **Colwich** (Staffs) and **Colwick** (Northants), metal-working in **Smethwick** (WMid; where smiths worked). It became particularly associated with salt manufacture, in **Droitwich** (H&W), **Nantwich**, **Northwich**, and **Middlewich** (Ches) and **Saltwick** (Nmbd).

Added as a separate element after a place name *Wick* means an outlying farm or settlement dependent on that place, as in **Hackney Wick** (GLon) and **Sutton Wick** (Oxon). Often it also has this meaning in **Berwick** (*bere-wic*, literally 'barley farm'; see p. 54).

On a coast or estuary *-wich* usually means 'harbour', as in **Ipswich** (Sflk), **Woolwich** (from which wool was exported) and **Greenwich** (GLon).

At least four *wics* remain 'sites of special interest': **Sandwich** in Kent is the oldest of the Cinque Ports, set up in the 11th century to defend the Channel coastline and granted special privileges by the Normans in return for providing the nucleus of the navy. **Gatwick** in Surrey changed from a dairy farm to a 'port', replacing its goats with 'jumbos'. It is now London's second airport. **Berwick-upon-Tweed** in Northumberland is both a *bere-wic* and a port. Argued over for many years by England and Scotland, it is now England's most northerly city. The area around **Wytch Farm**, between the Purbeck Hills and Poole Harbour, in Dorset has been a 'special site' since the Bronze Age. Famous at various times for its dairy farms, pottery, and beads and ornaments, today Wytch Farm is the largest onshore oilfield in Europe.

---

was used by the Romans for the smallest unit of self-government, and was often given to the settlements, consisting mainly of traders and retired soldiers, that grew up beside Roman forts. We know that **–ham** was an element used very early in the Anglo-Saxon period, but in general the archaeologists have not found very early Anglo-Saxon remains at the Wickham sites. It seems that the *vicus ham* names were given by people who did not live in the *vicus* but who knew the word and appreciated its meaning. The name would signify 'the *vicus* village which still exists over there', implying a degree of peaceful co-existence.

Much has been made of the fact that the Old English word for a foreigner, specifically a Briton, *w(e)alh*, also came to mean 'serf'. The word appears in numerous names; in various places called **Walcot(e)** or **Walcott**, some **Wallington**s, **Walford**s and **Walton**s, **Walmer** (Kent), **Wallasey** (Mers), and **Walworth** (GLon and Durham). In these names 'serf' or 'Briton' are both plausible, all that is certain is that the Anglo-Saxons felt the people there were 'not like us'. But there are some names where 'serf' seems unlikely. **Walsall** (WMid) and **Wallingford** (Oxon) both come from *w(e)alh*, used as a personal name, possibly a nickname for someone of British ancestry. It is hard to imagine such places, especially Wallingford which is on a river crossing and has always been an important settlement, being

identified with a serf or with anyone whose name was understood to mean serf. The people of **Wales** (from the plural *walas*) were certainly not serfs, although the villagers of Wales in Yorkshire may have been.

In **Cornwall** *walh* was added to the Celtic tribal name *Cornovii*, so that the name means '(the home of) the Britons of the *Cornovii* tribe'. Whatever *walh* may have meant in individual cases, a difference in attitude is implied by the other word for Briton that appears in place names such as **Cumberland**, **Comberbatch** (Ches), **Comberton** (H&W) and **Cumberwood** (Glos). Here the Anglo-Saxon word *Cumbre* is an adaptation of the name that the Britons called themselves, which suggests that no disrespect was intended.

Looking at the modern city of Halifax it is hard to believe that to the Anglo-Saxons it was 'a corner of land where coarse grass grows'. Many of our cities have such rural names. (IMAGE COLOUR LIBRARY)

Making themselves at home

After surveying the land they had found, the Anglo-Saxons set about making the place their own and exploiting its resources and possibilities. They defended it, travelled around it, and farmed it, all the time developing as a society. The names reflect these activities and this social development.

The in-comers, at every level, gave their names to places. Whole areas were named after the Saxons and Angles, and settlements after smaller tribes, family groups and individuals. Conversely, people were named because of where they lived. The relationship between personal names and place names can be complicated and it is not always possible to see whether the chicken or the egg came first. The North Folk and the South Folk of **Norfolk** and **Suffolk** belonged to the East Angles of *East Engle*. The northern Angles became known as the *Northhymbre* – the people north of the Humber – and gave their name to the ancient kingdom of **Northumbria** and the modern county of **Northumberland**. In the Midlands were the *Merce*, the 'boundary people' of the kingdom of **Mercia**. The reference is probably to the Welsh **Marches**, also from the word *merce*, but Mercia also had borders with other Anglo-Saxon kingdoms.

The origin of the word Saxon is uncertain; it may be from Old English *seax* 'knife' and refer to a type of sword. Whether or not this is true, a single-edged, broad-bladed weapon was adopted by some counties with Saxon associations for their coats-of-arms. The East Saxons lived in **Essex**, the South Saxons in **Sussex**, the West Saxons in the ancient kingdom of **Wessex**, and the Middle Saxons in the old county of **Middlesex**, now swallowed up in Greater London. **Surrey** was the *suther ge* (southern district) belonging to the Middle Saxons. The Middle Saxons were probably also the original 'Kentish Men' (the *Centingas*) living west of the River Medway and distinguished from the dominant Jutish 'Men of Kent' (the *Cantware*) east of the river. The Jutes do not seem to have had any large tract of land named after them, except that the word *Ytene* 'of the Jutes' was once included in the name of the area now known as the New Forest. The names of the areas they dominated, Kent and the Isle of Wight, are not even Anglo-Saxon (see pp. 22 and 30).

When names of races or tribes are given to large areas, or several places within a limited area, we can assume that they were the dominant group there. When such peoples appear in isolation the opposite is more likely; that they were an ethnic minority, and that what distinguished that particular place is the fact that these 'aliens' lived there. **Markingfield** and **Markington** – the open space and the settlement respectively of the Mercians – are both in Yorkshire, which was Northumbrian territory. Men of Kent strayed as far as **Canterton** (Hants), then in Wessex, and **Conderton** (Worcs) in Mercia. **Englebourne** (Devon) and **Englefield** (Berks) (the stream and open space respectively of the Angles), and **Exton** (Hants) (farm of the East Saxons) were in Wessex. **Saxondale** (Notts), **Saxham** (Sflk) and **Saxton** (NYorks) were in Anglian territory.

Sixpenny Handley (Dors) and **Pensax** (H&W) are in areas where the Saxons would have been in the minority at the time the places were named; the **pen** in each case is Celtic *penn* 'hill'. There are similar names, such as **Pennersax**, **Glensax** and **Glensaxon**, in southern Scotland, where Saxons would have been a long way off their home ground; the form of the words, with the descriptive element 'Saxon' coming after the words for 'hill' and 'valley', is Celtic. Perhaps there were isolated groups of Saxons, or perhaps the local Celts were not making any distinction between various Germanic peoples, just separating 'them' from 'us' much as their descendants separated Sassenachs (from Late Latin *Saxones* 'Saxon') from their own folk.

Some other peoples who never had great areas of land named for them are identified in town and village names. The Swabians appear in **Swaffham** (Sflk) and the Frisians in **Friston** (Sflk), **Frisby** (Leics), **Frieston** (Lincs), **Monk Fryston** (NYorks; Monk because it later belonged to Selby Abbey), **Frizington** (Cumb) and **Fressingfield** (Sflk). The last two names probably contain a personal name, Frisa, meaning 'the Frisian'.

Anglo-Saxon tribes which can be identified are the Hwicce in **Whichford** (Warks), the old forest of **Wychwood** (Oxon), preserved in the names **Milton-under-Wychwood** and **Ascott-under-Wychwood**, and **Whiston** (Northants). The Hreope are remembered in **Ripon** (NYorks) and **Repton** (Derbs), and the Wixan in **Uxbridge** (*Wixebruge*), **Uxendon** (*Woxindon*) and **Waxlow Manor** (*Woxeley*), all in Greater London, and **Whitsun Brook** (*Wixena broc*; Glos). (Waxlow Manor, in the London borough of Ealing, has long been built over. The name was formerly used for the telephone exchange serving Greenford, but is now found only in street names and one or two local businesses.) **Northill** (*Nortgivele*) and **Southill** (*Sudgivele*), both in Bedfordshire, were the north and south settlements of the Gifle tribe, who took their name from the Celtic river-name **Ivel**, meaning a forked stream. **Hitchin** (Herts) belonged to the Hicce.

There are hundreds – probably thousands – of place names based on the personal names of individual Anglo-Saxons. Sometimes we know who these people were, but in most cases the place name is the only record we have that they ever existed. No one of that name was ever important enough to be mentioned by historians or owned land mentioned in a charter document. There is only the name buried in the place name, subject to all manner of changes in spelling and pronunciation during the thousand or so years since it was first written down and the who-knows-how-many-years-before-that since it was given. This makes some people suspect that these names never did exist and that the experts simply make up a personal name rather than admit they have no idea what the place name means. Certainly there are scholars who will always favour a 'personal name' explanation if one seems reasonable, just as there are those who will admit the possibility only as a last resort if no other explanation can be found. Name specialists do make up personal names. These made-up forms are shown with an asterisk in most place-name books. While we cannot prove that these names ever existed, they are not simply imaginary. Enough is known about Anglo-Saxon names, and about sound and spelling changes, for the experts to be able to construct a plausible name and make a case for its existence. These names are particularly convincing when they appear in several place names. The name *Sunna forms a believable basis for **Sonning** and **Sunninghill** (Berks), **Sundon** (Beds), **Sunbury** (Surrey) and **Sunningwell** (Oxon). (**Sunningdale** (Berks) is a 19th-century parish name founded on Sunninghill.)

The Anglo-Saxons and Scandinavians were

Anglo-Saxon and Old Norse personal names

Many of the place names which come from Old English and Old Norse are made up of a personal name plus an ending indicating a farm, a house or some such feature, a naming system we still use informally when we say things like 'We're all going back to Joe's place'. However, few of the names that lie behind the old place names are familiar. Where did they come from? The Anglo-Saxons and the Scandinavians used a similar system of naming, so can be dealt with together. We know most about the aristocratic names, since they are more likely to be recorded in documents.

The Anglo-Saxon ruling classes used a system of names which were made up of two elements, each of which had a meaning, which did not necessarily make much sense when put together. These elements often ran in families, the sharing of a common element indicating that you were related. Thus Athelwulf 'noble wolf', King of Wessex, called his sons Athelbald 'noble bold', Athelbert 'noble bright', Athelred 'noble counsel' and Alfred (later known as the Great) 'elf counsel'. Alfred's daughter was Athelflaed 'noble increase' and his son Edward 'fortunate guard'. Edward called his children Athelstan 'noble stone', Edmund 'fortunate protection' and Edred 'fortunate counsel', and so it went on, down the generations.

So much for the nobility; but many of the people who gave their names to places had single-element names. These could arise in a number of different ways. Some people seem simply to have been given single-element names, others probably had their names shortened, just as a modern Edward might be called 'Ed'. Still others were given nicknames – there are a surprising number of uncomplimentary names preserved in place names, and a suspicious number of Ravens. Sometimes the nicknames could become quite formal and become an integral part of a name: one of Alfred's descendants is always known as Edmund Ironside, a nickname given in honour of his bravery, and Edmund's father has come down in history as Ethelred the Unready, a rather poor translation of the Old English pun *Athelred unred*, 'noble counsel uncounselled'. Similarly there was a Viking ruler of York called Ragnar Hairybritches and a king of Denmark known as Harold Bluetooth. Thus it is very likely that many of the personal names that have been preserved in place names are not those chosen by the parents, but bynames given by the owner's contemporaries.

fond of giving people nicknames, and these also appear in place names; **Ealing** (GLon) was the home of the followers of *Gilla (pronounced Yilla or Yella – the man with the loud voice), and **Scarborough** (NYorks) was probably the stronghold belonging to Skarthi (the man with a hare lip). Usually these names do not pose a problem, but some nicknames were based on the names of wild animals or birds, and no one can be sure which is meant. **Ramsbury** (Wilts) may well be the raven's fort (*hraefn*). Ravens and crows are often found in this kind of area and carrion-eaters and birds of ill omen are associated with battle scenes in Old English poetry. Alternatively the fort may have been associated with a man nicknamed Raven, perhaps because he had black hair. Some place-name books come down on one side or the other in individual cases; sometimes they contradict each other. Often it is not possible to tell who is right.

The element -**ing** is quite common in place names, often attached to a personal name. For many years everyone was confident that it meant 'the family or followers of x or y', and that names containing this element were the earliest Anglo-Saxon names. The names conjured up a picture of the days before the Anglo-Saxons were organized into great kingdoms and were simply small bands of people, a man with his extended family, slaves and hangers-on, or perhaps a larger group accepting him as their leader, coming across from the Continent and finding somewhere to live. However, some scholars began to have their doubts, and early in the 1960s John McNeill Dodgson compared the '-ing' names with archaeological finds of Anglo-Saxon pagan cemeteries. If the names were very early they should have coincided with the pagan remains, but in most cases they didn't. He concluded that the names were generally not from the very earliest period of settlement, and that the -**ing** element in itself was not a reliable guide to an early name. It was also realized that -ing was added to personal names to refer to something associated with a single individual, though not necessarily owned by him, rather than with him and his followers.

The problem for the non-specialist researching place names is that some dictionaries and books about place names, and many of the English Place Name Society's county volumes, were written when the old theory was taken for granted. Some '-**ing**' names were not looked at too closely because it was taken for granted what they meant, and assumptions were sometimes made about the age of a settlement because it was accepted that these were very early names. Most books on place names published before 1970 will maintain that misconception. A general rule to follow in these earlier works on place names is that if there is an early spelling containing -*inga(s)* or -*inge(s)*, which are plural endings, then the name refers to a group of people. So **Woking** (*Wocchingas*) in Surrey and **Wokingham** (*Wokingeham*) in Berkshire belonged to the family or followers of *Wocca. **Hastings** (*Hastinges*; ESx) belonged to the family or followers of Haesta's folk, **Reading** (*Reddinges*) in Berkshire to *Reada's, **Aldingham** (*Aldingeham*) in Cumbria to Alda's, and **Godalming** (*Godelminge*) in Surrey to Godhelm's.

When added to topographical terms, these plural endings could mean 'the people who live at'. **Great Salling** (*Salinges*) in Essex belonged

to the people who lived by the sallow-trees and **Wellingham** (*Uuelingheham*; Nflk) to the people who lived by the spring. **Wetheringsett** (*Weddreringesete*; Sflk) was probably the *sett* (stable or sheepfold) belonging to the Wetherings – the people who live at Wetherden. **Surlingham** (*Sutherlingaham*) in Norfolk may be the home of the people living to the south (of Norwich), or may mean 'South Herelingaham', named after *Herela's folk. If early spellings are all with -*ing*, which is a singular ending, then the name refers to a single person. **Paddington** (*Padington*; GLon) was associated with a man named Padda, **Aldingbourne** (*Ealdingburnan*; WSx) with Ealda, and **Benington** (*Benigtune*) in Lincolnshire with Beonna.

The suffix -*ing* could also be added to words other than personal names, with the meaning 'having a certain quality or character'. Place names containing -*ing* used in this way include **Deeping** (Lincs), the deep, probably boggy, place; **Clavering** in Essex and **Docking** in Norfolk where clover and dock plants grew respectively; and **Ginge** and **Lockinge** (Oxon). The last two were the names of small streams, transferred to settlements on their banks. **Ginge** means a turning, twisting stream and **Lockinge** a 'playful' one.

As an added complication, -**ing** in the modern version of the name may not represent Old English -*ing*. Some nouns in Old English added endings with -n in the genitive case (see box on p. 32), and some of these later became -ing, probably because -**ing** was such a common and familiar place-name element. **Abingdon** (Oxon), for example, was once *Abbandune* – Aebbe's hill, **Workington** (*Wirkynton*) in Cumbria belonged to Weorc, and **Bovingdon** (*Bovyndon*; Herts) and **Bovington** (*Bovintone*) in Dorset to men called Bofa. Nouns that already ended in -n could also be changed to -ing; as with *fearn* (fern) in **Faringdon** (Oxon) and **Farington** (Lancs). The process could also work in reverse: **Benson** (*Baesingtun* – farm or estate associated with *Benesa) in Oxfordshire, **Benenden** (*Bingdene* – woodland pasture associated with Bionna) in Kent, and **Ilfracombe** (*Alferdingcome* – valley associated with Aelfred) are disguised '-*ing*' names.

The individual whose name appears in a place name is the person most closely connected with the place at the time it was named – the one who sprang to mind when it was referred to. The relationship between the place and the person varies. At one time it was assumed that the person was the founder of the settlement or the one who snatched it from the British, and this may be so in some cases. Often it was the person who owned the property or was in charge when the name was first written down, which could be many years after the settlement was founded.

A surprising number of the Anglo-Saxon and Scandinavian personal names in place names belonged to women. This need not necessarily mean that the women actually owned the properties. The man of the house might be away at the wars or have some official position which frequently took him away from home. In his absence his wife might manage the land, or she might simply be the one that people associated with it. But the number of women's names in place names encouraged studies of Anglo-Saxon wills, which revealed that women did own and manage land, independently of husbands and fathers. Women's property rights were eroded after the Norman Conquest, although women continued as active managers of farms and estates; it was late in the 19th century before they regained their rights. Incidentally, one misleading example of a place seemingly owned by women, **Womenswold** in Kent, probably belonged to the family or followers of a man called ★Wimel.

Some places are associated with famous or legendary people, although the connection may be no more than wishful thinking. **Oswestry** (Shrops) means 'Oswald's tree' (*treow*), and some claim that this is St. Oswald, the 7th-century king of Northumbria, and that 'tree' here refers to a wooden cross erected to mark the site of the battlefield where Oswald was slain by the heathen king Penda of Mercia. This is by no means certain, but it is a nice legend. It is not uncommon for churches dedicated to a saint to give their names to the village. Sometimes 'saint' does not appear in the name, but a personal name followed by **church** or **kirk** (*cirice*, Norse *kirkja*), or **stow(e)** (place, specifically a religious site) usually indicates a church dedicated to a saint. **Oswaldkirk** (NYorks) was dedicated to Oswald of Northumbria, **Bridekirk** (Cumb) and **Bridestowe** (Devon) to the Irish St. Bride or Brigid, and **Instow** in Devon (*Johannesto*) to St John the Baptist.

Sometimes there is a personal connection with a local saint, but it is not safe to assume it. **Berinsfield** (Oxon) is named after St. Birinus, an early missionary to the pagan Anglo-Saxons. He was certainly active in the area and became the first bishop of the see based on nearby Dorchester-on-Thames; he may well have walked on these fields. The name, however, is modern, invented by a 20th-century historian.

Byland Abbey stands on the land belonging to the woman Beage. The fact that many Anglo-Saxon women owned land is reflected in a number of place names. (SPECTRUM COLOUR LIBRARY)

The social system, after the initial period of settlement, was based on communities of peasant farmers, each with their own homestead and bits of land in the village fields. Farmers had prescribed duties of military service and financial support to the king in return for his justice and protection. No doubt many personal names in place names belonged to these peasant farmers. Names beginning with **Charl-**, **Carl-** or **Chorl-** often indicate land farmed by free peasants (*ceorl* – the ancestor of 'churl'). Names with the first element **King-**, **Coning-** or **Conis-** (*cyning*, Norse *konungr* 'king') denote royal manors or estates, probably large Roman or British estates taken over as a unit.

However, from quite early on in the Anglo-Saxon period there are charters recording a king's grant of land to an individual or to the church as a gift, a reward, or in return for military services or political support. Increasingly the peasant owed money and services to an overlord, rather than directly to the king, and the land might be given the overlord's name although he probably had nothing to do with it, at least on a day-to-day basis. **East Garston** (Berks) (*Esgareston*) was held by Esgar; he was a high-ranking servant at Edward the Confessor's court and probably too busy to do more to his estate than count the revenue. This situation foreshadowed the more formalized feudalism introduced by the Normans.

Sometimes land, or the income from it, was set aside for a particular office-holder or institution, indicated in names such as: **Preston**, **Prestwich** and **Preswick** from *preost* 'priest' and **Aldermaston** (Berks) from *ealdorman* 'chief officer of the shire'. Other examples are names beginning with **Bishop-** and some with **Bush-**, as in **Bispham** (Lancs), **Bisham** (Worcs), and **Biscathorpe** (Lincs) from *biscop* 'bishop' – the see, rather than the individual. **Athelney** (Som), **Aldingfleet** (Lancs) and **Allington** (Lincs) came from *aetheling* 'prince, nobleman' and **Chilton** from *cild* 'prince, young nobleman'. The word *hiwan* referred to the members of a household or a religious community. The communities of such places as **Hindon** (Wilts), **Hinstock** (Shrops), **Hainault** (Essex), and some places called **Hinton** may have farmed or managed the land themselves or just collected the rent.

After the Norman Conquest the name of the individual or institution holding the estate was often tacked on to the existing name (see pp.87–92).

Living off the land

Anglo-Saxon agricultural settlement

FIRST ARABLE FIELD
Grows OATS this year
Lies FALLOW next year
Grows BARLEY third year

Grove for grazing pigs

River

Track

MOOT PLACE

Ford

SECOND ARABLE FIELD
(Cut into strips)
Grows BARLEY this year
Grows OATS next year
Lies FALLOW third year

MEADOWS
Owned in strips like the arable fields

Track

THIRD ARABLE FIELD
Lies FALLOW this year
Grows BARLEY next year
Grows OATS third year

Brook

COMMON or WASTE
For grazing horses, cattle, sheep etc.

For clarity, the number of strips on each field is greatly reduced. Each man should have four times the number shown. This is just one of the ways Anglo-Saxon settlements were arranged.

Once the land was theirs, the Anglo-Saxons had two things in mind – to keep it, and for it to keep them. The land had to be farmed, and defended against invaders, wild beasts and the neighbours. Exploitation of the land is, of course, a continuing process; many farms and estates would already have been in existence, and there is archaeological evidence to suggest that some boundaries may date back to the Bronze Age. We know that the Anglo-Saxons evolved systems for land use that lasted beyond the Norman Conquest and continued to evolve until the Enclosures, which began in the late medieval period and gained momentum in the 16th and 17th centuries. Some place names containing Old English elements were not recorded until the 13th century or even later. Land use would also have been affected by local differences in geology, climate, and ethnic traditions. Because of this we have not tried to differentiate here between the Anglo-Saxon period and the later Middle Ages, and we have not specifically drawn attention to regional differences.

The usual picture of an Anglo-Saxon village is of three fields in which the crops were rotated, surrounded by common land and pasture, with the fallow land being grazed and manured by the livestock. However, in some places the same crop was grown on the same land over and over again, with half the land allowed to lie fallow in alternate years. In others, for example in Kent, the pasture land could lie well away from the village. **Tenterden** in Kent was the woodland pasture belonging to the men of Thanet, some 30 miles away. We can only sketch in the broad outlines of flora, fauna and their exploitation. Detailed research, especially into field names reveal a lot about local conditions.

Wildlife

Wildlife would have been plentiful in a land which was underpopulated by modern standards. A number of names refer to birds. **Foulness** (Essex), **Foulden** (Nflk), **Foulmere** and **Fulbourn** (Cambs) and **Fulmer** (Bucks) all contain *fugol* (fowl), at that time the usual term for any sort of bird. *Hana* (cock, wild bird) appears in **Hanwell** (GLon), **Hampole** (SYorks), **East & West Hanney** (Oxon), and **Great Hanwood** (Shrops), and *bridd* (bird, specifically a young bird) in **Birdbrook** (Essex) and **Birdham** (WSx). **Birdlip** (Glos) is probably 'steep place where birds are found', despite the more colourful derivation of 'bride's leap', often served up with a poignant legend to account for it. **Altam** (Lancs), **Eltham** (GLon), **Iltney** (Essex), **Elveden** (Sflk), **Elvet Hall** (Dur), and **Elvetham** (Hants) all contain *(i)elfetu* swan. **Elterwater** in Cumbria combines the Norse form *elptr* with Old English *waeter*, lake. **Swan** in place names can refer to the bird, but can also mean 'swineherd'. Owls (*ule*) were noticeable at **Ulcombe** (Kent), **Ulgham** (Nmbd) and **Ulley** (SYorks). Cuckoos (*geac*, Norse *gaukr*) were common at **Yagdon** (Shrops), **Yaxham** (Nflk), **Yaxley** (Cambs and Sflk) and **Goxhill** (Humb), and the presence of larks (*lawerce*) has given rise to **Laverstock** (Wilts), **Laverstoke** (Hants), and **Laverton** (Glos and Som).

Some creatures were useful: ducks (*ened*) were found at **Enmore** (Som), **Anmer** (Nflk) and **Enford** (Wilts) and at **Dukinfield** (GMan) (from *ducena*, genitive plural of *duce*, duck). Geese were found at **Gosford** and **Gosforth**, **Gosbrook** (Staffs), **Gostrode** (Surrey), and **Goosey** (Oxon). **Goostrey** (Ches), however, means 'gorse tree'. Snipe (*snite*) were present at **Snitterfield** (Warks) and **Snydale** (WYorks). No doubt many ended up in the pot, particularly around **Fullerton** (Hants), the home of the fowlers or bird-catchers.

The crane is no longer found in Great Britain but was once very common. The Old English words for it, *cran* and *corn*, form the first elements of many place names such as the various **Cranford**s, **Cranbrook**s and **Cranbourne**s, **Carnforth** (Lancs), **Coreley** (Shrops), **Corley** (Warks) and **Conksbury** (Derbs). Place-name experts are undecided as to whether *cran* could also refer to the heron. Whether we are dealing with one species or two, the *cran* names are probably the most common 'wildlife' names, which suggests that these birds were not only widespread but important in some way. We know that cranes and herons were hunted for food and sport, and the presence of herons might have indicated another important food source, fish and eels.

Fish (*fisc*) are obvious in names such as **Fishbourne**, **Fishburn** and **Fishlake**. Fishermen lived at **Fisherwick** (Staffs) and **Fiskerton** (Lincs and Notts). Pike (*pic*) were caught at **Pickmere** (Ches) and **Pickburn** (WYorks), and eels (*ael*) at various **Elton**s and at **Ely** (Cambs) (eel district), where the catch was measured in tons and formed an important part of the revenue of the cathedral until late medieval times.

Crayfish were found at **Crabwall** (Ches). **Cowpen Bewley** in Cleveland has nothing to do with cows; it comes from *cupum*, the dative plural form of *cupe*, a basket or wickerwork trap for catching fish. 'Bewley' was added when it belonged to the manor of Bewley. In some places weirs and dams were built to improve the catch; **Ware** (Herts), **Wareham** (Dors), **Warfield** and **Wargrave** (Berks), and **Warham** (Nflk) contain one Old English word, *were* or *waer*. **Yarpole** (H&W), **Yarwell** (Northants)

Wild or tame – how do you tell?

In medieval times man exploited wild animals by hunting and trapping, and some creatures, like bees and deer, became domesticated to some extent. Both wildcats and household moggies were found, and horses existed as wild, tamed, and completely domestic animals. How do you tell? As usual with place names, there is no definitive answer, but we can have a good guess – in this case by looking at the accompanying element. One denoting some kind of farm or enclosure is probably where the beasts were raised. On the other hand a hill, stream, wood or marsh name is more likely to mean where they were found. This of course still leaves you with *leah*, where a clearing could be natural or man-made, or *hamm*, where a natural enclosure might have been made more secure to keep livestock.

and **Yarm** (Cleveland) contain another Old English word, *gear*. Off the coast there were mussel beds at **Musselburgh** (Lothian) and oyster beds at **Oystermouth** (WGlam).

Creatures other than birds and fish had uses: beavers (*beofor*) at **Beverley** (Humb), **Bewerley** (NYorks), and **Bevercotes** (beaver lodges) (Notts) were almost certainly caught for their fur, as were the otters (*oter*) found at **Otterbourne** or **Otterburn**, at **Otterham** on the River **Ottery** in Cornwall, and at **Ottershaw** in Surrey. Badgers (*bagga*) were found at **Bagley** (Shrops) (still present in **Bagley Wood** in Oxfordshire), **Bagshot** (Sur), and at **Brockhall** (Northants; *brocc-hol* badger hole, sett), **Brockley** (Avon and GLon) and **Broxbourne** (Herts). **Bawdrip** (*Bagetrep*) in Somerset means badger trap. The hares (*hara*) at **Harnham** (Wilts), and probably also at **Harley** (Shrops), **Harnhill** (Glos) and **Harewood** (WYorks) would have provided both meat and skins, as would the wild boar (*eofor*) found at various places beginning with **Ever-**. **Wookey** (Som) is from *wociga* meaning noose or snare, although there is no mention of the quarry here or at **Snargate** (gate or gap where snares were laid) in Kent.

Wild bees (*beo*) were found at **Beoley**

Wild or tame – who's right?

The Oxford English Dictionary says that 'cock' and 'hen' first referred to domestic fowl, and that the use of these words to refer to wild birds did not arise until the Middle English period. But most place-name experts insist that these words in names such as **Cockfield** (Sflk) and **Henlow** (Beds) referred to wild birds. So who's right? A lot of research into place names has been done since the first edition of *The Oxford English Dictionary* was compiled, and evidence is available now that its editors did not have. The second edition, published in 1989, did not revise the early meanings of words. We shall have to wait for the third edition, some time in the next century, to find out.

(H&W), **Beeleigh** (Essex) and **Beeford** (Humb) and bumblebees (*dora*) at **Dorney** (Bucks). Bees' nests (*bic*) helped name **Bickleigh** and **Bickley**, and swarms (*imbe*) helped name **Empshott** (Hants). Honey (*hunig*) could be gathered at **Honeybourne** (H&W) and **Honiley** (Warks). In time bees became domesticated and from about the 10th century onward honey was an important export. **Beeby** (Leics) was 'the bee farm', **Honington** (Warks) and **Hunnington** (Worcs) were farms where honey was produced. Beekeepers (*bicere*) lived at various **Bickerton**s and at **Bickerstaffe** (Lancs). Wax (*weax*) was a useful by-product, collected in the valley at **Wexcombe** (Wilts), produced at **Wexham** (Berks) and **Waxholme** (Humb).

Deer were also widespread. They were hunted and may also have been 'farmed' to a certain extent. **Buckden** (NYorks) and **Buckfast** (Devon) contain *bucc* (buck, stag). **Hart** (Clev), **Hertford** and many names beginning with **Hart-** come from *heorot* (hart), and **Hindhead** (Surrey), **Hindley** (GMan) and **Hendon** (GLon) from hind. *Deor* often refers to deer, although it was also a blanket term for any wild beast. It appears in **Deerhurst** (Glos), **Dordon** (Warks), **Durleigh** (Som), **Durley** (Hants) and **Dyrham** (Avon). **Derby**, **Darton** (SYorks), **Dearham** (Cumb), and **Dereham** (Nflk) all have names suggesting 'farm where deer are kept', although they may just have been seen nearby.

Some animals and birds were less welcome. Minor nuisances included ants at **Ampthill** (Beds) and snails at **Snailham** (WSx) and **Snailwell** (Cambs). Various places beginning with **Cat-**, as well as **Castlett** (Glos), may refer to wildcats, which were much more widespread in those days. They could also refer to feral cats, who could have been a nuisance but at least kept down the mice which infested **Mowsley** (Leics), **Moseley** (Worcs), **Muscoates** (NYorks), **Muscott** (Northants), and **North & South Muskham** (Notts).

There were martens or weasels (*mearth*) at **Maresfield** (Leics), snakes at **Wormley** (Herts), **Wormsley** (H&W) and **Wormwood Scrubs** (GLon), and adders (*naeddre*) at **Netherfield** (ESx). Ravens (*hraefn*) were found at **Rainow** (Ches), **Great & Little Raveley** (Cambs) and many places beginning with **Raven-**, and rooks (*hroc*) nested at **Rockley** (Wilts), **Rookley** (IoW), **Ruckinge** (Kent) and **Ruckland** (Lincs). Crows (*crawe*) were sighted at many places beginning with **Crow-** or **Craw-**, at **Cromer** (Nflk) and **Cranoe** (Leics). Eagles (*earn*) at **Eridge** (ESx), **Earnley** (WSx), and **Yarnfield** (Staffs and Wilts), and buzzards (*wroc*) at various **Wraxall**s and at **Wroxall** (IoW) could all pose a threat to crops or livestock. **Fox-** in place names usually means what it says. **Barbon** in Cumbria, **Barmer** in Norfolk and some instances of **Barford** were the stream, lake and fords respectively of the bear (*bere*), and **Lostford** (Shrops) was the ford

of the lynx (*lox*). Wolves (*wulf*, Norse *ulfr*) were a problem at **Woodale** (NYorks), various places called **Woolley**, at **Ullock** and **Ulpha** in Cumbria and **Wolborough**, Devon. You would have been slightly safer at **Woolpit** (Sflk) ('wolf pit', where they were trapped) and in Warwickshire where they seem to have been better prepared: **Great & Little Wolford** (*Wolwarde*) and **Wolvey** (with the second element from *hecge* 'hedge') mean 'place protected from wolves'.

Fields and farms

With all the dangers from wild animals, not counting marauders, it is hardly surprising that so many Anglo-Saxon names refer to an enclosed piece of ground. The common elements **-ton**, **borough** and **-stead** or **-sted** had this meaning, among others (see box on p. 42). Hamm (see p. 38) usually means land enclosed in some way.

Other elements in place names that refer to enclosed land are:

camp, a word borrowed from Latin *campus* 'field' meaning an enclosed piece of land. The land was originally one of the open fields surrounding a Romano-British settlement. A reference is found in **Castle & Shudy Camps** (Cambs; 'Shudy' probably means a shed or hovel), **Campsey Ash** (Sflk), **Broad & Chipping Camden** (Glos), and also in field names such as **camp** or **comp**. It sometimes appears as **-combe**, when it can be confused with **-combe** from Old English *cumb*, 'valley'. Sometimes the position of the place will tell you which it is, but there is no reason why a **camp** shouldn't be in a valley, and in this case you need an early spelling with *camp* or *comp*, as in **Barcombe** (ESx; *berecampe* 'barley field'), **Ruscombe** (Berks; *Rothescamp* – belonging to Rot) and **Addiscombe** (GLon; *Addescompe* – Aeddi's camp).

croft, a small enclosed (arable) field is seen in **Croft** (Lincs and NYorks) (for **Croft**, Leicestershire see p. 58), and some **Crofton**s. It is also referred to in field and street names, often with a crop: **Bancroft** (beans) and **Peachcroft** (which in early names refers to peas rather than peaches).

edisc, an enclosed pasture or field, in some

dialects also meaning stubble field. It is referred to in **Edgefield**, **Brockdish** (*Brochedisc* 'pasture by the brook'), **Thornage** (*Tornedis* 'enclosed field with a thorn tree') all in Norfolk, **Standish** (GMan; stoney pasture), and in field names, usually as **Eddish**.

geard, an enclosed patch, yard appears in **Bromyard** (H&W; *brom* 'broom') and **Yorton** (Shrops).

haecc, a hatchway, gate, is revealed in **Heckfield** (Hants), **Great Heck** (NYorks), various places called **Hatch**, **Hatch End** (GLon), **Brands Hatch** (Kent), and in field names, usually as **Hatch**, **Hatchgate**, **Hatchet** or **Hacket**.

(ge)haeg, an enclosed land, fence referred to in **Haynes** (Beds), **Haywards Heath** (WSx), various **Haywood**s, **Harpurhey** (GMan; *Harpour's*), **East Woodhay** (Hants), and **West Woodhay** (Berks).

haga (Norse *hagi*), an enclosed land, hedge found in **Haigh** (GMan and SYorks), **Haworth** (WYorks), **Thornhaugh** (Cambs), and **Wellow** (*Welhag*; Notts).

hecge, a hedge revealed in **Heacham** (Nflk), **Hesset** (Sflk), **Wolvey** (Warks) (see above).

loca, a fold or pen referred to in **Challock Lees** (Kent; *cealfa locum* 'enclosures for calves'), **Porlock** (Som; *Portloca* 'enclosure by the harbour'), and some names beginning **Lock-**.

pen(n), an enclosure for animals found in **Pencombe** (H&W), **Ipplepen** (Devon) (**Ipela's*), **Owlpen** (Glos; *Olla's*), and **Great & Little Pan** (IoW). However, beware, most 'pen' names are from the Celtic *penn* 'hill'.

(ge)set, a stable or pen for animals, but can also mean 'dwelling'. It is referred to in

Letheringsett (Leodhere's folk) and **Stradsett** (on a Roman road; Nflk), and **Wintersett** (used in winter; NYorks).

worth, worthig(n), an enclosed land or settlement seen in **Worthen** (Shrops), **Worthing** (Nflk) (**Worthing** in West Sussex is from an Anglo-Saxon personal name), and many names ending in -**worth**, -**worthy** or -**wardine**.

Outside the enclosed areas were open fields and woodlands. The Anglo-Saxons would not be at all impressed by what we think of as a field. To them, *feld* usually meant a sizeable stretch of open country without trees, marsh or other obstructions. The sense of 'field' as we know it developed in the late Old English period, applied to the large common fields in which each villager owned a share. **Heathfield** means a heath or open land where heather grows, as do **Hatfield** and **Hadfield**. **Sheffield** (SYorks) was the open land beside the river **Sheaf** (the river name comes from Old English *sceath*

meaning a boundary – the Sheaf once formed a part of the boundary between Mercia and Northumbria). **Sheffield** (ESx), on the other hand, was the open land where sheep grazed. **Wakefield** (WYorks) was where 'wakes' or festivities took place. A wake was a period where no one got much sleep, either because of a festival or a vigil; hence the wake which accompanied a funeral, and the 'Wakes Weeks' when a factory or a whole town took its annual holiday. *Feld* can occasionally appear as -**vil(le)**; **Enville** (Staffs) was 'even' – smooth and level – and **Clanville** (Hants) and the various **Clanfield**s were 'clean' – free from weeds. **Leafield** is first recorded in the 13th century as *La Felde*, with the French for 'the' before Old English *feld*. The district of **The Fylde** (Lancs) comes from a closely related Old English word *filde*, meaning 'plain'.

Aecer (Norse *akr*) meant a plot of cultivated land, and seems to have referred to land which was next to rough pasture or marshland; possibly land which had only recently been brought into use. The element is also common in field names, and here it is usually closer to its modern meaning as a measure of land; originally the area that a team of oxen could plough in a day. It appears in **Alsager** (Ches; Aelle's), **Bicknacre** (Essex; Bicca's), **Benacre** (Sflk; where beans were grown), **Cliviger** (Lancs; by the cliff), and the unfortunate **Weddiker** (Cumb; 'weedy' *aecer*). **Halnaker** (WSx) is from *healf aecer* 'half acre', and field and street names such as **Broad-** or **Bradacre** and **Longacre** describe the shape of the plot.

Brec or *braec* meant land newly 'broken' for cultivation. It appears in the Norfolk settlements of **Breckles** and **Great Bircham**, **Bircham Newton** and **Bircham Tofts** (**Tofts** is Norse *toft* 'homestead'). It also appears in some instances of **Bratton**. The best-known example is the **Brecklands**, also in Norfolk. This is a 19th-century name, from the dialect word 'breck' meaning a patch of cultivated land or, in a broader sense, a patch of land which stood out in some way from its surroundings. *Br(a)ec* is also fairly common in field names, appearing as **breach**, **breech**, **break**, **brake** (which can be confused with 'brake' meaning thicket) or **breck** (which can also come from Norse *brekkr* 'slope').

Land (in Old English and Norse) had several meanings, as it has today, and stayed in use as a place name element long after the Anglo-Saxon period. It meant 'district' in names like

---

Hundreds, wapentakes and things

A student of place names in England would not get far before running into *hundreds* and *wapentakes*. A *hundred* was an Anglo-Saxon unit of local government consisting of approximately a hundred 'hides', and a hide was the amount of land needed to support one free family and its dependants, or as much as could be ploughed by one plough team in one year – notionally about 120 acres. **Hyde Park** was one hide; **Piddletrenthide** (Dors) was an estate on the River Piddle consisting of 30 (French *trent*) hides. The equivalent of a *hundred* in some areas with a large Scandinavian population was called a *wapentake* (Old English *waepentaec*, from Norse *wapnatak*, the act of taking up a weapon, perhaps referring to the brandishing of weapons to show acceptance of a decision).

The householders got together every so often for a '*moot*' – a meeting to sort out matters of local interest. The words *maethel* and *mot* both mean 'meeting', *spel* refers to speech; they appear in names such as **Matlock** (Derbs), **Matlask** (Nflk), **Modbury** (Devon), **Motcombe** (Dors), **Mottistone** (IoW) and **Spellow** (Lancs). The meetings often took place at a local landmark or boundary marker, such as the *hlaw* in Spellow, the stone at Mottistone, or trees such as the oak in Matlock and the ash in Matlask. A 'landmark' element such as -*stan* or -*stone* (stone), -*tree* or a kind of tree, following a personal name, often denotes a meeting place, as in **Coventry** (WMid; Cofa's tree) and **Lillingstone** (Bucks; boundary stone of *Lytel's folk).

A *thing* in Old English was a public meeting or a court of justice. The word is found in such names as **Thinghill** (H&W), **Finedon** (Northants), **Fingest** (Bucks) and **Tingrith** (Beds), all with topographical elements. Norse *thing* meant a public assembly or parliament and usually appears as *thingvollr* – assembly field – as in **Dingwall** (High), **Thingwall** (Ches and Lancs) and **Tynwald Hill** (IoM) – still the site of the annual Manx parliament.

Old English *run* meant a secret discussion or council. One of the most famous of all meeting places is the 'council island meadow' – *run ey maed*, Runnymede – where King John signed the Magna Carta.

---

the **Brecklands**, **Cumberland** (see p.43), **Northumberland** (see p. 44), **Cleveland** (district of 'cliffs' in the sense of hills). It sometimes simply meant a piece of land; in field names often a strip in the common field. It can refer to an estate, and this is probably the case in names like **Buckland** (land granted by royal charter), **Copeland** (Cumb) and **Coupland** (Nmbd) (from Norse *kaupland* 'bought land'), **Sunderland** (*sundor-land* – land which has been 'put asunder' or detached from the ori-ginal estate), and **Threapland** (Cumb) ('disputed land' – the estate was close to the parish boundary). However, in many places land seems to have meant specifically 'newly cultivated land'. It is more likely to have the latter meaning when the topography, or the surrounding names, suggest heath, moors, marsh, or woods, and of course in the various places called **Newland** or **Newlands**.

Leah originally meant a forest, then a piece of lightly wooded country or a forest clearing, whether natural or man-made. In late Old English it developed the meaning meadow or pasture. It is a very common element in settlement names and in field names; perhaps the most common after *tun*. It can appear alone, as **Lea**, **Lee** or **Leigh** or, very rarely, as a first element; **Lyhan** (Nmbd) is one example. As a final element it appears as **-ley**, **-leigh**, **-le**, or **-low**, combined with personal names, animals, plants, or topographical elements; in short, with almost anything you can think of. The interpretation of *leah* in any individual name is often a combination of common sense and guesswork, using evidence from its location, the first element, and the date of the name. In a case like **Thundersley** (Essex), where the first element is the name of the pagan god Thunor, it may mean a sacred grove. Associated with tree names, such as **Oakleigh** or **Haseley**, the element probably means 'wood'; with the names of wild animals 'clearing', with domesticated animals 'meadow' and with crops 'field'. With a name like **Stanley** (stony *leah*), or with a personal name, it could have any one of its range of meanings. Where the main interest is in the first element *leah* is sometimes not translated in place-name books.

Another 'clearing' element which should be mentioned is *rod*; not because it is particularly common but because it gives rise to names which are easily confused with modern English 'road' and Old English *rod*, *rood* 'cross'. It appears in **Rode** (Som) and **Roade** (Northants), **Rodd** (Herts), **Roddam** (Nmbd), various

Padstow Harbour. The word 'stow' simply means 'a place' but was often used for a religious site. Padstow comes from 'St Petroc's stow', an unusual combination of a Cornish saint with an Anglo-Saxon ending. (FRED MCDONALD)

Metathesis – why Birmingham is full of Brummies

Metathesis is a term used for something which often happens in language: two sounds or two letters in a word, or two words in a sentence, change places. There are many English words where r and a vowel have changed places at some stage in the word's history, for example third comes from Old English *thridda*.

Birmingham is first recorded in the Domesday Book as *Bermingeham*, the village of *Beorma's or Beornmund's folk. In later documents it appears as *Bremingeham*, *Burmingeham* and *Brimingeham* and various other combinations of r + vowel or vowel + r. The semi-humorous modern spelling Brummagem reflects the local pronunciation, and the official name might well have turned out very similar if it had been left alone. However, it seems that the local aristocracy thought the popular version rather vulgar (especially because 'Brummagem' was a slang term for a counterfeit coin) and 'corrected' the name to Birmingham. A native of the city will write his address as Birmingham, and may even speak of Birmingham, but using, of course, a 'brummy' accent.

Rodes, and **Ormerod** and **Huntroyde** (Lancs). It is also found as **Rode**, **Rood** or **Royd** in field names.

Other elements in place names that refer to pasture land are:

laes, found in **Leasowe** (Ches), **Lissett** (Humb) and **Beccles** (Sflk). It is also found in field names as **Lease**, **Leaze**, **Leaser** or **Leasure** and it is often very difficult to separate from names coming from *leah*.

maed, a modern 'mead, meadow' referred to in **Medbourne** (Leics), **Metfield** and **Shipmeadow** (Sflk; for sheep), **Madehurst** (WSx), and **Bushmead** (Beds). It is also in field names.

denn, a woodland pasture, usually for pigs, although **Horsmonden** is associated with horses and **Cowden** with cows. **Smarden** contains *smearu* 'fat, grease, butter' and may refer to a dairy farm or to rich and productive land. All the previous examples are in Kent, where the element is very common. It also appears in East Sussex and a few minor names in Surrey, but not elsewhere. It appears as -**den** and so could be confused with names from *denu*, valley, but fortunately *denu* usually takes the form -**dean** in this region.

These enclosures, fields, and clearings provided the Anglo-Saxons with their needs and livelihoods. History books in general do not tell us much about what they produced, but the place names are a ready source of information. They grew cereals such as wheat (*hwaete*) referred to in many places called **Wheatley** or **Whaddon** (usually containing *dun* 'hill', occasionally *denu* 'valley'), in **Wheatacre** (Nflk),

and **Wheddon** (Som). Oats (**haefera*, Norse *hafri*) were cultivated at **Haverhill** (Sflk), **Haverigg** (Cumb), **Market Harborough** (Leics), and rye (*ryge*, Norse *rugr*) in **Ryal** (Nmbd), **Ryarsh** (Kent), **Rydal** (Cumb), **Reydon** (Sflk), **Royton** (GMan) and **Roydon** (Nflk).

Barley (*baer*, *bere*, Norse *barr* or *bygg*), from which they made ale as well as bread, is referred to in **Barleyhill** and **Barhaugh** (Nmbd), various places called **Barford** and **Barforth**. The names **Barton** and **Berwick** mean 'barley farm', but often came to mean an outlying farm or settlement dependent on the main farm. Pulses were a good source of protein which could be dried and stored for the winter. Beans (*bean*, Norse *baun*) were found in **Benacre** and **Benhall** (Sflk), **Bandon**, **Banstead** and **Benhilton** (Sur), and various **Binste(a)d**s. Peas (*peose*) were cultivated at **Peasemore** (Berks), **Peasenhall** (Sflk), **Pishill** and **Pusey** (Oxon), and **Pishiobury** (Herts). Vegetables were also grown; the general Old English word for vegetable was *wyrt*, which appears in **Wortley** (SYorks) and **Worton** (Wilts and GLon). The latter, a small settlement near Isleworth, survives only in street names.

Leac specifically meant leek or garlic, but may also have had the general meaning of potherb. It appears in **Lackford** (Som), **Leckhampstead** (Berks and Bucks), **Letton** (H&W) and various town and field names **Laughton**, **Latton**, **Layton**, and **Lawton**. **Laughterton** (Lincs) and **Leighterton** (Glos) contain *leahtric* 'lettice'. Celery (*merece*) grew at **Marcham** (Oxon) and **Marchington** (Staffs), and watercress (*caerse*) was gathered at various **Cresswell**s and **Carswell**s, **Craswall** (H&W), **Carshalton** (GLon), **Carsington** (Derbs), **Kerswell** (Devon), **Kearsley** (GMan) and **Kesgrave** (Sflk).

We also know, however, that crops were grown that are not recorded in place names. Pollen samples from excavations in the Thames valley show that coriander and other herbs were grown in Roman times and perhaps even earlier, but herb names appear in only a few place names. Dill (*dile*) at **Dilham** (Nflk), **Dillicar** (Cumb) and **Dulwich** (GLon), and rue (*rude*) at **Rudyard** (Staffs) are among them. This could mean, of course, that herbs which were not native to northern Europe were allowed to die out by Anglo-Saxons who did not recognize their value, yet we know that some were grown in the herb gardens of monasteries. It seems more likely that individual species were lumped in with *wyrt* (vegetable) and *leac* (leek or garlic). Another group conspicuous by its absence is the root crops. The Anglo-Saxons grew two kinds; beet (*bete*) and turnip (*naep*, the source of Scots and dialect 'neep', now usually applied to the swede). Neither appears in settlement names; perhaps they too were simply *wyrt*s, or perhaps a study of local field names may reveal them.

Many place names contain the names of individual species of trees. Usually such names are quite straightforward and translate as the valley, farm, field, etc. where that sort of tree grows, or the tree belonging to a particular person. But referring to a particular tree in a name can suggest that it was significant in some way, probably because the fruit or timber was valuable, or because it was used as a landmark or meeting place (see box on p. 52).

The most common place-name elements that refer to species of trees are:

alder (*alor*, Norse *elrir*), found in **Albourne** (WSx), **Aldridge** (WMid), **Aller** (Som), **Alrewas** (Staffs), **Awre** (Glos), **Ellerton** (Humb), **Ollerton** (Ches and Notts), and **Orleton** (H&W).

apple (*aeppel, apuldor*, Norse *epli, apadr*), referred to in **Apperley** (Glos), **Apperknowle** (Derbs), **Appley** (Glos), **Apuldram** (WSx), **Applegarth** (Dumfries and NYorks). In the latter's case there is a reference to the Middle English *garth* or Norse *garthr* 'orchard'.

ash (*aesc*, Norse *askr*), seen in **Ashurst** (Kent and WSx), **Esh** (Dur), **Esher** (Sur), **Askwith** and **Askrigg** (NYorks), **Monyash** (Derbs), and various places called **Nash** (Middle English *atten aesc* 'at the ash').

aspen (*aespe*), referred to in **Aspenden** (Herts), **Aspley End** (Beds), **Aspull** (GMan).

beech (*bece, boc*, Norse *bok*), referred to in **Buckhurst Hill** (Essex), possibly **Boxted** (Sflk) and **Buxted** (ESx), although these may refer to box trees.

birch (*beorc, birce*, Norse *bjork*), found in **Bartley** (Hants), **Bartlow** (Cambs), **Berkeley** (Glos), **Little Berkhamsted** (Herts), **Berkley** (Som). (**Great Berkhamsted** is from Old English *beorg* 'hill'.)

box (*box*, plural *byxen*), referred to in **Bexhill** (ESx), **Bexington** (Dors), and **Bix** (Oxon).

elder (*ellern, ellen*, Norse *eldre*), found in **Elstead** (Sur) and **Elsted** (WSx).

elm (*elm*) referred to in **Elmdon** (Essex), **Elmbridge** (H&W) and **Elm** (Cambs).

hawthorn (*hagu-thorn* – the 'g' was pronounced as something like a modern 'w'). It is referred to in **Hatherleigh** (Devon), **Hathern** (Leics).

hazel (*haesel*, Norse *hasl*), revealed in **Hasfield** (Glos), **Haselor** (Warks), **Haselmere** (Sur), and **Haslington** (Ches).

lime (*lind*, Norse *lindr*), referred to in **Lindale** (Cumb) and **Linwood** (Hants, Lincs).

maple (**mapel, mapuldor*), found in **Mapperley** (Derbs), **Mapperton** (Dorset), **Mappleton** (Humb) and **Mappowder** (Dorset).

oak (*ac*, Norse *eik*), referred to in **Acklam** (Clev, WYorks), **Acle** (Nflk), **Acol** (Kent), **Acomb** (NYorks), most **Acton**s and **Aughton**s, **Eyke** (Sflk), **Aikton** (Cumb), **Noke** (Oxon) and **Rock** (H&W). (Middle English *atten, atter oke* 'at the oak'.)

pear (*peru, pirige, pyrige*), referred to in **Great Parndon** (Essex), **Parbold** (Lancs), **Perry Barr** (WMid), **Pirbright** (Sur), **Pirton** (H&W, Herts), **Pyrford** (Sur), **Waterperry** and **Woodperry** (Oxon).

plum (*plume*, Norse *ploma*), found in **Plumbland** (Cumbria), **Plumpton** (Cumbria, ESx, Lancs), **Plungar** (Leics), **Plympton** and **Plymtree** (Devon).

sallow (*sealh, salh*, Norse *selja*), referred to in some instances of **Salford** (others are fords on salt roads), **Great & Little Salkeld** (Cumbria), **Salle** (Nflk), **Salton** (NYorks), **Selborne** (Hants), probably **Sellafield** (Cumb), **Selwood** (Som), **South Zeal**, **Zeal Monachorum** (Devon), and **Zeals** (Wilts).

thorn (*thorn, thyrne*, Norse *thyrnir*), found in **Thorley** (Herts, IoW), **Thorington** (Sflk), **Thornage** (Nflk), **Copthorne** (WSx), **Thirn** and **Thrintoft** (NYorks), and **Thurnscoe** (SYorks).

willow (*welig, withig*), referred to in **Welford** (Berks), **Welhamgreen** (Herts), **Wellow** (IoW), probably **Widecombe in the Moor** (Devon), **Widdington** (Essex), **Widford** (Essex and Herts), **Willen** (Bucks), **Willington** (Beds), and some instances of **Willey** and **Wilton**.

Pasture for the beasts was vitally important. Grass (*gaers*, Norse *gres*) is referred to at **Garsdale** (Cumb), **Garsdon** (Wilts), **Greasbrough** (SYorks), **Gresham** (Nflk) and around **Grasmere** in the Lake District. (**Garsington** in Oxfordshire and **Grassendale** in Merseyside were 'grassy'.) Clover (*claefre*) was found at various places beginning with **Claver-** or **Clare-**

and at **Clarborough** (Notts); and hay (*heg, hieg*) at many places with the first element **Hay-** or **Hey-** and at **Clayhidon** (Devon; *hieg dun*, with 'clay' added later).

The animals reared in those far-off times were much the same as those that are kept today; different varieties, smaller, hardier, and probably more scruffy, but familiar. Pigs (*swin*, Norse *svin*) were important for leather and meat and were found at **Swindon** (Wilts), **Swinton** (Mayo) and at many other places beginning with **Swin-**, at **Swilland** (Sflk), **Swingfield Minnis** (Kent) ('Minnis' is from the Old English *maennes* 'common land'), and **Somborne** (Hants). Usually these would graze on common land or in the woods, watched over by the swineherd (*swan*, the ancestor of 'swain', originally meaning a young male servant but later developing the sense 'herdsman'). The word is an element in **Swanley** and **Swanscombe** (Kent), and various **Swanton**s. *Hlose*, meaning pig sty, appears in **Loose** (Kent), **Loosley Row** (Bucks), and possibly in **Loseley** (Surrey) and **Lostock** (GMan and Ches). Acorns (*aecern*), presumably winter food for the pigs, were stored at **Accrington** (Lancs).

Cattle were raised for meat, leather, milk and cheese, and as draught animals. **Ox-** in place names usually refers to oxen (*oxa*, Norse *oxi*). Another Old English word for an ox or for cattle, *hryther*, appears in **Rotherfield** (ESx and Oxon) and **Rotherwick** (Hants); the word 'rother' still exists in some dialects. Cows (*cu*) are referred to at **Cowarne** (H&W), **Cowden** (Kent), **Stow cum Quy** (Cambs; in the Domesday Book 'Quy' is *Coeia*, from *cu eg* 'cow island'), and in some instances of **Cowley** (although Cufa's *leah* is a more common derivation).

The genitive singular form *cy* 'of a cow' appears in **Keele** (Staffs), **Keyhaven** (Hants) and **Kyloe** (Nmbd). Bulls (*bula*) are referred to in **Boulmer** (Nmbd) and **Bulmer** (Essex and NYorks), in **Bulley** (Glos), and in the street names **Bull Green** (Halifax) and **Bollo** ('bull hollow') **Lane** in Acton, Greater London. In street names 'bull' may refer to bull baiting rather than to where the village bull was kept. Calves (*cealf*, Norse *kalfr*) were raised at **Chaldon** (Surrey), **Chawleigh** (Devon), **Calverton** (Bucks and Notts), **Callerton** (Nmbd), **Kilpin** (Humb) and **Kelloe** (Durham). The element **-wic** often refers to a dairy farm in names such as **Butterwick**, **Cheswick** (Nmbd; *cese* or *ciese*

'cheese'), **Chiswick** (GLon) and **Keswick** (Cumb).

Goats (*gat*, Norse *geit*) were also kept, providing milk, meat, leather and hair for weaving into cloth, and have some connection with **Gatcombe** (IoW), **Gateforth** (NYorks), **Gastard** (Wilts), **Gayton** (Mersey and Nflk), **Gatwick** (WSx) (where 'jumbos' are now more common) and **Gotham** (Notts). The Old English words for ram were *ram(m)* or *bucca*, and probably occur in some names beginning with **Ram-** or **Buck-**, but in each case other meanings or personal names are also likely. Kids (*ticce*) were raised at **Ticehurst** (ESx), **Tisted** (Hants), **Tixover** (Leics) and around **Tixall Wide** (Staffs).

Various words for horse are common in place names. We cannot always say for certain whether these were domestic horses or wild ponies, as there was no separate word for pony in Old and Middle English. *Hross* (the same in Norse) or *hors* was a general word for horse; it came to be used specifically for a stallion in Middle English. It appears in various names beginning **Hors-**, in **Rosley** and **Rosgill** (Cumb; with Norse *gill* 'ravine'), in **Rossall** (Shetland), **Roishnish** (WIs) and **Rosedale Abbey** (NYorks).

The word for a stallion was *hengest* (Norse *hestr*) and is found in **Henstridge** (Som), **Hinksey** (Oxon), **Hinxhill** (Kent) and **Hestaval** (WIs). *Horsa* and *Hengest* were both used as personal names. According to legend the first Saxon arrivals employed by Vortigern were not led by 'a Man called Horse' but by two. The word for foal (*fola*) forms the basis of **Follifoot** (NYorks), **Foulridge** (Lancs) and **Fowberry** (Nmbd). *Stod*, a stud or a herd of horses, is found in various places beginning **Stod-** or **Stud-**, and in **Stadhampton** (Oxon), **Stoodley** (Kent), and **Stotfold** (Beds; the horses' fold or pen). In **Stottesdon** (Shrops) the basis may be *stod* or, as it is in the street name **Stott Hill** in Bradford, *stot*, meaning a draught animal, either a horse or an ox. Horsemen or grooms appear in **Horsington** (Som) and perhaps in **Horsmonden** (Kent).

Sheep (*sceap*, *scep* or *scip*) provided meat, milk, and wool, by far the most important cash crop. It is hardly surprising that names referring to them are so widespread, such as many names beginning with **Sheep-**, **Shep-**, or **Ship-**, **Shefford** (Beds and Berks), and **Skipton** and **Skipwith** (NYorks). Lambs were grazed on **Lammermuir** in the Borders, at **Lamesley**

(T&W), various **Lambley**s, **Lambrigg** (lamb ridge; Cumbria), and **Lamberhurst** (lambs' wooded hill; Kent). Wethers were grazed at **Wetherall** (Cumb), **Wetherby** (WYorks), **Wetherden**, **Withersdale Street** and **Withersfield** (Sflk). Sheep were probably dipped at **Sheepwash** (Devon) and at various **Lambourn(e)**s, and there were shelters for them at **Sapcot** (Leics; with *cott* 'cottage or shelter') and at **Austerfield** (SYorks), **Good & High Easter** (Essex), **Osterley** (GLon) and **Osborne** (IoW; from *eowestre* 'sheepfold').

At the beginning of the Anglo-Saxon period the smallholdings, villages and estates would have been able to grow, raise or gather much of what they needed. Building and craft materials were just as important as food. Timber (the same word in Old English) appears in **Timberland** (Lincs), **Timberscombe** (NYorks), **Timperley** (GMan) and **Timsbury** (Avon; *timber bearu*). **Timsbury** (Hants) is from *timber burh*, a fortified building made of timber. Boards (*bred*) are referred to in **Bredhurst** (Kent) and **Bradley in the Moors** (Staffs; most **Bradley**s are 'broad *leahs*'), **Bradbury** (Nmbd), **Bredenbury** (H&W) and **Burdale** (NYorks; *Bredhalle* 'board hall').

Bampton usually means a farmstead made of beams (the same in Old English). Willow trees (see p. 55) were pollarded to yield thin branches for hurdles and basketware. **Staple**- (*stapol* 'post') and **Stave**- (*staef* 'staff, stave') combined with a 'wood' element usually denotes a clearing or grove where the staves were obtained. **Yardley** means a *leah* where rods or spars (*gyrd*) could be gathered. Reeds (*hread*, *hreod*) for thatching and making baskets were gathered in the wetlands of **Reedham** (Nflk),

Redworth (Durham), and **Rowde** (Wilts). **Ridgewell** (Essex) and **Rodbourne** (Wilts) were reedy springs and **Radipole** (Dorset) a reedy pool. **Redmire** (NYorks), **Rodmarton** (Glos) and **Redmarley** (Worcs) come from *hreadmere* 'reedy lake'. *Beonet* and *beos* both meant coarse grass or bent-grass; a name given to various kinds of reeds, rushes, or similar stiff-stemmed plants, also useful for thatching etc. *Beonet* appears in many places beginning with **Bent-**, *beos* in various **Beeston**s, in **Bestwood** (Notts) and **Bessacarr** (*beos aecer*; SYorks). Coarse grass (*feax*) grew at **Halifax** (WYorks) and possibly also at **Faxfleet** (Humb).

Flax (*fleax*, Norse *lin*) was grown to make cloth at **Flaxley** (Glos) and **Flaxton** (NYorks), at various places with the first element **Lin-** (although some are from Old English *lind*, Norse *lindr* 'lime tree') and at **Lilley** (Herts), **Lyneham** (Oxon and Wilts) and **Lyford** (Oxon). Other plants were grown or gathered for dyes; woad (*wad*) is referred to in various places beginning with **Wad-** and at **Odell** (*Wadhelle*; Beds), and madder (*maeddre*, Norse *mathra*) at **Mayfield** (Staffs) and **Matterdale End** (Cumb). The Old English word *croh*, borrowed from the Latin *crocus*, appears in **Croydon** (GLon), and perhaps also in **Croughton** (Ches) and **Crofton** (Lincs). It refers to a particular species of autumn crocus, *Crocus sativas*. The stamens yielded what we now call saffron (from Old French *safran*), used as a dye, in cooking and in medicine. In the late medieval period the same plant was grown at **Saffron Walden** in Essex and at the Bishop of Ely's gardens around Holborn in Central London. The street names **Saffron Hill** and **Ely Place** mark the site.

Trade and industry

The popular image of Anglo-Saxon life centres around the self-sufficient village, with each family owning its strips of land in the arable fields and grazing enough livestock on the common land for its needs. Spinning and weaving were tasks undertaken in almost every household. Certain specialists, like the miller and the smith, might spend little time on the land, being paid in kind by their neighbours for

the work they did. However, there was probably never a time when families or villages were totally self-sufficient. Some swapping and bartering between neighbouring settlements for things that were more easily produced in one place than another was probably always essential. As the Anglo-Saxon period progressed trade became more important, a cash economy developed, and from about the 8th century onwards names reflect industries and specialized products.

Every settlement would have its own mill (*myln*); larger ones might have several, often driven by water. As you would expect there are dozens of **Milbo(u)rn**s, **Milburn**s, **Millbrook**s, and **Milford**s. **Milton** can sometimes be a tun with a mill, although 'middle tun' is the more common meaning. Other 'mill' names include **Mellis** (Sflk), **Mells** and **Milverton** (Som). **Millichope** (Shrops) possibly means 'valley by the mill hill', which suggests a windmill; so do the various **Mill Hills**, although some of these are not recorded until much later. **Croft** (Leics) was first recorded as *craeft* 'a machine', possibly referring to a kind of mill.

Each settlement would also have its smith who could take care of people's day-to-day needs, making and repairing tools, weapons, fish hooks, etc. and shoeing horses and oxen. Old English smith appears in **Smeaton** (NYorks), and **Smethwick** (WMid). **Smisby** (Derbs) contains Norse *smithr*, and **Smeethe** (Kent) Old English *smiththe* 'smithy'. **Smitha** (Devon) is Middle English for 'at the smithy'; in the 13th century it was the home of a man called Roger de la Forge. Later inhabitants were called '*le smythe*' or '*Smythe*'. As well as the local smiths, there were also specialized craftsmen who made high-quality metalwork such as weapons, armour, and jewellery. These were much prized and an important export in the later Anglo-Saxon period. **Faversham** (Kent) comes from Latin *faber* 'smith, craftsman'. We do not know why the Latin word was used, and this is the only example of it in a place name. The town was a major centre for fine metalwork, especially for jewellery. **Goldonscott** (Som) means 'goldsmith's cottage'.

There was one essential product which most settlements would have needed to import. Salt was needed for cooking and particularly for preserving food for the winter. It was obtained by evaporating seawater around the coast, and from brine at inland sites which had brackish springs. Obvious place names are **Salt** (Staffs), **Salter** (Lancs; salt-maker or -merchant), and **Woodbury & Budleigh Salterton** (Devon). Places like **Saltburn** in Cleveland and **Saltfleetby** in Lincolnshire refer to salt streams, while **Salcombe** in Devon means 'salt valley'. **Salcott** (Essex) and **Salthouse** (Nflk) had buildings where salt was made or stored, and at **Saltcoates** in Strathclyde there were cottages for saltworkers. **Prestonpans** (Fife) refers to the salt pans belonging to the priests' *tun* (on the foreshore of the Forth estuary).

Harpham in Humberside may refer to a salt-harp, a kind of sieve. The briny springs of Worcestershire and Cheshire gave rise to a group of famous salt towns; **Nantwich** (*Nametwihc* – the odd spelling probably a scribal error) in Cheshire contains *named*, used in Middle English to mean 'famous'. **Northwich** and **Middlewich** (Ches) were the northern and middle salt towns, and **Droitwich** (H&W) contains *drit* 'dirt, mud'. All four of these were simply *Wich* in the Domesday Book, and this element often refers to a salt works (see box on p. 86). **Salperton** (Glos) was probably a *tun* on a road (*herepaeth* see p. 61) along which salt was transported, and some places called **Salford** were fords on salt roads.

Other industries reflected in place names of the Anglo-Saxon and early Norman period include:

charcoal or *coal*. Old English *col* could mean either charcoal or coal, and it is often not possible to tell which is meant. It is referred to in **Colwich** (Staffs), **Colerne** (Wilts), **Coldred** (Kent), and **Coldridge** (Devon). **Colsterdale** (NYorks) and **Colsterworth** (Lincs) were the homes of *colestres*, 'charcoal burners'.

Pottery gave its name to **Potterne** (Wilts), **Pottersbury** (Northants), **Potter Heigham** (Nflk), **Potton** (Beds), and is possibly the reference in **Crockerton** (Wilts) and **Crockenhill** (Kent). There were kilns (*cyln*) at **Kilham** (Nmbd), **Kilnhurst** (SYorks), **Kilnsea** (Humb), **Chatcull** (Staffs; Ceatta's *cyln*) and **Yarkhill** (H&W; *geard* 'yard' + *cyln*). These may have been for pottery or perhaps for lime-burning, as at **Limekilns** (Fife), and **Limehouse** and **Lime Street** (GLon)

Quarrying is referred to in **Standhill** (Oxon;

Very little that glitters is actually gold

Anglo-Saxon jewellery and fine metalwork was famous throughout Europe, but 'gold' and 'silver' names seldom refer to the metals. **Golder** (Oxon), **Golding** (Shrops) and **Goldhanger** (Essex) are where marsh marigolds (*golde*) grew. **Goldcliff** (Gwent) and **Silverdale** (Lancs) are from the colour of the local stone, and **Silverley** (Cambs) probably from silver-leaved plants. **Goldsborough** (NYorks), **Goldsthorpe** (SYorks), **Goldshaw Booth** (Lancs), **Goldstone** (Shrops), **Goldington** (Beds) and **Silverstone** (Northants) are from personal names. **Silverton** in Devon is probably the tun by the ford in the gulley (*sulh*). **Golden Valley** (H&W) refers to the metal, but that is a mistake; the Old Welsh name *Istratour* was believed to contain the word for gold, *our*, but the name really meant 'valley of the River Dore'.

ENGLAND AT THE END OF THE 9th CENTURY

SAXON EARLDOM OF BAMBURGH

• Bamburgh

YORK

• York

THE FIVE

Lincoln
•

Derby • • Nottingham

BOROUGHS

• Stamford

MERCIA

• Tamworth   Leicester •

EAST

• Bury St. Edmunds

ANGLIA

WESSEX

• Winchester

stan 'stone' + *gedelf* 'digging, pit'). **Quarndon** (Derbs), **Quarrington** (Lincs), **Quernmore** (Lancs), and **Quorndon** (Leics), all came from *cweorn* 'millstone'; **Wharncliffe Side** (WYorks) was once Querncliffe 'millstone hill', with 'side', as in hillside, added later. Various places called **Wheston** or **Whetstone** contain *hwetstan* 'whetstone', probably because suitable stone could be found there.

Shoemaking (*sutere*, Norse *sutari* 'shoemaker'), is referred to in **Sutterby** and **Sutterton** (Lincs).

Soap-making (**sapere* 'soap maker, soap merchant') was carried out at **Sapperton** (Glos and Lincs).

Tile-making was an industry in **Tilehurst** (Berks), **Tyler Hill** (Kent), and **Tyley** (Glos).

The products of such industries, as well as agricultural produce, livestock, and other goods would have been sold or bartered in the market towns. Bede (see p. 30) speaks of a fisherman selling his catch in town, reporting that he could sell much more if he could catch it. The Old English word for trade was *ceap*, with *ce(a)ping* referring to a market. **Chipping** (Lancs) was a market town, and the same word was often added to the names of villages which had a market, such as **Chipping Norton** (Oxon) and **Chipping Ongar** (Essex). (Later 'market' was used in a similar way in such names as **Market Drayton** in Shropshire and **Market Harborough** in Leicestershire.) **Chipstead** (Kent and Surrey) were market places (*ceap stead*) and **Chipperfield** (Herts) was probably the open land where traders (*ceapere*) met. The same word is found in **Chipper Lane** in Salisbury, Wiltshire. Many towns have a **Cheap Street** or **Cheapside** where the market was held, although some of these are much later imitations of London's Cheapside.

Getting around – roads and travel

Farmers and tradesmen going to market, servants, tax-collectors, troops, churchmen and aristocracy inspecting their estates, and the King surveying his realm all needed to travel. There were two ways of doing this; by road and by water.

The Anglo-Saxons had inherited a good road system, most of which is still in use. The position of roads was rarely arbitrary as it usually represented the best route across a marsh, through a gap in the hills, or between crossing points of rivers, and many roads used since prehistoric times now lie beneath the trunk roads and motorways of today. It is only in recent years, with the need for traffic to avoid centres of population, that we have really had to change them. However, the Romans were not afraid to run a new road through the most unpromising terrain if that was where they wanted to go.

The Anglo-Saxons had the benefit of the paved Roman roads and of the ancient tracks, some running for many miles. They may not have appreciated what they had. In the early years of settlement most travel would have been in the local tribal area; in later years within the travellers' own kingdom. England was not united as a nation until the 10th century, and before then few people would have had much call to travel the length and breadth of the land. Hence the Roman roads and the ancient tracks often did not receive names that reflected their purpose as long-distance highways.

Watling Street ran from Dover to Wroxeter via London, but the name originally belonged just to the stretch of it near St Albans, where the Waeclingas (Wacol's folk) lived. Similarly **Ermine Street**, originally applied to the road near **Arrington** (Cambs), the home of Earna's people, was only later applied to the road from Pevensey to York. In recent years, with motorways and bypasses changing the long-distance routes, we have reversed the process. Watling Street for most of its length is now known as the A2 or the A5, with its old name surviving attached to streets in various towns along the old route.

The Old English word *straet* is borrowed from Latin *via strata* 'a paved road', and it usually refers to a Roman road. It is the ancestor of the word 'street', which in modern names usually refers to a roadway bordered by buildings in a town or village rather than a road (a highway from one town to another). There is a good chance that a road, referred to as a 'street', was originally a Roman road. (Two words of warning: the fame and importance of Roman roads have resulted in their names being adopted for stretches of road elsewhere that have no connection with the original, and some people have a romantic longing for 'their' road to be ancient, so that a 'street' name may be merely wishful thinking.)

The Anglo-Saxons used *straet* in the names of settlements near Roman roads, in such names as **Street** and **Strete**, **Stratfield**, **Stratton** and **Stretton**, **Streatham** and **Streetham**, **Streatley**, **Streetley** and **Strelley**. **Stratford**, **Stretford** and **Strefford** refer to fords where a Roman road crossed a waterway; so does **Old Trafford** (see box). Occasionally, **street** in a village name may mean a linear village straggling along a roadway, but in general names like these are 'Roman road' names until proved otherwise. The element **Stan-** (*stan*, Norse *steinn* 'stone'), as in **Stanway** and **Stane Street**, denotes a paved road, almost certainly Roman.

The general Old English term for a road was *weg*. It appears in **Whaley** and **Whaley Bridge** (*weg leah* – clearing, etc. by a road), but is usually a second element. The first element may describe the road – **Broad Way**, **Hollow Way** ('eroded or sunken road', or 'road in a hollow'), or **Ridge Way**. It may describe where it leads as in **Port Way** (to a town, Old English *port* from Latin *porta* 'gateway'), and **Maiden Way** (Cumb; from the former Maiden Castle, now destroyed) or what it was used for: **Malt Way**, **Salt Way**. Similarly it may describe who used it: **Pilgrims' Way**, **Peddars Way** (Sflk; from dialect pedder, 'pedlar'). 'Way' names can appear as one word, especially when applied to farms, villages, etc. along the route such as **Broadway** (H&W and Som) and **Bradway** (Derbs), **Holloway** (GLon) and **Holway** (Som), **Stantway** (Glos) and various **Stanway**s.

Highway (Wilts; *heg weg*) stood on a road along which hay was carried, but usually 'highway' simply means the main road. Yet another word of warning; **way** has never gone out of use as a naming element, and it has recently become quite fashionable. There are now several long-distance footpaths which have the name 'way', such as the **Pennine Way** and **King Alfred's Way** (from Portsmouth to Oxford via Alfred's capital at Winchester). These often use ancient paths and tracks, and you may well be treading in the footsteps of our remote ancestors for most of your walk, but the

route may not have existed as a single entity until this century and parts of it may be quite new; the name almost certainly is.

Old English *paeth* (path) was applied to an unmade road, particularly to one that led across open country such as moor or heathland. Lane was applied to a narrow track between buildings in town and hedges in the country. Neither appears very often in the names of settlements. **Gappah** (Devon; *Gadepade* – 'goat path'), **Horspath** (Oxon), **Morpeth** and **Dupath** (see box on p.64), **Pateley Bridge** (NYorks; *leah* by the path), **Laneham** (Notts; dative plural *lanu* 'at the lanes'), and **Lenwade** (Nflk; where the lane crossed a *gewaed* 'ford') are among the few examples we have. Both are of course quite common in the names of roads; 'lane' particularly in names of small roads in towns.

In the south and west of England *herepaeth* seems to have been a common term for a major road. It meant a road wide enough for an army (*here*) to use. **Harpenden** (Herts) may mean *herepaeth denu* (valley), and could refer to part of Watling Street here. (The alternative root would be *hearpere* 'harper' – the name is not recorded until the 12th century so the 'early' forms are inconclusive. The Old English words for 'harp' or 'harper' do appear in other names: **Harpham** (Humb), **Harpsden** (Oxon), **Harpswell** (Lincs)). **Harptree** (Avon) is probably the 'tree by a *herepaeth*'. **Harepath** appears in the names of farms in Devon and Wiltshire, and **Herepath** is an alternative name for the length of ancient track between Avebury and Marlborough, usually called Green Street. **Hare Lane** (formerly Hare Street, now part of the A38 between Worcester and Gloucester) is on the route of an old Roman road.

None of these roads, paths and tracks could go very far without crossing a river or stream, usually by means of a ford. There are several places simply called **Ford**, and a few names refer to the river being crossed: **Brentford** (GLon) and **Ilford** (Essex; see box on p.65) are

Although there has been a bridge at Eynsford for hundreds of years, on hot summer days people still wade through the ford that gives the village its name. (IMAGES COLOUR LIBRARY)

examples. Hundreds of names end in -ford or -forth coupled with the name of the owner, or with the plants and animals found nearby (the Ashfords and Applefords denoting types of trees, the Gosfords and Gosforths geese, Bramford (Sflk) and Brampford (Devon) broom, and buntings at Buntingford in Hertfordshire). Some are named for the animals driven across them to market or to and from pasture: the various Sheffords and Shiffords denoting sheep; Oxford, Oxenford near Godalming in Surrey, Rutherford (NYorks) denoting cattle, the Gat(e)fords or -forths goats, and the Swinfords pigs. Others are associated with the goods most commonly taken across them. Where these are seasonal, like the Heyfords and Barfords which denote hay and barley, it may be that the crossing itself was used mainly at harvest time, perhaps because there was a quicker route if you were not moving a heavy load. Harpford in Devon lay on a *herepaeth*; Hereford had a ford wide enough for an army to cross without breaking ranks. Stafford was a ford by a landing place (*staeth*).

A less common term for ford is *gewaed* (related to modern 'wade') referred to in Biggleswade (Beds; *Biccel's) and Iwade (Kent; *iw* 'yew'). The Norse equivalent *vath* appears alone in three places called Wath in Yorkshire and in Waithe (Lincs), and as a final element in such names as Langwith (Notts and Derbs) and Langwathby (Cumb; 'long' ford), Sandwith (Cumb) and Stenwith (Lincs; 'sandy' and 'stoney' fords).

In early medieval times there were few bridges even on major routes, although the Romans had built some. Those that existed would have been landmarks; Bridge (*Brige* in the Domesday Book, from Old English *brycg*) was sufficient to identify the site of the village in Kent. In some cases the name was originally simply 'bridge' but the owner's name was added later: in Bridgerule in Devon, Ruald was the tenant recorded in the Domesday Book. Bridge Sollers (H&W) was owned by the de Solers family, and Bridgwater (Som) by Walter de Dowai. Names with *brycg* forming the first, descriptive element, such as Breighton (Humb), Brigsley (Lincs) and Bristol (Avon) (the *tun, leah* and *stow* by the bridge) suggest that the bridge existed at quite an early date. If the second element of Bridgham (Nflk) and Brigham (Cumb and Humb) is *ham*, which was used only in early Anglo-Saxon names, the bridges could even be Roman. Bridge is more common as a second element, and many names ending in -bridge describe what the structure was made of: Stambridge in Essex and various Stanbridges suggest stone; Woodbridge (Sflk) and Trowbridge (Wilts; *treow* 'tree') mean wooden. Market Rasen (Lincs) had a plank bridge (*raesn* 'plank'). Thelbridge in Devon and Elbridge in Kent (*thelbrycg*; the 'th' mistaken for 'the' and dropped) come from another word for plank, *thel*. Felbrigg (Nflk) comes from the Norse equivalent *fjal*. Some bridges were merely a treetrunk (*stocc*) or a beam (the same in Old English) as in Stockbridge (Hants), and Bamber Bridge (Lancs). Stockwell (GLon) and Benfleet (*Beamfleote*, 'stream with a beam') in Essex probably refer to streams crossed by such rudimentary bridges.

In time most fords were replaced by bridges. Usually the name of the place was firmly established in people's minds and did not change. Occasionally -bridge was added to a 'ford' name, as in Stamford Bridge (Humb) and Fordingbridge (Hants; the bridge of the Fordings, the people who lived at Ford). A ford did not necessarily go out of use when a bridge was built; at Eynsford in Kent the bridge is narrow and steep and the ford, well-maintained with a good, solid bed, is still used by riders of horses and mountain bikes, and by less intrepid cyclists and pedestrians on hot summer days. In some cases an old ford would have been an attractive alternative to a new tollbridge.

It is sometimes worth looking at early forms of a place name ending in -**bridge** for some indication of when the first bridge was built. For example, **Redbridge** (Hants) was *Hreutford* or *Hreodford* ('reedy ford') in a document c. 890 but *Hreodbrycg* in a document dated some sixty years later. This method is not foolproof, of course; the name in the 9th-century document may have been copied from an earlier one by a scribe who did not know that the bridge had been built in the meantime, or 'bridge' may not have been added to the name until some time after it was built. But, assuming that the later document is genuine, you can confidently say that the bridge was there by the time it was written.

A 'bridge' element in a place name can also mean a causeway across marshy ground; this is certainly the case in **Bridgend** (Lincs) which stands at one end of a causeway across the Fens. **Slimbridge** (Glos) means a causeway across muddy ground (*slim* 'mud, slime'). **Bracebridge** (Lincs) may contain an element meaning small branches or brushwood, and in several counties there are names of farms etc. which are variations on **Rice-** or **Risebridge**, probably from the more common word for brushwood, *hris*. A 'brushwood causeway' may seem unlikely, but the use of this type of material to stabilize a marsh was already old. Traces of such causeways have been found in the Somerset Levels under the peat. As late as the 19th century substantial causeways, some even supporting railways, were built on such 'floating' foundations.

Theale (Berks and Som) means 'the planks' and there is archaeological evidence of a plank causeway across wetlands near Theale in Somerset. **Grandpont**, now a small district in Oxford, was a more substantial road, built on stone arches across the Thames water meadows in about 1085. The name is Norman French and means 'great bridge'. The word 'causeway' itself comes from *cauci weg*, originally a 'way' along a *cauci* (a Norman French word meaning a mound or embankment). The word 'causey' still exists in Scotland and northern England, meaning a paved road, and is still occasionally used for a causeway across wet ground. It appears in **Causey Park** (Nmbd) and in street, field and farm names.

The third method of crossing water was by boat, and regular ferry services existed in some places in the early medieval period. The one that ran between the end of **Horseferry Road**

in Westminster and Lambeth probably dates from the 7th century. The word 'ferry' comes from Norse *ferja*. It is not common in village names, although there are a few examples. **Ferriby** means 'the farm by the ferry'; North and South Ferriby face each other across the Humber. **North & South Queensferry** refer to the ferry itself, across the Firth of Forth. This was instituted by St Margaret, wife of Malcolm Canmore (the son of the ill-fated King Duncan in *Macbeth*), in the 11th century and ran for 900 years until the Forth Road Bridge was opened in 1964. There are Ferry Streets, Roads etc. in many towns. Usually these streets once led to a ferry and pinpoint the site quite accurately, but some are modern names where a bit of poetic (or developer's) licence may be suspected.

Travel was not easy. **Denver** (Nflk) and **Laver** (Essex) contain *faer*, meaning a difficult passage, and **Malpas** (Ches, Cornwall and Mon) is a Norman French name with the same meaning. **Fenny Stratford** (distinguished from **Stony Stratford**, both now part of Milton

Pagans and Christians

The pagan Anglo-Saxons were fairly tolerant about Christianity. Cynics might say that they had so many reasons for beating up the British and each other that there was no need for religious bigotry. One of the few words they adopted from Latin, either directly from the Romans or through British intermediaries, was *ecclesia*, which they used for a Romano-British Christian church in the early days of settlement. It usually appears as Eccles, either alone or in such names as **Ecclesfield** (SYorks), **Eccleshall** (Staffs) and various **Eccleston**s, and in **Egglescliffe** (Clev). A disguised example is **Eaglesfield** (Cumb); perhaps the inhabitants thought an eagle more dignified than a character from the Goon Show.

The arrival of St. Augustine in 597 was the beginning of the end for the Old Religion. One by one the Anglo-Saxon kingdoms accepted Christianity, either from conviction or for political reasons. King Raedwald of the East Angles, took a 'belt-and-braces' approach to worshipping at Christian and pagan altars in the same building. Once the king had been baptized then the whole kingdom was officially Christian, although no doubt some people stuck to their pagan beliefs in private. There are a few names that show the survival of pagan practices. *Hearg* and *wigg* or *weohg* were both names for a heathen temple. They are referred to in **Harrowden** (Northants), **Harrow on the Hill** (GLon) and **Peper Harrow** (Surrey), and in **Wysall** (Notts), **Wye** (Kent), **Weeford** (Staffs), several **Weedon**s and perhaps also **Weyhill** in Surrey.

Thundersley in Essex and **Thursley** in Surrey were dedicated to the god Thunor, **Tuesley** in Surrey and **Tysoe** in Warwickshire to the god Tiw. **Wensley** (Derbs) and **Wednesbury** and **Wednesfield** (WMid) to Woden. Some of these names were first recorded surprisingly late, when the whole country had been officially Christian for many years. There are a remarkable number of such names, and similar field names, in Surrey. In *Signposts to the Past* Margaret Gelling suggests that Farnham Abbey may have been established to sort out a load of particularly obstinate pagans.

Keynes) suggests a boggy ford on a Roman road. There is a **Mudford** in Somerset, and **Fulford**s (foul fords) in several counties. **Defford** (H&W), **Dipton** (Devon) and **Deptford** (GLon and Wilts) had deep fords. Various **Somerford**s and **Summerford**s were passable only in summer, several **Efford**s only at the ebb tide. The common name **Twyford** denotes a place where two streams had to be forded one after another. **Islip** (Northants and Oxon) denote respectively a slippery place (*slaep*) by the River Ise and the River *Ight* (now called the Ray). **Ruislip** (GLon) either means a slippery place where rushes grow, or a rushy 'leap' – a place where you had to leap across a stream.

Roads in various parts of the country contain words such as featherbed, honey or honeypot, meaning that the going was deep, soft and sticky rather than comfortable and sweet. Pudding can mean the same, although in a town it may simply be the street where puddings, originally referring to kinds of sausages, were made and sold. It has been suggested that the village of **Pease Pottage** (a late name, first recorded in 1724 as Peasepottage Gate) may have been at a place on the road where the consistency was like that of pease pudding.

At the end of a long and probably tedious day you would have to find a bed for the night; if you were lucky in a monastery or inn. If not, well, there are **Caldecote**s and **Caldecott**s in several counties, meaning 'cold shelter', and many towns have **Coldharbour** as a district name or in a street name. This has a similar meaning; it was often by an open area on the outskirts of town, probably where drovers could graze their animals overnight and you bedded down as best you could in whatever rudimentary shelter might have been provided.

The respectable townsfolk would probably regard you with the deepest suspicion, and the 'cold' could have as much to do with the welcome as the temperature.

It wasn't all bad news: there is a **Fairford** in Gloucestershire, and a few **Fairmile**s dotted around the country. **Shawford** (Hants), **Shadforth** (Dur) and **Scalford** (Leics) had shallow fords, and **Bridford** in Devon had a shallow ford 'suitable for brides'. **Shereford** (Nflk) and **Sherford** (Devon) had fords where the water was clear. You could cross without paying at **Freeford** (Staffs), and presumably also at **Tetford** (Lincs) and at **Thetford** (Nflk and Cambs) – the names mean 'public ford' (*theod* 'people, nation'). **Wangford** in Suffolk, **Wainfleet** (Lincs), **Wainforth Wood** (WYorks) and **Wainlode** (Glos) were at places where the stream could be crossed by a wagon (*waegn*). **Glandford** (Nflk; *gleam* 'merriment'), **Playford** (Sflk) and **Plaitford** (Hants) were associated with sport or merry-making.

Waterways were a means of travelling as well as an obstacle. Rivers were major routes inland from the coast and many earlier settlements were along the river valleys. Of all the words that the Anglo-Saxons had for rivers and streams, none refer specifically to whether a watercourse was navigable or not, and the river name itself will give no clues about its use. However, a look at the names along it will.

The most common modern name for a landing place, wharf, comes from Old English *hwe(a)rf* meaning a wharf or shore, but appears in very few medieval names (**Wherstead** in Suffolk is one). It is of course very common in modern names, especially in new developments in and around dockland areas.

There were two main Old English words for a landing place, *hyth(e)* and *staeth* (Norse *stath*). Both usually refer to a landing place on a river; but flat-bottomed boats with very shallow draught were used for punting about the wetlands, and in some cases 'dry place' may be meant, rather than a nice neat wharf on a recognizable channel. To decide which is the most likely look out for 'wet' names nearby, especially on the earliest map available.

Hyth can appear alone, as in **Hythe** in Kent and in minor names such as **Hythe Bridge Street** in Oxford, or as a first element as in **Huyton**, Merseyside. As a final element the form can vary quite a lot: in Greater London **Rotherhithe**, **Erith**, **Lambeth**, **Putney** and

---

Crime and punishment

As if the discomforts of travelling weren't enough, there were muggers – and worse – along the way. **Dupath** in Cornwall means 'thief path'. **Shootersway** in Berkhamsted, Hertfordshire, **Shacklerley** and **Shakerley** in Lancashire, and the sweet-sounding **Sugar Way** (between the North Berkshire Downs and the Marlborough Downs) contain *sceacere* 'robber'. **Morpeth** (Nmbd) means 'the path where a murder took place'.

But they didn't all get away with it. Gallows stood at **Galphay** (NYorks) and **Gawber** (WYorks). **Wrelton** (NYorks) probably comes from *wearg* 'criminal', *hyll* 'hill', and *tun*, indicating a *tun* by the hill where criminals were hanged. A similar fate awaited them at **Dethick** (Derbs), the 'death oak'. **Warnborough** (Hants; *Wergeborne*) was the stream where criminals were drowned.

Chelsea are all 'hyth' names; so are **Maidenhead** in Berkshire and **Stockwith** in Nottinghamshire. **Erith** and **Earith** (Cambs) were muddy or gravelly landing places, **Greenhithe** (GLon) presumably had green vegetation round about, and **Aldreth** (Cambs) had alder trees. The landing place at **Stockwith** was made of tree trunks or logs. Some names refer to domestic animals, probably as cargo. **Bolney** (Oxon) refers to bulls, **Rotherhithe** and **Riverhead** (Kent), to oxen (*hryther*), and **Lambeth** to lambs. **Chelsea** was probably a landing place for chalk or limestone. Maidens gathered at **Maidenhead** (we are not told why!). **Putney** may be the *hyth* where kites were seen (compare Pitshanger on p.32), or have belonged to a man called Putta; **Stepney** belonged to Stybba.

In contrast to the variety of descriptive elements that appear with *hyth*, most of the *staeth* names refer to their owners or their situation. **Toxteth** (Mersey), **Croxteth** (Lancs) and **Brimstage** (Ches) belonged to Toki, Croc and Bryni respectively, and **Bickerstaffe** (Lancs) belonged to the beekeepers (*bicere*). **Brancaster Staithe** (Nflk) and **Flixborough Stather** (Humb) were the landing places for those settlements. **Staithes** (NYorks) was once *Setonstathes*; the landing places for the *tun* by the sea. **Burnham Overy Staithe** was the landing place for **Burnham Overy**, the village *ofer ea* (over the river) from Burnham.

One last Old English element should be considered, partly because it gives rise to some very common names and partly because a lot has been written about it over the years. *Draeg* is found only in place names, and its meaning has had to be deduced from them. It appears in various **Drayton**s and **Draycott**s and seems to mean, in very broad terms, a place where a load could be or had to be dragged. Eilert Ekwall, in the *Concise Oxford Dictionary of English Place-Names*, said that this was especially 'a "portage", a place where boats are dragged over a narrow piece of land or past an obstruction in a river', although he gave other explanations as well.

Other writers tended to latch on to the 'boats' sense and to apply it as a general rule whenever there was a river anywhere near, sometimes in places where it would have taken far more time and effort to drag a boat overland than to row it round. There is at least one instance where a writer has justified this explanation merely by saying 'Drayton lies by a river bend', ignoring the fact that the bend skirts a steep hill. Unless the river had been blocked somewhere on the bend, and for long enough for the name to become established, it would have been madness to haul any load over the hill. Kenneth Cameron and others have related it to 'dray', which originally meant a sled. David Mills, in *A Dictionary of English Place-Names*, gives the meaning of **Drayton** as 'farmstead at or near a portage or slope used for dragging down loads' or 'farmstead where drays or sledges are used' which seems to cover most eventualities. Here, as so often, we have to follow the 'golden rules' of amateur place-name interpretation – look at the site, take all known factors into account, including the experts' opinions, and opt for the common-sense solution.

Backformation

Collins English Dictionary defines backformation as 'the unwitting invention of a new word on the assumption that a familiar word is derived from it'. It often happens in place names, particularly with the names of rivers and settlements along their banks. **Plympton** in Devon looks straightforward – the farm on the river Plym. Actually it means 'plum-tree farm', and the river is named after it – a backformation. **Plymstock** is the outlying farm dependent on Plympton, but **Plymouth** means 'the mouth of the Plym', taking its name from the river.

There is a more complex example in Essex. The Hrothingas (the family or followers of Hrotha) gave their name to several settlements, now called the **Rodings**†, along a valley. The valley became known as the Roding valley and the river as the Roding. In this case part of the river already had a Celtic name, *Hyle*, meaning 'trickling stream'. This was replaced by Roding, but not before giving its name to **Ilford**.

† The Rodings are **Abbess Roding**, once held by the Abbess of Barking, **Aythorpe**, **Beauchamp** and **Berners Roding**, named for their Norman owners, and **Barwick Roding** (*berewic* meaning barley farm, but often meaning an outlying farm or village dependent on a larger one nearby). **Leaden**, **Margaret** and **White Roding** are named from their churches; Leaden from its lead roof, Margaret from its dedication, and White from its colour.

The Vikings –
Raiders, Traders and
Settlers

One version of the Anglo-Saxon Chronicle for 787 recalls that 'In this year . . . came for the first time three ships of Norwegians from Horthaland [around Hardanger fjord in south west Norway] . . . these were the first ships of the Danes to come to England.' In the following years Scandinavian pirates raided settlements, particularly monasteries, around the coast of England, making off with their treasures and butchering or enslaving their inhabitants. In 850 a Viking army wintered in England and from then on they sought not only plunder but also land. There were already Scandinavian settlements in the Highlands and Islands of Scotland. In Ireland, as in England, they raided around the coasts and later set up winter camps. The camps became bases from which to go raiding in the summer when they were joined by others from Scandinavia and northern Britain. More permanent settlements followed.

The two main groups of raiders and settlers were the Danes and the Norwegians. As we saw in the Chronicle entry, the Anglo-Saxons tended to lump them together, usually as 'the Danes' or 'the heathens'. The two groups were culturally similar, spoke related dialects of Old Norse, and while they sometimes fought they often co-operated. However, we can deduce from place-name and archaeological evidence that the Norwegians settled mainly in the Shetlands, northern and western Scotland, Ireland, the northwest of England and Wales, while the Danes settled in the north and east of England.

Viking longship. (WERNER FORMAN ARCHIVE)

The fortunes of the Scandinavians fluctuated according to the strength and determination of their 'hosts', and from time to time they had to pack their ships and move. In particular there was much coming and going across the Irish Sea. Early in the 10th century the Irish fought back and many Scandinavians withdrew to Scotland, northwest England, the Isle of Man and South Wales. A few years later the Anglo-Saxon king Athelstan brought northern England under his rule and some Scandinavians went back to Ireland. Others settled in southern Scotland. A century later Brian Boru defeated the Vikings at Clontarf; forcing some of them back across the water. In the late 10th century Danish raids on England began again after a century of more or less peaceful settlement, and from 1016 to 1042 Danish kings sat on the English throne. Had things gone slightly differently Britain might have become a Scandinavian rather than a European nation. With all this movement the period of Scandinavian immigration, and therefore name-giving, stretched from the beginning of the 9th century in Shetland until perhaps as late as the 14th century in some places.

Place-name elements

The most important Norse place-name elements appear on the chart on pp. 70–71. As indicated, some elements appeared only in certain areas, while others took on different forms in different places. We have already seen that many Norse place-name elements were very similar to Old English ones, and it is not always possible to tell one from the other. We have dealt with some closely related elements in the Anglo-Saxon chapter and they are not included on the chart.

A few place-name elements that are similar in Norse and Old English can cause confusion because they give rise to names very similar to those with quite different meanings, or indicate a Scandinavian origin for a settlement when this is not the case. These elements include:

brekka meaning 'slope, hill' appears alone in **Breck** (Lancs), but usually as the final element -**breck**, as in **Norbreck** and **Warbreck** ('beacon hill') in Lancashire. In some instances the vowel has changed, as in **Haverbrack** (where oats grew; Cumb) and **Scarisbrick** (Lancs), which may mean 'slope by a hollow (Norse *skar*)' or 'Skari's slope' – an interesting combination – as *brekka* is Norwegian and *Skari* is Danish. 'Breck' names in Norfolk are from Old English *br(a)ec* (see p. 52).

bryggja means 'landing place, jetty' and appears as **Brig**- or -**brigg**. It can be confused with names from Old English *brycg* 'bridge, causeway'.

by or *byr* means 'farm, village'. Its equivalent in Old English is *tun*, and -*by* may have replaced *tun* in some names where the first element is an Anglo-Saxon word, for example **Welby** (Lincs) and **Walby** (Cumb; near the Roman wall). It appears as the first element in a few names such as **Bicker** (Lincs) and **Byker** (T&W) (both with Norse *kjarr* 'marsh'), but is usually found as the final element -**by**, often with a Scandinavian personal name or with a feature of the landscape. Occasionally -**by** has replaced Old English *burh*, as in **Badby** and **Naseby** (Northants) and **Rugby** (Warks), all with personal names. If the site makes *burh* a possibility, especially if the place is near the edge of Scandinavian territory, check early spellings. A few of the names in Devon end in -**by** from Old English *byge* 'bend'; these have been mistakenly cited as Scandinavian names.

fjorthr, meaning 'estuary, inlet', appears as -**ford** or -**forth**, and so could be confused with Old English and modern 'ford'. The site will usually decide matters.

holmr, meaning 'small island, dry ground in a marsh', is the source of most places called **Holme** or **Hulme**. It is the first element in such names as **Holmpton** (Humb), **Holmesfield** (Derbs; with Old English *feld*), and the final element in names such as **Levenshulme** (GMan; Leofwine's). **Holme** can come from Old English *holagn* 'holly', and occasionally -holm(e) names outside Scandinavian territory may be from Old English *hamm* (see p. 38).

kirkja means 'church' and usually appears as **kirk**, sometimes with a saint's name. It forms the basis of various **Kirklands** (estates belonging to a church) and **Kirbys** (village with a church). It can be added to a name of any derivation, sometimes replacing Old English *cirice* or Gaelic *Kil-*.

lundr, meaning 'grove, small wood', appears alone as **Lound**, **Lund**, or **Lunt**; in **Londonthorpe** (Lincs), **Lumby** (NYorks) and **Lunnasting** (Shetland). As a second element it is often -**lund**, in which case it gives no trouble, but it can appear as -**land**, as in three instances of **Rockland** (Nflk), **Snelland** (Derbs), **Swanland** (Humb) and **Toseland** (Cambs). An early spelling of -*lund* or -*lunt* gives it away.

saetre, meaning 'shieling' (see the chart for the forms it takes), is often indistinguishable from the related Norse word *setre* 'dwelling, house' in the Highlands and Islands. There is no sure way to tell, but in general, if the settlement is small and isolated and the first element is the name of a domestic animal, suspect a *saetre*. A more prosperous settlement on a good site is likely to be a *setre*. In England it can be confused with Old English *(ge)set* 'dwelling, place for animals', which also appears as -set(t) or -side. In East Anglia most of these names are from *(ge)set*.

thorp means 'secondary or outlying farm or village'. It can appear as a later addition to a village name, as in **Ixworth Thorpe** (Sflk) –

the thorp dependent on Ixworth (which is an Anglo-Saxon name, 'Gicsa's worth'). But it often appears alone or with a personal name, with no indication of the settlement it belonged to. A Danish element – a 'thorp' name outside Danish territory will be from Old English *throp*, with the same meaning. An early spelling may give the game away. **Swanthorpe** (Hants) had early spellings with -*drop* and -*thrope*. Most 'throp' names have avoided metathesis (see p. 54) and appear as **Throop(e)** or **Thrupp**, or as the final element -**rop** or -**rip**, as in **Astrop**, **Eastrip** (eastern *throp*), **Hatherop** (Glos; high *throp*) and **Souldrop** (Beds; *throp* near a *sulh* 'gully').

vik means 'bay, inlet, creek'. It appears alone in **Wick** (High), as the first element in **Wigtoft** (Lincs), and as the final element in **Lerwick** (with Norse *leirr* 'mud'; Shet) **Blowick** (Norse *blar* 'dark'; Lancs) and **Lowick** (Norse *lauf* 'leaf'; Cumb). It is rare in England, where -**wick** is usually from *wic* (see p. 43), and more common in Scotland and the Islands. Suspect *vik* if there is an early spelling with v- or -k and the accompanying element is Norse. An apparently Scandinavian name outside the areas where they are known to have settled should be treated with suspicion: always look for another explanation rather than 'stray' Vikings.

Scandinavian settlements

Scandinavians settled in various areas of the British Isles at different times and apparently for different reasons, and it is worth looking at these areas separately to see what the names tell us about each. Books on place names will tend to talk about the effect of Scandinavian settlement on Anglo-Saxon names, and it would be wise to remember that in Scotland, Ireland and Wales the chronology is turned around – 'Anglo-Saxon' names are likely to be from Middle or modern English and later than Scandinavian ones.

The Highlands and Islands of Scotland

To many people in Britain the Northern and Western Isles are remote places; good for holidays but not for making a living and not on the way to anywhere except perhaps the ends of the Earth. To the Norwegians they looked quite different. Their climate and conditions for agriculture were at least as good as those at home, and they were easy to get to. They provided handy staging posts for voyages between Norway and Ireland, Iceland, and Green-

Scandinavian Elements

The following shows the most important Scandinavian elements, the areas in which they are found, and the forms they usually take in these areas. Because of the small number of names in Wales and Ireland these have not been included: elements labelled 'all' may not be represented there.

Element	Appearing as	Area(s)	Meaning	Notes
a	A-, -a, -ay-, -ey	all	river, stream	related to Old English ea* usually final element of river names.
bekkr	beck	NW England SW Scotland	stream	has replaced 'burn' in some cases. long-lived†
bolstathr	-bist, -bust -bister -bost -bo, boll, -poll -bster, -pster, -mster	Orkney Orkney, Shetland Lewis, Skye Highlands NW Scotland	dwelling, homestead, farm	see p. 71
both/buth	-booth	all	hut, temporary shelter	see p.77
breithr	Bray-	all	broad	
brekka	Breck, -breck	NW England, IoM	slope, hill	see p. 68
bryggia	Brig-, -brigg	all	landing place, jetty	can be confused with 'bridge' names; see p. 68
byr	-by, -bie	all	farm, estate	see pp. 68, 76–77
dalr	-dale	Highlands & Islands	valley	see p. 31
eith	-a, -ay	Orkney & Shetland	isthmus	
erg	see p. 78	NW England	shieling	see p. 78
ey	-ey, -ay, -a	all	island	related to Old English e(i)g*
ferja	Ferry(-), -ferry	all	ferry	see p. 63 – long-lived†
fiall	Fell, -fell -val Field Fiold	NW England, IoM, S Scotland Hebrides Shetland Orkney	hill, mountain	see p. 78 – long-lived†
fjorthr	-ford, -forth	all	estuary, inlet	ancestor of Middle English 'firth'†
garthr	-garth -gaard	all Shetland	enclosed land, yard	
gata	Gate, -gate		road, street	see p. 135
gil	-gill	N England, SW Scotland	steep valley, ravine	see p. 78
hof	Hov-	Orkney, Shetland	pagan temple	
holmr	Holme, Hulme, Holm-, -holm(e), -hulme	all	island, dry ground in marsh	see p. 68 – long-lived†
kirkja	Kirk(-), -kirk	all	church	see pp. 47, 68–69, 79 – long-lived†
kvi	hwei, kwei -quoy Qui-	Shetland Orkney, Shetland Hebrides	cattle pen	'quoy' forms are later than 'hwei' or 'kwei'
leir	Lar-, Lear-, Ler-	Highlands & Islands	clay, loam, mud	
lundr	-lund, -land	all	grove, small wood	see p. 69
myrr	-mire	all	wet moorland, mire	also first element in Myerscough (Lancs) – long-lived†
nes	Ness, -ness, -nish	all	headland, promontory	related to Old English ness*
saetre/ setre	-set(t) -setter, -ster -(s)hader -side	all except E England Orkney, Shetland Hebrides NW England, SW Scotland extreme NE Scotland	shieling dwelling, house	

Element	Appearing as	Area(s)	Meaning	Notes
skali	-skaill	Orkney, Shetland	shieling	
	-scale, -scole	Danelaw		see p. 78
sker (1)	Sker-, Skeir, Skerry	Highlands & Islands	small rocky island	long-lived†
(2)	Scar, -scar	N England, S Scotland	ridge, crag	
skogr	-skew, -scoe, -scough	all	small wood	
slakki	Slack, -slack	all	shallow valley	see p. 78
sletta	-sleat, -slat	Highlands & Islands	level field, plain	
stakkr	-stack, -staca	Highlands & Islands	steep hill, column of rock	long-lived†
stathir	-sta	Shetland, Orkney, Hebrides	dwelling place, farm	see p. 71
	-ston	Orkney		
storr	Stour(-), Stor(-)	Shetland, Orkney	strong	
thing	–	–	–	see p. 52
thorp	Thorp(e)	England	secondary farm	see p. 69
thveit	-thwaite	England	clearing, meadow, paddock	
	-that, -what	S Scotland		
	Twatt	Orkney, Shetland		
toft	Toft(s), -toft	England	homestead, enclosed land around a house	see p. 77 – long-lived†
vagr	-wall, -way, -vagh	Shetland, Orkney, Hebrides	bay, inlet	
vath	Waith, -wath, -with		ford	see p. 62
vik	-wick	all	bay, inlet	see p. 69
	-wig, -aig	Highlands & Islands		
	Voe	Shetland		
vra	Wray(-), Wrea, Wreay, Wra(-), -wray	all	nook, corner of land	

* names outside areas of Scandinavian settlement may come from Old English element
† only early names (to c. 1300) definitely show Scandinavian settlement

land, from which the more intrepid mariners might even get to Vinland (North America). Shetland lay more or less at the centre of the northern world (see map).

The first settlements were set up about AD 800, perhaps even earlier. In *Scottish Place-Names* W.F.H. Nicolaisen has used place-name elements to estimate the probable sequence of events. Assuming that the best sites were the first to be settled and hence had the oldest names, and looking at similar names in Scandinavia, he decided that the oldest place-name element was *stathir*, followed by the two related elements *setre* and *saetre*, and then *bolstathr*. By plotting the names containing these elements on the map, he concluded that the Shetland Isles were the first to be settled, then the Orkneys, the Outer Hebrides, northern Skye and the northeast tip of Scotland between Wick and Thurso, followed by the area south of this to the Dornoch Firth, the Inner Hebrides and the northwest coasts of highland Scotland.

Most of the Scandinavian names in the Highlands and Islands area refer to agriculture.

There are few elements referring to crops, but many based on 'cattle' and 'sheep' names. Some reflect farming practices suited to the northern climate. For example there are many 'shielings' – hill pastures used in the summer, with a hut or temporary shelter for the shepherds. Names such as **Quoy Ness** (Shet) and **Quinish** on Harris and Mull, (*kvi nes* 'cattle fold headland'), **Hestival** ('horse hill'; Shet and Orkn) and **Lamba Ness** (Shet) may also refer to summer pastures. The many names combining 'livestock' with 'island' may simply be islands where such livestock was reared, or outlying islands used as summer pasture, the creatures being rowed across in the spring. **Fair**

The Western (or Southern) Isles

The Vikings called the Hebrides the *Suthreyar* 'southern islands' – which immediately gives most of us a totally different perspective. The Norse name survives in the name of the Anglican diocese of **Sodor and Man**, which originally included the Hebrides. Sodor will also be familiar to the many fans of the Rev. Awdry's *Thomas the Tank Engine* books, although the allusion must surely be to the 'little trains' of Man.

Isle, **Fara** (Orkn) and the **Faroes** all contain *faer* 'sheep'; **Soay**, **Soa** and **Saay** (WIs) all contain another word for sheep, *sauthr* – so Soay sheep are 'sheep island sheep'. **Lampay** (WIs) and **Lamb Holm** (Orkn) mean 'lamb island', **Hestam** 'horse island' and **Haversay** 'goat island' (the last two both in the Western Isles). **Calva** may mean 'calf island', but calf can sometimes refer to a small island off a larger one, as in the **Calf of Man**.

There are also, as you would expect, some names referring to shipping. **Scalpay** (WIs) means 'boat island' (Norse *skalpr* 'boat', also found in **Scapa Flow** in Orkney). **Flodigarry** (WIs) is from *flotti garthr* 'fleet enclosure'– perhaps a harbour or anchorage, and **An Acairseid** (High) is a Gaelic transformation of Norse *akkarsoeti* 'anchorage'. **Stornoway** (WIs) contains Norse *stjorn* 'steerage, rudder', although it is not certain exactly what the significance of this was. **Stroma** (High) and **Stromness** (Orkn) both give warning of strong currents (Norse *straumr*). **Cape Wrath** (High) does not refer to stormy weather, however appropriate this may be, as 'wrath' is from

Position of The Shetlands

ICELAND

Faroe Is.

NORWAY

Shetland Is.

Hebrides

Orkney Is.

SCOTLAND

North Sea

Uig Bay (Uig means 'bay') on the Isle of Lewis is typical of the shallow tidal bays into which the flat-bottomed Viking longships could sail. (FRED MCDONALD)

Norse *hvarf* 'to turn', and the headland would be the landmark where you turned south for the Western Isles and Ireland.

A large number of names refer to high ground: headlands, cliffs, rock formations, etc. **Hoy** (Orkn) is from *ha ey* 'high island', **Muckle Flugga** (Shet) from *mikill* 'great' and *flugi* 'cliff', and **Habost** (WIs) is from *ha bolstathr* 'high

farm'. These might simply be descriptive names, but some of these high places might provide the intrepid voyagers with their first sight of land. From the sailors' viewpoint, only a foot or two above the water, land might also be heralded by the birds (*fugl*) flying around **Foula** and **Fogla** (Skerry), and **Fugla Ness** and **Fugla Stack** (Shet). There might also have been some economic significance to these birds: gulls' eggs are edible and were certainly still being gathered within living memory in the Western Isles and the Firth of Forth (where the **Isle of May**, Norse *ma ey* 'gull island' is still a major nesting site). The cormorants (*skarfr*) at **Scarskerri** (High) and the gannets (*sula*) at **Sullom Voe** (Shet) might have been eaten (salted gannet is an acquired taste) or might have shown where the fishing was good.

Ireland

The picture of Vikings in Ireland is quite different from the farmers of the Highlands and Islands. The Irish Vikings established a fort at **Donegal** (Irish *Dun na Gall* 'fort of the strangers'), and powerful settlements at Dublin, Cork, Limerick, Wexford and Waterford. Only the last two of these cities now have Scandinavian names. **Wexford** is from Irish *escir* 'ridge, sandbank' and Norse *fjorthr* 'inlet, fjord', from the spit of land north of Wexford harbour. **Waterford** comes from '*wether* (*vethr*) *fjord*', from which sheep were exported. These settlements were not just raiding bases; the Scandinavians were also merchants with trading links throughout the known world. There are very few Norse names in the country as a whole; those that exist are mainly on the coast or clustered around their strongholds and do not give much clue to their activities. **Wicklow** (*vikingr lo* 'Viking's meadow'), **Arklow** (Wick; Arnkel's *lo*); **Bardsey** (Bardr's island), **Dalkey** (*dalkr ey* 'thorn island'), and **Howth** (*hofuth* 'headland') are all around Dublin.

Carlingford (Louth) is from *kerling* ('hag') *fjorthr*, the 'hags' probably being three hills that serve as markers for ships coming into the loch – now known more charitably as the **Three Nuns**. **Strangford** (Down), at the mouth of Strangford Loch, is from *strangr* 'strong, violent' and *fjorthr*. It has been suggested that *strangr* referred to the current at the entrance to the loch. The Irish name **Loch Cuan** means 'haven lake', and it seems just as likely that the reference is to a strong (safe and secure) inlet, once you got past the strong (violent) current.

In Scotland and northern England there are many names showing Gaelic, often specifically Irish, influence, but this type of name seldom occurs in Ireland itself. The exceptions are **Ulster**, **Leinster** and **Munster**, which are Scandinavianized names showing some understanding of the Irish language. These contain the name of Irish tribes (the Ulaid, Lagin and Mumu), with the Irish *tir* 'territory', but with the Norse possessive ending *s*, giving the equivalent of 'Ulaid's *tir*'. They also show acknowledgement of who was in power. Judging from place-name evidence in Ireland, the Vikings seem to have regarded it as a place to raid and trade from, rather than a place to settle and farm. However, the district of **Galloway** in southwest Scotland has a Gaelic name, no doubt given by its inhabitants, representing Gall-Ghoidil, the name given to the 'stranger Gaels', of mixed Irish and Norse descent, who settled in the area. Other place names in northwest England and southwest Scotland provide evidence that when the Vikings left, some Irish went with them.

Wales

Wales was always open to raiding and trading by the Vikings from Ireland, and the pattern of Scandinavian names in Wales is very much the same as that in Ireland: mainly confined to coasts and islands and with a few hybrid names. There are a number of islands with the ending -holm (*holmr* 'small island') such as **Grassholm** (grass island), **Gateholm** (goat island), **Skokholm** (a corruption of *stokkr* 'stock, log'), **Steep Holm** and its neighbour **Flat Holm** (nothing to do with its shape; 'Flat' is from *floti* 'fleet', the island having been used as a Viking naval base). Others such as **Bardsey**, **Caldey**, and **Ramsey** contain the Norse *ey* 'island', as

A replica of a Viking
longship sailed from
Trondheim to the isle of
Man in 1979 to
celebrate the millennium
of the Tynwald, the
Manx parliament.
(POPPERFOTO)

do **Anglesey** (*Ongull's*), **Lundy** (Norse *lundi* 'puffin') and **Skomer** (Norse *skalm* 'split' – the eastern and western parts are joined by a narrow neck of land). **Green Scar**, **Sker Point** and **The Skerries** off Gwynned contain Norse *sker*, a small rocky island or crag. The main Scandinavian towns were **Fishguard** (*fiskr garthr* 'fish yard'), **Milford Haven** (*melr fjorthr* 'sand inlet', with 'haven' added later), and **Haverfordwest** (see p. 99), all in Dyfed, and **Swansea** (W Glam; *Sveinn's ey*). **Tenby** (Dyfed) is a Scandinavian rendering of Welsh *din bych* 'little fort'.

Recent studies have shown that the 'natives' in parts of Dyfed and of the Conway Valley in North Wales are genetically closer to the Norwegians than to their Welsh neighbours. In the 12th century, when the area around Pembroke, still known as 'Little England beyond Wales' was colonized by Normans and Anglo-Saxons the no-man's-land between the English and Welsh territories was known as the *landsker* – a Norse word meaning 'frontier'. We know that some Scandinavians settled in Wales after being thrown out of Ireland, and it seems as though their influence was greater and more prolonged than the place-name evidence suggests.

England

The Anglo-Saxons in the 8th and 9th centuries were still squabbling among themselves. In the Chronicles for these years, tales of battles with the 'heathens' are interspersed with stories of fighting between neighbouring Anglo-Saxon kingdoms and between factions within those kingdoms. From time to time an Anglo-Saxon ruler would succeed in defeating the Vikings,

A reconstruction of a homestead in Viking York. Although very different from Roman *Eboracum*, York was once again a major centre of industry and commerce during the Viking years.
(ARCHAEOLOGICAL AND HERITAGE PICTURE LIBRARY, YORK)

and a strong united effort might have seen them off altogether if the Anglo-Saxons could have buried the hatchet for long enough to make one. They didn't and the Vikings got the upper hand and began to settle in parts of England.

Only King Alfred of Wessex managed to hold the Vikings to a draw; in 886 he and the Danish leader Guthrum divided the country between them. North and east of a line running along the Thames, the Lea, the Ouse and Watling Street to Chester, the Danes were the acknowledged rulers and Danish law and customs prevailed; the area became known as the Danelaw. This opened the way for more peaceful colonization, and although in the years that followed Alfred and his successors gradually won control of the whole of England, the Scandinavians were allowed to stay and to run their own affairs to a large extent.

Of the 'five boroughs' from which the Danelaw was administered (Lincoln, Nottingham, Stamford, Leicester and Derby) only Derby has a Scandinavian name. The name **Derby** ('deer farm') is first recorded in 917 and appears in other 10th-century documents. The Anglo-Saxon name, *Northworthig*, is recorded in a document dated c. 1000; presumably the original name hung on in Anglo-Saxon memory. But most Anglo-Saxon place names in the Danelaw survived, though sometimes slightly changed.

There are several reasons for the survival of Anglo-Saxon names. Some settlements would have stayed in Anglo-Saxon hands as there were not enough Danes in Guthrum's army to populate the area they controlled. The names were already firmly established, and some already recorded in writing. The Scandinavians in general were a cosmopolitan lot, used to visiting foreign lands and coping with strange names. Perhaps the most important factor is that the language spoken by the Scandinavians was quite close to Old English. There were differences in grammar, particularly in the grammatical endings used, but many of the words were similar enough to be recognizable, and a good degree of communication would have been possible between the communities right from the start. There are many hybrid names, containing an Old English and a Norse element, but few of the 'Pendle Hill' type (see p. 97) that suggest a lack of understanding between the two parties.

The nature of settlement in the Danelaw has been explored by Kenneth Cameron, whose work was followed up by Gillian Fellows Jensen, both distinguished scholars. They took various kinds of Scandinavian names and hybrids and plotted them against the geology of the regions in which they occurred. We have already seen in the first part of the Anglo-Saxon chapter the combination of factors needed for a desirable settlement: a dry site with access to water, fertile land and some woodland, all dependent on the underlying geology.

They found that most instances of a particular type of hybrid, consisting of a Scandinavian personal name plus Old English *tun*, were on good sites which the Anglo-Saxons must have used, and perhaps even took from the British. A few such names would come from the later medieval period when Scandinavian personal names pop up all over the place, even well outside the Danelaw. But they concluded that this type of name recorded in the Domesday Book or before probably denotes an Anglo-Saxon estate with a new master. The survival of *tun* suggests that these names were given by the Anglo-Saxons rather than the Danes, who would have used the equivalent *-by*. These names come from the very earliest days of the Danelaw, and the new owners were probably members of Guthrum's army rewarded for a job well done. Despite the

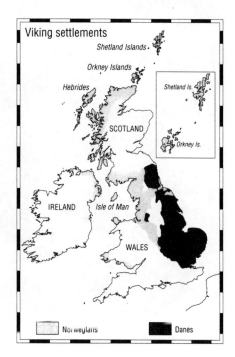

Viking settlements

change of ownership most of the Anglo-Saxon peasantry would have stayed on their land, paying their dues to a new lord of the manor.

These surveys revealed something else; most names ending in -**by** were on poorer land, often amid better sites with Anglo-Saxon names. This suggests that the owners were not bloodthirsty Vikings with horns on their helmets but farmers breaking new ground, making the best of what was available. Later work by John Dodgson showed a number of -**by** names and other wholly or partly Scandinavian names on poor soil in the Wirral, again with Anglo-Saxon names on the better sites. The Wirral was one of the places settled by the Scandinavians thrown out of Ireland, with the permission of Athelflaed, King Alfred's formidable daughter. There are also several places in England and southern Scotland called **Sowerby** or **Sorbie**, where the name means '*by* on sour ground'. These findings need treating with caution – we have already seen that a change of ownership

did not always entail a change of name – but it does seem that after the first period of colonization by a victorious Danish army subsequent settlement was less aggressive.

Further evidence for the relationship between the Anglo-Saxons and the Scandinavians is in the sheer number of hybrid names of all kinds. There are hundreds, far more than the Celtic/Old English hybrids. They show much more understanding and meaningful communication between the races, and there are a large number with an Anglo-Saxon personal name, showing Anglo-Saxons in possession of a *tun* or *holt* even if it was now called *by* or *skogr*. Names containing an Old English topographical term with a Scandinavian personal name show that there were Anglo-Saxons around to name the place, even if they no longer owned it. Whatever they were like, the Scandinavians did not swamp the Anglo-Saxons and wipe out their culture as the Anglo-Saxons had done with the Celts.

Danish and Norwegian settlement

We have already said that the Danes settled in the east and northeast and the Norwegians in the northwest. As usual it is not as simple as that; there were pockets of Norwegian settlement in northeast England and a few Danes in the northwest, and York was in turn a Danish and a Norwegian city. We also cannot draw a line between northern England and southern Scotland as far as place names go: 'England' must be taken as extending as far as the Clyde in the west and, more tentatively, as far as the Forth in the east (we hope our Scottish readers will forgive the liberty).

Most Norse words that appear in place names were used by both Norwegians and Danes; some were slightly different in the two

dialects but were close enough to give indistinguishable place names. Others differ slightly, a difference sometimes not discernible in modern names but traceable in early spellings. Norwegian *buth* and Danish *both* 'hut, temporary shelter' (the ancestors of modern 'booth' and Scots 'bothy') can both give rise to names containing booth, but the Norwegian *buth* often has early spellings such as *bouthe* or *buthe* while the Danish word will be spelt just with an o. **Bootham** (*Buthum*) in York is Norwegian, **Boothby** (*Bodebi*) in Lincolnshire is Danish.

However, there are some elements that were used only by one or the other and, where both groups settled, these can be used to tell them apart.

Danish elements

Thorp(e), -**thorp(e)**, when of Scandinavian origin, is always Danish (see p. 69).

Toft means a homestead or a piece of enclosed land around a house. It appears in various places called **Toft** or **Tofts** and as the final element in such names as **Bratoft** (Lincs; 'broad'), **Nortoft** (Nmbd; 'north'), and **Willi-**

toft (Humb; by the willow trees). It was the final element with personal names such as **Lowestoft** (Sflk), **Sibbertoft** (Northants) and **Antofts** (NYorks; Aldwine's). In field names it lasted into the later medieval period and spread outside the Danelaw, so that only early names are certain indicators of Danish presence.

Norwegian elements

Romantic nonsense

'A bit of romantic nonsense' is how James Graham-Campbell, in *The Viking World*, described the name **Jarlshof** on the southern tip of Shetland. The site has been inhabited since the Bronze Age, and the outlines of several Norse buildings can still be seen. Jarlshof, meaning roughly 'Earl's Mansion', was invented by Sir Walter Scott in his novel *The Pirate*, and it stuck.

Another piece of romantic nonsense is the word *ghyll*, found in the name **Gaping Ghyll** (WYorks) and also in books about the Lake District. The word is Norse *gill*, meaning 'ravine' (see text), as spelt by William Wordsworth in his poem *An Evening Walk* – there is no historical or linguistic justification for it, and it survived only because of the poet's popularity.

erg, meaning 'shieling', is a word adopted from Irish. It appears as the final element in **Birker** (birch), **Mosser** and **Mozergh** (with Old English *moss* 'bog, morass'), all in Cumbria, and in **Golcar** (WYorks; *Guthleikr's*) and **Grimsarch** (Lancs; *Grimr's*). In **Argam**, **Arram** and **Arras** (all in the east of Yorkshire, on the edge of Norwegian territory), and in **Arrowe** (Ches) it appears alone, the second syllable being due to inflectional endings. **Airyholme** (NYorks) and **Arkholme** (Lancs) look as though they are '*holmr*' names; actually they are from *ergum*, the dative plural form of *erg*, so the names mean 'at the *ergs*'.

fjall means 'rough hill, mountain'. Appearing as **Fell** or -**fell**, it is very common in names of hills and mountains in northern England, Scotland and the Isle of Man, occasionally in settlement names such as **Whinfell** (Cumb; where whin or furze grew). It has stayed in use as a word for hills or high moorland and so some names may be late. **Hampsfell** (Lancs) is a genuine Norse name, containing the Norse

personal name Hamr, but in **Great** & **Little Mell Fell** in Cumbria 'fell' has been added to earlier names; Great Mell Fell was originally *Mell* (Welsh *moel* 'bare hill') and Little Mell Fell was *Meloc* (Welsh **moelog* 'small moel').

gill, meaning 'ravine, steep narrow valley', is common in the names of valleys and is sometimes found in settlement names such as **Skell Gill** (WYorks; gill of the River **Skell**, from *skiallr* 'noisy, resounding'), **Scargill** (Durham; Skakari's, or where seabirds – Norse *skraki* – were found), **Howgill** (deep gill, with Old English *holh* 'deep, hollow'), and **Garrigill** (Cumb; with the Norman personal name Gerard). **Gaping Ghyll** in West Yorkshire is a swallow hole; for the unusual spelling see box.

skali means 'hut, shed, temporary shelter' and appears alone in several places called **Scales** or **Scholes** and in **Scole** (Nflk). It appears as a first element in **Scaleby** and **Scafell** (Cumb) and **Scawton** (NYorks), and as the final element in **Winscales** and **Winskill** (Cumb; in a windy place), **Summerscales** and **Winterscales** (WYorks) (used in the summer and winter respectively). The huts at **Portinscale** (Cumb) were presumably used all the year round; the first element is Old English *port-cwen* (literally 'town woman') meaning prostitute.

slakki, meaning 'shallow valley', appears alone in a few places called **Slack**, or as the final element in names such as **Witherslack** (Cumb; with Norse *vithr* 'wooded'). It is more common in field and minor names.

Breck, -breck, when of Scandinavian origin, is always Norwegian (see p. 52).

Norwegian/Celtic hybrids

As well as the elements themselves, there are other clues to Norwegian settlements as opposed to Danish ones. Some Norwegian names show Celtic influence, probably because these places were settled by Norwegians from Ireland, or people of mixed descent. There are two kinds of evidence for this. One is the appearance of Irish personal names: **Great Corby** (*Corc*) and **Glassonby** (*Glassan*) in Cumbria, and **Duggleby** (*Dubhgall*) and **Yockenthwaite** (*Eogan*) in North Yorkshire.

The second and more intriguing is in the order of elements. The position of the descriptive element after the thing being described is distinctly Celtic, as in **Kirkoswald** in Cumbria, which means the same as **Oswaldkirk** (NYorks) – St. Oswald's church. These are known as 'inversion compounds' and are a feature of place names in Cumbria and Dumfries and Galloway. Others are **Gilcambon** (Kamban's gill) and **Aspatria** (Patrick's ash), both in Cumbria, and **Torthorwald** (D&G; Thorwald's hill). There are also a few 'strays' in other areas; **Corstorphine** (Thorfinn's cross) is in the suburbs of Edinburgh. The largest group of inversion compounds contain 'kirk' followed by the name of a saint; **Kirkandrews** (Cumb), **Kirkbride** (Cumb and D&G), **Kirkconnel** and **Kirkcormack** (D&G) and **Kirksanton** (Sanctan; Cumb) are examples. Many of these refer to Irish saints, and in some cases the '**Kirk-**' seems to have replaced the Gaelic '*Kil-*'.

There are also place names which contain the name of an ethnic group, similar to the ones we looked at in the Anglo-Saxon chapter. As we have seen, the Anglo-Saxons were not necessarily reliable about nationalities, but the Scandinavians presumably could tell each other apart, and wholly Scandinavian names like **Denby** or **Danby**, **Denaby** and **Danthorpe**

in Yorkshire should be good indicators. (Beware *Dan-* or *Den-* names, and even such 'obviously Danish' names as Dane Court Kent and Danehill in East Sussex as they can also be from Old English *denu* 'valley'.) **Normanton** and **Normanby** come from Old English *northman*, usually referring to Norwegians. The Scots at **Scottow** (Nflk), **Scotby** (Cumb), **Scotforth** (Lancs) and **Scothern** and **Scotter** (Lincs), and the Irish at various places called **Ireby** and **Irby**, **Ireleth** (Cumb), **Irton** (NYorks) and **Kirk Ireton** (Derbs) may have been Norsemen who came to England from Scotland and Ireland, or Scots and Irish travelling with them. However reliable the Scandinavians might be as a rule, there were no Romans at **Romanby** in North Yorkshire, only the Scandinavian farmer, Rothmundr.

Pagans and Christians

Just as the patterns of settlement were different in the various areas, so relationships between pagans and Christians, and the conversion of the pagans, appears to differ. An Irish monk wrote a poem in praise of the storms that brought a temporary respite from Viking raids:

'The wind is rough tonight, tossing the white hair of the ocean; I do not fear the fierce Vikings, coursing the Irish sea.'

The monk had plenty to fear. Religious houses were a tempting and easy target, providing treasure, food, and the monks themselves, who could be ransomed or used as good-quality slaves if the church did not pay up. (The communion wine probably went down quite well too.) There is no doubt that, as pirates, the Scandinavians were a pretty grim lot. Anglo-

Saxon literature tells horrific stories. King Edmund was tied to a tree and had spears thrown at him until they seemed 'like a hedgehog's bristles' (he is buried at **Bury St. Edmunds** in Suffolk, although the name means his *burh* or town rather than his burial place), and the 11th-century bishop Aelfheah was pelted to death with ox bones by a pack of Danish mead louts.

Some Scandinavians accepted Christianity for political reasons. The Anglo-Saxons were Christians, and as they reconquered the Danelaw baptism was often a condition of peace treaties. It is said of one Scandinavian leader that 'he had been a heathen more genuinely and more often than a Christian', and no doubt this was the case with many early 'converts'.

The Orkney experience

On Orkney, so the story goes, conversion was carried out in 995 by the newly-Christian King Olav Tryggvason of Norway, who offered Earl Sigurd of Orkney the choice between Christianity and death and took Sigurd's son as hostage.

But the islands had been visited long before

the Vikings came by Celtic monks, known as the *Papae* (fathers), who came to spread the Gospel to the Picts. Norse place names such as **Papa Stour**, **Papa Westray** and **Papa Stronsay**, as well as **Papdale** – the valley of the Papae – near Kirkwall suggest that the Papae were still around and were left unmolested, though whether the Norsemen took any notice of their strange beliefs is another matter. Another name that may be relevant is the island of **Egilsay**, for which the usual explanation is 'Egil's island'. However, the church on the island is architecturally similar to early Irish churches. It dates from about the 12th century, but if it replaced an earlier building which predated the Vikings, the name might derive from *eaglais*, a Celtic word for church derived from Latin *ecclesia*. This is very tenuous, but would provide an interesting parallel with the Anglo-Saxon *eccles* names (see p. 63).

From Lindisfarne to Kirkcudbright

The Celtic Christians seem to have had some effect on their pagan neighbours, and it is interesting that most of the Scandinavian place names which specifically refer to a church or to a saint are in the northwest of England and Scotland. It is possible that this concentration of names reflects an Irish influence reinforced by the native Celts. **Kirkcudbright** (D&G) refers to St. Cuthbert, the 7th-century Northumbrian saint who made several missionary journeys to this area. This was the same Cuthbert whose bones had been moved from Lindisfarne to Durham because of repeated Viking raids. He might have been gratified to know that the word of God had reached the heathen after all.

Scandinavian legacy

What difference did the Scandinavians make to Britain? Well, first and foremost they were merchants and traders, and they developed trade between different parts of the British Isles and between Britain and the rest of the world. Towns, cities and ports grew up partly because the Scandinavians developed them as trading centres, and partly because the Irish and the Anglo-Saxons fortified and strengthened their settlements to defend them. Alfred set up a string of fortified towns in Wessex, and later others were created or strengthened in recaptured territory. This is not to say that Britain was completely isolated and rural before the arrival of the Vikings. There was trade with the continent and there were towns, but the Scandinavians fostered developments that were already taking place. They woke the Anglo-Saxons up to their weaknesses, and the unification of England was a long-term result of the Viking raids.

The Scandinavians also affected the English language. We have already seen that they affected the pronunciation of English in the places where they settled. In one way they prevented or reversed change; Old English *sc* came to be pronounced *sh* in the Wessex dialect, but *sk* in other dialects, partly because the *sh* sound did not exist in Norse. Similarly the *ch* sound developed in Wessex but not in areas under Scandinavian influence, where *c* was pronounced *k*.

They added a number of words to the language, from nautical and legal terms such as reef and the word law itself, not all of which survived the Normans, to useful everyday words like both and same. Perhaps the most radical change was brought about, at least partly, through Scandinavian influence. Their vocabulary was similar to Old English, but some grammatical constructions and the range of inflectional endings were different. To communicate, the two communities had to concentrate on what they had in common, and the differences were gradually eroded. As the endings were lost new grammatical patterns had to evolve to replace them. There were other factors, and the Norman Conquest brought yet another language which had to be accommodated, but the change from Old to Modern English began partly as a result of the Vikings.

1066 and All That –
the Norman Heritage

When the Normans took over the administration of England in the late 11th century they found a naming system firmly in place. They were a conquering elite and not a nation of peasant farmers who needed to use a name for every hill and ditch like the Anglo-Saxons and Scandinavians. They were in general content to let the conquered people they ruled get on with their farming without interfering. Their effect on place names, therefore, was more like that of the Romans, or of the British in India, than of the Germanic invaders. Moreover, while there were still some areas of England only lightly inhabited, the best land had already been heavily settled for generations, and most of the naming had already been done.

As a result there are few names that come directly from Norman French, and even fewer for large settlements. (New towns were established in the Middle

Ages, but like many modern new towns, such as Milton Keynes, they tended to take their names from places that already existed.) Of the names that did come from French, most are names given to new manors or castles, which were founded as a part of the system of government that the Normans introduced.

A favourite name element was Bel- or Beau-, 'fine, beautiful'. It often becomes Bew- or Bea- in modern names and is occasionally mangled beyond recognition. **Beaulieu** (Hants), meaning 'beautiful place', has kept its French spelling, but not the pronunciation. The same name is recognizable in **Beauly** (High) and two villages called **Bewley**, but is less obvious in **Beadlow** (Beds) and **Bewdley** (H&W). **Belper** (Derbs) and particularly **Bearpark** (Dur) have moved beyond the easily recognizable, although 13th-century records prove that they originally had the same name as **Beaurepaire** (Hants) meaning 'fine retreat'. Similarly, few would easily find the French beau trouvé, 'beautiful find' in **Butterby** in Durham, which looks more like a Norse name.

Other names with beau are **Beauchief Abbey** (SYorks; 'fine headland') which is also the source of **Beachy Head** (ESx) where the extra 'Head' had been added in modern times. **Beaufront Castle** (Nmbd; 'beautiful brow'), the various **Beaumont**s 'beautiful hill', **Beaumaris Castle** (Gwyn; 'beautiful marsh'), a number of places spelt variously **Bellasize**, **Bellasis**, **Bellasice** and **Belsize** all meaning 'beautiful site' and **Belvoir** 'beautiful view' are others from this group. As ever, it is not wise to assume that any name with this sound comes from French. The very French-looking trio of villages called **Belchamp** in Essex is Old English belc + ham, and means 'homestead with a vaulted roof', and **Beausale** in Warwickshire is 'nook of land owned by (the Anglo-Saxon) *Beaw'. Even more deceptive is **Belleau** (Lincs), which was first recorded as Norse Elgelo, 'Helgi's meadow', but which has since been respelt to look like the French for 'beautiful water'. **Belgrave** (Ches) started out as the Old English Merdegrave 'marten's grove', but sounded too much like the French merde, 'shit', to the Normans, so had its first part changed to Bel. When the Duke of Westminster developed some of his land in London, he named Belgrave Square after his estate in Cheshire, and the area became known as **Belgravia**. Similarly the new owners of **Beaumont** in Essex changed the name to something pleasanter than the Old English name of Fulanpettae, 'foul pit'.

The Normans also used mal-, the opposite of bel-, as a name element, most notably in **Malpas**, 'bad passage'. It is used in at least eight places, usually where a route goes through marshy ground and would be difficult to pass without getting muddy in wet weather.

Other French names are: **Blanchland** (Nmbd; 'white glade'), **Bruern** (Oxon), **Bruera** (Ches) and **Temple Bruer** (Lincs; 'heath'). **Devizes** in Wiltshire means 'place on the boundary' and **Egremont** in Cumbria means 'pointed hill'. **Freemantle** (Hants) was recorded as Frigid Mantell in 1200, meaning 'cold cloak' a common name in France. **Grosmont** (Gwent and NYorks) means 'big hill', and in **Kirmond le Mire** (Lincs) the first part is formed from the French place name Chèvremont, 'goat hill', and obviously used with direct reference to the French place as the English place is actually in a valley (the second part refers to the wet land it is on). **Mold** in Clwyd has come a long way from its original Monthault, 'high mount', and **Montacute** in Somerset is a Latinized form of the French place name Montaigu, 'pointed hill'. **Mountsorrel**

The French language in Britain

The Norman Conquerors of England brought their own dialect of French, and naturally expected those they had defeated to communicate with them in the same tongue. As a result French became the language of administration, fashion and learning, and anyone who hoped for financial or social success had to know the conqueror's language – a situation not unlike that in India and Africa under the British Empire. The ruling classes spoke French and French speakers took over the top jobs, particularly in the legal system and in the equivalent of the civil service, and it became necessary for tradesmen to be able to communicate in French as well.

Thus almost all writing was either in Latin, the language of scholars and the Church, or in French, and this destroyed Old English as a language of learning, which it had been until then. The English who had to learn French would mostly have gone on speaking English at home, and the ordinary peasants would have had to learn only a smattering of their masters' tongue. Gradually, however, the two languages began to fall together, a process that can also be seen in the ex-Empire. The British rulers of the Indian Raj soon adopted words like jodhpurs and bungalow from the Indian languages, and the English spoken in India today is not quite that of Britain. The words and form of the Indian languages have been carried over into English.

French continued to be influential for about three centuries. The first Royal edict in English was in 1258, and French continued to be the language of the law courts until 1362 (and indeed law reports were written in legal French until about 1600). There was a flourishing tradition of literature in what came to be known as Anglo-Norman which only ended with the death of John Gower in 1408.

The term 'Norman French' or 'Anglo-Norman' is rather a loose one. In fact, many of William the Conqueror's followers were Breton, and spoke either their own Celtic language or their local variety of French, rather than the dialect of Normandy. There was no standard form of the language in the Middle Ages, and each region spoke its own form, just as each region in England spoke its own dialect. Features which distinguished the Norman's French and which have left a mark on modern English were such sound differences as the use of a 'g' where modern French has 'j' (hence English 'garden' and French 'jardin'). As a consequence where French had 'g' the Normans had to use a different sound, 'w', giving 'William' from French 'Guillaume' and 'wardrobe' instead of 'garderobe'.

The North Yorkshire town of Richmond acquired its name from the French *riche mont* meaning 'strong hill'. The Richmond in Surrey is named after it. (IMAGES COLOUR LIBRARY)

(Leics) means 'reddish hill' and **Pleshy** in Essex 'an area surrounded by a hedge of interwoven branches', another common name in France. **Ridgemont** (Beds, Humb) comes from *Rougemont*, 'red hill', and **Tilts** (S Yorks) means 'lime trees'. The **Richmond** in North Yorkshire is from the French name *riche mont* 'strong hill', but the Richmond in London is only indirectly French. When Henry VII rebuilt the great palace at Sheen which had burnt down in 1501 he gave it a new name after his earldom of Richmond. Again, we must beware of false friends; **Little Hautbois** (Nflk) looks as if it must be the French for 'high wood' but actually comes from Old English *Hobbesse*, 'marshy field full of tussocks'.

An interesting sub-group of French names is found in some of our most famous Abbeys. Norman clerics were determined to reform what they saw as the sometimes lax English church. As a part of their take-over a building programme was started (which explains why so many of our great cathedrals are Norman) and a number of new monasteries were founded. As French foundations they tend to have French names, particularly as wild and sparsely-inhabited areas were sometimes deliberately chosen as places of retreat, where the founders would have been free to impose their own names. These new Abbeys include those jewels of the Yorkshire Moors **Fountains**, named after the springs found there, **Rievaulx**, first founded as *Rievall*, a French translation of the English name *Ryedale*, 'valley of the Rye', and **Jervaulx**, a magnificent French distortion of the name of the place on which it was built, the Ure valley. Others are **Gracedieu** (Leics; 'Grace of God'), **Landieu** (Dur; 'glade of God'), **Vaudey** (Leics; 'valley of God'), and **Battle** (ESx), founded to commemorate the battle of Hastings, which may look thoroughly English, but 'battle' was a word introduced by the French.

Norman influence on English place names

Although the number of new names introduced by the Normans was not great, the Normans profoundly influenced the history of place names in other ways. As we have seen from what happened to some of the French names above, the English could have difficulty with French pronunciation, and altered the French names to suit themselves. The same problem existed the other way. We are all familiar with the way in which the French today have problems pronouncing certain sounds in English. The same sort of problems existed then and it is easy to imagine the problems that could arise.

In the Domesday Book and in later charters it is often difficult to tell if the written form of the word represents the sounds of Old English, French or Latin, and the scribes sometimes had great difficulty trying to write down Old English sounds which did not exist in their own speech. If you imagine a Frenchman today trying to pronounce English names, and then writing them down as if they were French, you can get a very good idea of the problems these scribes faced. French was written and more importantly spoken in England for some three hundred years after 1066, and the changes introduced in the pronunciation of English names is the most marked effect the Norman Conquest had on place names.

The main problems the Normans had were with consonants, particularly with the sounds represented by 'ch' and 'th' and with the Old English liking for groups of consonants together. 'Ch' often became an /s/ sound so that many of the Roman -chester names became -cesters. Spellings such as *Chirenchester* and *Glouchestre* became **Cirencester** and **Gloucester**, while **Diss** (Nflk), from Old English *dic*, 'a ditch' (and pronounced with a /ch/), shows the same process at the end of a word. Often it was chance that dictated whether or not the English or the Norman pronunciation won. Thus we have two **Chippenham**s (Cambs and Wilts), but also a **Cippenham** (Berks), all meaning 'river-meadow belonging to *Cippa'. The same situation exists with /th/: **Therfield** (Herts), from the Old English meaning 'dry open land' and written *Derevelde* in the Domesday Book, has kept its English form, while **Turville** (Bucks) from exactly the same source not only has Norman 't' for 'th', but has also had the English 'field' changed to the similar-sounding French *ville*.

The combination of consonants also presented a challenge. Consonants were often simplified so that *Snotingeham*, 'settlement of Snot's followers', became **Nottingham** and *Dunholm* 'island with a hill' became **Durham**. Durham also shows the Norman problem of distinguishing between English 'n', 'r' and 'l'. Sometimes this could lead to quite extreme changes; for a time the form *Nicole* was quite common for **Lincoln**. **Salisbury** is a prominent example of this process. It started life as the name of a small Roman settlement called *Sorviodunum*, the second half meaning 'fort', the first probably from the river on which it stood. The Anglo-Saxons changed the second element to *their* word for 'fort', and identified the first half with their word for armour, *searu*, and the name became *Searobyrg*, later *Searobyrig*. When the Normans came along they confused the 'r' with an 'l' to give us the modern Salisbury. However, when the city was moved from its ancient fortified site to its present location the old 'r' form survived in a shortened, Latinate form and we can still visit the original site, now known as **Old Sarum**.

Another pronunciation problem was pre-

The Domesday Book

As well as being great fighters the Normans had a genius for administration and the law. One of the most important sources of information on early place names, the Domesday Book, owes its origin to this. The Domesday Book is the results of a survey covering most of England and finished in 1086. It was carried out so that the new King, William the Conqueror, could find out what income he was entitled to, and also, as one contemporary chronicler tells us, 'what and how much each landholder in England had in land or stock and how much money it was worth. He ordered such a searching investigation that not a single yard of land nor – I am ashamed to write this, but he was not ashamed to do it – an ox, a cow or a pig that was not put down on his list; and all this information was brought to him afterwards'. This investigation seemed so like the searching enquiry expected on Judgement Day – Doomsday – that the native English nicknamed it the Doomsday or the Domesday Book. The survey was conducted by royal officers who would have been French speakers on the whole, trained to write in Latin, but who were receiving their information from native Old English speakers. This explains some of the strange forms that the place names in it can take, although considering these difficulties the work is remarkably competent.

sented by the names beginning with the sound spelt in Old English 'Ge-' 'Gy-' or 'Gi-', and pronounced /y/. The Normans tended to replace this with the sound found in 'judge'. A surprising number of these have stuck as in **Jarrow** (T&W) Old English *Gyruum*, 'settlement of the fen people', **Jesmond** (T&W) earlier *Gesemuthe*, 'mouth of the Ouseburn (formerly called the *Yese*)', where the French 'mont' or 'mond' has also replaced the English 'mouth'; and **Jevington** (ESx) 'farmstead of a man called Geofa'. This last should be compared with **Yeaveley** (Derbs) which escaped Norman influence and developed regularly from its Old English name meaning 'Geofa's clearing in the wood'.

Finally, the French language has left some direct influence on the formation of place names. A few relics have survived in street names such as Cambridge's **Petty Curry** 'little kitchen' and London's **Petty France** 'little France', the old French quarter. However, it is most obvious in those names where a little bit of French has crept into otherwise English names such as **Chester le Street** (Dur), 'Roman town on the Roman road', **Chapel en le Frith** (Derbs), 'chapel in the wood', **Hutton-le-Hole** (NYorks), 'in the hollow', and **Ashby de la Zouche** (Leics) where the common place name Ashby has been distinguished from others by showing that it is the property of the Zuche family.

This last name brings us to an important naming habit introduced by the Normans: the use of two-part names, one element of which indicates possession of the land or describes it in some other way. Although there are Old English names which indicate ownership, the Norman system of land tenure, Feudalism, was much more formal and systematic than the Anglo-Saxon one was (see box). Moreover, there had been such a profound shake-up of ownership after the conquest that most of the old estates had disappeared. The two-part names come in several forms: the most common is the simple place name plus the family name of the land-holder, and the other type can have a descriptive word added either from one of the languages of record, French or Latin (the latter being particularly common in properties owned by the church) or in English. This type of name is found most frequently where the basic name is a common one, especially if there are neighbouring villages with the same name. Obviously if a village has a rare name it needs no

The feudal system

The historian Christopher Brooke has tried to explain in one of his books the ordering of Norman society and the system of land tenure. He has written about the difficulty of trying to 'find one's way about what is so unhappily called the feudal system, which I prefer to think of as the feudal labyrinth.' He points out that one important step is to understand the differences between our attitude to land ownership and that of the Normans. They had no sense of owning land in the way we do. Except for the King, who nominally owned much of the land, everyone else was a tenant. The King had the right to grant the use of land, usually in a unit called a manor, to someone who could in turn pass the right to use the land to someone else.

At each stage the person receiving the land from his superior would in return owe fealty (duty and loyalty, and above all military service) to his superior, and is said to 'hold' the land from him. On payment of what was in effect a form of death duty this land could pass from father to eldest son, so the land could remain in the same family for many generations. As a result the holder's name or title could be used to distinguish one manor or village from another of the same name, although a change of the family or person holding the land could mean a change in name, at least until the work of lawyers and map-makers fixed the names.

Thus, the group of Dorset villages which share the name **Caundle** are now called after one-time overlords **Bishop's Caundle**, **Purse Caundle**, **Caundle Marsh** and **Stourton Caundle**, but this last has a varied history. It is first recorded in the Domesday Book as simply *Candel*. In 1178 a Latin document calls it *Candel Henrici Budde* and in 1202 it is both *Candel Danielis de Brueria* and *Caundle Malherbe*. In 1256 it is *Candle Joce*, presumably the first name of a member of the Malherbe family, for we have another record of Robert Malherbe granting some land to Henry de Haddon, and in 1270 the village is recorded as *Candel Hadden*. It is *Caundle Pyle* in 1335 and *Caundel Chidiok* 1483–5. Finally the Stourton family were lords of the manor from the 15th century until 1727.

further identification, but a common one needs these extra names, technically called 'affixes', to distinguish them.

Milton is a very common name, usually a shortened form of *Middle-ton*, 'middle farm', but sometimes from a village with a mill. There are at least 30 places just called Milton, and nearly as many more with affixes. These include **Milton Abbas** in Dorset from the Latin meaning 'of the Abbot', referring to the abbey there, while Devon's **Milton Abbot**, which was owned by the abbey of Tavistock, shows the English form of the name. **Milton Bryan** (Beds) had a Lord of the Manor descended from someone called Brian by 1303, while **Milton Clevedon** (Som) was held by the de Clyvedon family from c. 1200. **Milton Damerel** (Devon) was held in 1086 by Robert de Albermarle, and **Milton Ernest** (Beds) acquired its name from the Erneis of Middelton mentioned in 1193. Lucas de Kaynes held the manor of **Milton Keynes** in 1221 and one

Chepstow is Old English for 'market place', and the Norman castle, the oldest in Wales, is referred to in the Welsh name *Cas-Gwent*, 'castle of Gwent'. The Norman name *Strigull* has yet to be explained. (BRITISH TOURIST AUTHORITY)

Walter de Lillebon held **Milton Lilbourne** in 1242. **Milton Malsor** (Northants) was held by a family recorded at the beginning of the 13th century in Latin as *Mala opera* and in French as *Malesoures*, both meaning 'bad deeds'. The earliest records we have of these family names is not necessarily the date at which they first took control of the land.

If we turn to another common name, **Hinton**, which can either be 'high farm' or 'monks'/nuns' farm' (both from Old English), we find **Hinton Admiral** (Hants) comes from the same name which gave us Milton Damerel. **Hinton Ampner** (Hants) gets its name from the almoner (person responsible for charitable donations) of St Swithun's Priory at Winchester, and **Hinton Blewett** (Avon) from the Bluet family, their name originally being a nickname meaning 'bluish'. **Hinton Charterhouse** (Avon) is named after the monastery founded there in 1232, **Hinton Daubney** (Hants) was held by the d'Aubeny family, and **Hinton Martel** was held by the Martell family from the 13th century. **Hinton Waldrist** was held by a man called *Thomas de Sancto Walerico* in a Latin document of 1192, the name being Latin for the French town of St Valery. Alongside these feudal names we find such English names as **Great Hinton** (Wilts), **Cherry Hinton** (Cambs) from its cherry trees, and **Hinton in the Hedges** (Northants) and **on the Green** (H&W).

An equally rich range of place names have been formed from other common names such as **Stoke**, **Thorp**, **Hutton**, **Steeple** or **Ashby**.

If we look at these affixes more systematically, we will find that they can be divided up to give us different types of information about places. First of all there are those that tell us about the geography of a place. These can come from any of the place-name languages, but English is the most common language. Thus **Water Eaton** (Oxon) is on the river, and distinguished from nearby **Woodeaton**. **Eaton upon Tern** (Shrops) and **Eaton under Haywood** (Shrops) describe what they are near, and **Church Eaton** and **Castle Eaton**, both in Staffordshire, are named from their most prominent buildings. **Brent Eleigh** (Sflk), meaning 'burnt', must have had its fire before 1254 when the name first occurred. Crops can form part of these names. Three places in the middle of beanfields use three different languages; **Barton in the Beans** (Leics) is pure English, **Barton in Fabis** (Notts) is the Latin

version of the name, while **Thornton le Beans** (NYorks) has a touch of French. This range of languages is not uncommon. **Aston Subedge** (Glos) 'under the edge (of a ridge)' combines Latin and English, while **Thorpe sub Montem** and **Thorpe under Stone** both mean 'at the bottom of the hill', in contrast to another Yorkshire settlement **Thorpe on the Hill**.

Sometimes a place will have alternative names in different languages, so that **Bradwell-on-Sea** in Essex can also be known by the Latin version of its name **Bradwell juxta Mare**. **Weston super Mare** is also on the sea, while **Barnoldby le Beck** (Humb) 'by the stream' mixes French and Old Norse. In names such as **Chester le Street** (Dur), 'Roman town on the Roman road' the 'street' part usually refers to a Roman road, while the 'le' is all that is left of the French for 'in the'. The full form survives in names such as **Alsop en le Dale** (Derbs). Another example of alternative Latin and English names are **Walton Inferior** and **Superior** (Ches) which can be called by their English translations **Higher** and **Nether Walton**. Many pairs of villages likewise situated at different heights are distinguished by 'Upper' and 'Lower', while names such as **High Wycombe** (Bucks) are also found. **Ault Hucknall** in Derbyshire seems to be the only name from the French for high, *hault*.

The size of the village is also a common source of affixes. 'Great' and 'Little' are too common to need illustration. Rarer are names such as **Mickle Trafford** (Ches), and **Much Wenlock** (Shrops) or **Muckle Flugga** (Shet) as alternatives to 'Great'. (The last name is from the Old Norse meaning 'Large Cliffs'.) The Latin equivalents are found in **Appleby Magna** and **Appleby Parva** (Leics). **Tolleshunt Major** in Essex also looks as if it should be another Latin 'big' name, but actually gets its name from a man called Malger who held it in 1086.

Other apparently obvious names can be misleading. **Compton Greenfield** (Avon) actually comes from the name of the Grenville family, **Norton Hawkfield** (Avon) from the Hauteville family, and **School Aycliffe** (Dur) gets its name from someone with the Scandinavian name Scula, who was given land there c. 920. Popular etymology has been at work in all these cases. Some names that look as if they must be family names, on the other hand, are actually descriptive. Thus **Ainderby Quernhow** (NYorks) has a second half meaning 'mill hill', **Barton Bendish** (Nflk) means 'Barton within the ditch' (it is west of the Devil's Ditch), while **Thorp Thewles** (Clev)

means 'immoral' – the reasons for this are unknown and must be left to the reader's imagination.

Other affixes can tell us about the social position of the people who held the land. The power and wealth of the medieval church is amply reflected in place names. **Abbot's Bromley** (Staffs) belonged to Bromley Abbey, while **Stoke Abbot** and **Bradford Abbas** (both in Dorset) were held by the Abbot of Sherborne. The 'Abbas' in **Itchin Abbas**, however, comes not from the Latin for 'abbot', but is a reduced form of Latin *abbatissa*, 'abbess', for the village belonged to the nunnery of St Mary at Winchester. Nuns also held **Nun Appleton** (WYorks) and **Nuneaton** (Warks), as well as **Barrow Minchin** (Som) which gets its name from the Old English *mynecen*, 'a nun'. **White Ladies Aston** (H&W) comes from the Cistercian nuns at Whitstones who wore white robes, while **Brewood Black Ladies** (Staffs) was held by black-robed Benedictine nuns.

Monks are also to be found at the many **Monkton**s, and at places with names like **Monk's Eleigh** (Sflk) and **Monk Fryston** (NYorks). In Latin they appear in **Zeal Monachorum** (Devon) 'of the Monks' and **Toller Fratrum** (Dors) 'of the Brothers'. (The naming of the neighbouring village **Toller Porcorum** 'of the pigs' must surely have been done tongue in cheek.) Less obviously **Wimborne Minster** in Dorset gets its second half from the Old English for a monastery, just as many other places have 'church', 'kirk', 'chapel' or 'capel' or 'steeple' or have the saint to whom the parish church is dedicated as part of their name. **Tooting Bec** (GLon) gets its name from the Abbey of Bec in Normandy that held it. Names like **Fryer Mayne** (Dors) refer not to the mendicant Friars who were not permitted to own property, but to the Knights Hospitallers of St John.

'Bishop' in names such as **Bishop Auckland** (Dur), **Bishop's Stortford** (Herts) and **Eaton Bishop** (H&W), or the Latin **Huish Episcopi** and the contradictory **Kingsbury Episcopi** (Som) usually mean that the property was owned by the see rather than the individual bishop. Other members of the church are found in **Stoke Canon** (Devon) or the Latin **Whitchurch Canonicorum** (Dors), **Ash Priors** (Som), **Stoke Prior** (H&W), **Hinton Ampner** (Hants; see above), **Priest Hutton** (Lancs) and **Sacriston Heugh** (Dur). **Stour Provost** in Dorset is misleading for it is

From Baghdad to Baldock – the Knights Templars

The Knights Templars or, to give them their full name, the Poor Knights of Christ and of the Temple of Solomon, were one of the two chief Christian military orders in medieval times. Founded in 1119 with the intention of protecting pilgrims in the Holy Land, they became extremely wealthy, owning property throughout Christendom. The Order was suppressed by the Vatican in 1312 after accusations, almost certainly false, of heresy and corruption.

The word 'temple' in a place name usually marks property owned by the Templars. They had religious houses at **Templ**e (Cornwall and Lothian), and at **Templeton** (Berks and Devon). The remains of their castle and monastery can be seen at **Templemore** in Tipperary, although the name is Irish *teampall mor* 'big church'. They owned estates at **Templecombe** (Som) and at various places where **Temple** has been added to the settlement name, as in **Temple Bower** (Lincs), **Temple Dinsley** (Herts), and **Temple Normanton** (Derbs).

The Temple church in central London dates back to 1185, when the Templars acquired the site and built the church to the same design as their headquarters in Jerusalem. After the suppression of the Order the precincts were leased by lawyers and formed two of the four Inns of Court, the Inner Temple and the Middle Temple. The old Temple Bar, once a gateway to the City of London, stood just outside the precincts in Fleet Street; Temple Place and Temple Avenue are nearby.

The Templars owned land in many towns and cities; Bristol has a Temple Gate, Temple Street, Temple Bridge and, of course, Temple Meads station. A pub called the Temple at nearby **Temple Cloud** marks the site of a Templar's hospice.

As a source of names the Templars have proved surprisingly durable. Queen Matilda gave them land in Oxford in 1139, and the area was known as Temple Cowley by 1200; Templar Road was named in 1935 and a new shopping precinct in the area was named Templars Square in 1992. Temple station on the London underground stands at the south west corner of the old Temple precincts.

Any name containing 'temple' may well have a connection with the Order. The original meaning may soon be lost, however. Hindu and Sikh communities in many parts of Britain now have their own religious meeting places and it is only a matter of time before a 'temple' name refers to one of these.

The Templars wore a badge depicting two knights riding one horse; a symbol of the vow of poverty taken by individual knights, if not by the Order, and this sign probably appeared outside their hospices. After the Order was suppressed the sign became corrupted, often being depicted as a winged horse. Some pub names such as the Flying Horse, the Pegasus or the Winged Horse may indicate a connection with the Templars, if there is a long history of an inn on the site. Much of the Templars' property was granted to a similar order, the Knights Hospitallers of St John. They used the emblem associated with John the Baptist, usually shown as a lamb holding a banner. A pub called the Lamb and Flag may be connected with them if the name is recorded early enough (their lands were confiscated by Henry VIII in 1540).

And **Baldock**? This was a 'new town' founded by the Templars in the 12th century. They called it Baldac, the Old French name for the city of Baghdad.

a corruption of the name of the Norman Abbey of Préaux that held it. **Ashby Puerorum** in Lincolnshire means 'of the boys' (choirboys), while **Childer Thornton** (Ches) 'of the young men' refers to the young monks at Chester's St Werburgh's Abbey. Names containing 'child' need to be treated with care for in **Child Okeford** (Dors) the name is thought to refer to the old meaning of 'child', 'prince, young nobleman'.

The names of more worldly possessors of the land also feature in place names. As the major landholder, names such as **Kingston** are ten-a-penny, but are sometimes dressed up in Latin as in **Lyme Regis** (Dors) and **Letcombe Regis** (Oxon). **Bognor Regis** is a latecomer to this list, having acquired its title after a stay there by George V in 1929. **Queenborough** in Kent was named from Queen Philippa in the 14th century, but West Yorkshire's

Pontefract

Pontefract, meaning 'broken bridge', is a Latin name recorded as early as 1090. The name looks very straightforward, but the local pronunciation of the name, 'Pomfret', is rather different from the spelling. Pomfret is a longstanding pronunciation, for the town's name was spelt *Pumfrate* in about 1190, and it was once the general one, for in Shakespeare's play *Richard II* the defeated king is told 'You must to Pomfret, not unto the Tower'. But where does it come from?

The local pronunciation is the French form of the name, which would be something like *pont freit*. This was probably the original form, but the Latin would have been used in documents and may have been felt to be more dignified and thus became the official name. Obviously, as a French name it could not have been in use before the Conquest, although the town is much older. Its Old English name was *Taddenescylf*, 'Taedden's shelf of land', which is still in use today as Tanshelf to the west of Pontefract, and it had already been renamed once by the Scandinavians who called it *Kyrkebi*, 'church village'. Obviously it must have been a very significant event, this broken bridge, to change the name once more and to stick. Perhaps even more remarkable than the wide range of names this town has had is the fact that there is no real evidence about the events that gave the town its name.

Saffron Walden was originally called just Walden, Old English for 'valley of the Britons'. It acquired the first part of the name from the French word saffron, a popular medieval flavouring that was grown in Britain from the 14th century.
(POPPERFOTO)

How Shrewsbury became Shropshire

Shrewsbury is first recorded in 1006 as *Scropesbyrig*, an Old English name which probably means 'the fortified place in the area called The Scrub'. The development of the ending -*byrig* to -bury is quite regular, but the first half and its development into Shropshire and Salop need explaining.

The Normans found it difficult to pronounce groups of consonants together, so the opening /skr/ was a problem. In addition they could not always register the difference between /r/ and /l/ in English names (a common phenomenon world wide: some Eastern languages do not differentiate between the two sounds at all). The 'r' became an 'l', the 'sk' was simplified to a /s/ and an 'a' inserted to avoid a consonant group giving a name something like *Salopesberi* which is the sort of form usually found in official (i.e. Norman) documents in the 12th and 13th centuries. It is from this that the form Salop comes.

The county name Shropshire is a less radical altering of the first part of the name, with the 'r' kept and the 'sc' merely softened to /sh/ and the term for 'district' added to it. Meanwhile, back in Shrewsbury, the English had carried on using *their* form of the name, but the middle 'p' had gradually been softened first to a /b/ and then a /v/, possibly influenced by the sounds used by neighbouring Welsh speakers. Once reading and writing become widespread, it is remarkable how easily people allow their ideas of what is correct to be influenced by it, and this seems to have happened next. In medieval writing a /v/ or a /u/ in the middle of a word were both written as a 'u', a source of much confusion. A spelling such as *Shrousbury* seems to have led to the 'u' being thought of as a vowel, which led to the alternative spelling *Shrowsbury*.

The final change of Shrow- to Shrew- is an even more bizarre case of the townspeople changing their habits to suit written forms. Through the 15th to 18th centuries many words beginning 'sh' and with 'w' after the vowel could be spelt either 'shrew-' or 'shrow-' and could be pronounced in either way. Thus 'shrewd' was also found as 'shrowd' and 'show' could be 'shew', while we still have 'sow' and 'sew'. This confusion seems to be the cause of the change in vowel. It is worth noting finally that although most people pronounce the name, ignoring this final spelling change, so that Shrewsbury's first vowel sound rhymes with 'owe', in the town itself the pronunciation with the vowel sound of 'food' is also found.

Queensbury was named in 1863 from a local pub, the Queen's Head. Local legend connects **Queen Camel** (Som) with Camelot and Guinevere, but this cannot be, for the oldest form of the name is *Cantmael*, possibly from Celtic words meaning 'district' and 'bare', and it only gained its 'Queen' after it came into the hands of Queen Eleanor in the 13th century. Likewise **Princethorpe** in Warwickshire was *Prandestorpe* 'hamlet of Praen or Pren' in 1221, but **Princes Risborough** was held by the Black Prince. Among the aristocracy we find **Countessthorpe** (Leics), **Erlestoke** (Warks), **Earls Colne** (Essex) and **Collingbourne Ducis** (Wilts) from the Latin 'of the duke'. Lower down the social scale there is **Tolleshunt Knights** (Essex), **Sheriff Hutton** and **Thornton Steward** (NYorks) and the humble **Thorpe Acre** (Leics) which gets its name from a corruption of the Hawker who held it.

Although this long list is by no means exhaustive, the majority of other affixes will be family names. Many of these are only slightly changed from those of their owners, but others can be deceptive: **Theydon Bois** in Essex looks as if it gained its name from the French for 'wood', but this is only indirectly the case for the manor was held by the de Bosco or Boys family by the 12th century, although their surname could have come from the word for 'wood'. Similarly **Stoke Farthing** (Wilts) has nothing to do with money, but is a delightful corruption of the name of Rois de Verdun who held the manor in 1242.

Castles, forests and chases

Castles, forests and chases were all Norman introductions. The Anglo-Saxons had had a few fortified buildings which we might call proto-castles, but the Normans and their heirs were the great builders of these fortresses, at first earth mounds with a wooden structure on top, then increasingly complex stone buildings. These were important buildings which needed royal permission to be built, and could be a useful way of distinguishing one village from another, as in **West Bromwich** and **Castle Bromwich** in the West Midlands. They could also give their name to a place, as in **Barnard Castle** (Dur), built by someone called Bernard in the 12th century, or in the common name **Castleton**.

However, not all 'castle' names actually come from castles. Once they became a common feature of the landscape, folk etymology could cause other names to change to 'castle'. So **Castleford** (WYorks), first recorded as *Ceaster forda*, illustrates the way in which *caester*, 'Roman camp' can become 'castle'. **Castley** (NYorks) shows the danger of confusion between Old English *ceastel*, 'heap of stones' and 'castle', while **Castlett** (Glos) is simply a corruption of the name *Cateslat*, 'valley of the

wild cats', found in the Domesday Book. In addition 'castle' may be used of ruins and mounds from earlier times, as in the great Iron Age hill fort of Maiden Castle.

William the Conqueror, like so many Normans, was a very keen huntsman, and loved the deer, one chronicler tells us, as if they were his own children. It is to this Norman passion for hunting that we owe the terms forest and chase. Nowadays we tend to use the term forest as a term for a large wood, but this is not its original sense. It was uncultivated land, and thus often wooded, but included areas of scrub and pasture, but most important of all it was an area set aside for the king to hunt in, and had its own laws and officers to see that no one infringed his rights. Thus Nottingham's **Sherwood** ('shire-wood') **Forest** is not a repetitive name as it seems at first, and when William the Conqueror created the **New Forest** in Hampshire it was a very new idea indeed, for such things had not existed under the Saxons. A chase was an alternative term for a royal hunting enclosure, and is referred to in **Cannock Chase** (Staffs), the first part meaning 'hillock', and **Cranborne Chase** (Dors and Wilts) meaning 'crane-brook'.

Cambridge and Grantchester

The university town of **Cambridge** and its suburb of **Grantchester** both owe their name to the same source, the river on which they stand. This was originally called the Granta, and the earliest record of Cambridge's name is c. 745 as *Grontabrioc*, 'bridge on the river Granta'. However, this name presented the Normans with a number of problems of pronunciation and the name started to change. The initial 'Gr' was first changed to a 'cr' which they found easier to pronounce, and then simplified to a 'c'. The resulting *Cantbridge still had a cluster of four consonants in the middle, a major problem for French speakers, so these then drifted towards an easier pronunciation. First of all the 't' was swallowed, and then, because it is easier to say, the 'n' became an 'm', leaving us with Cambridge. The Normans could now pronounce the name, but they were left with the apparently nonsensical situation of a town named from its river crossing, but with a river name that did not match. It was almost inevitable that the process called backformation (see p.65) should come into play, and that the river should be re-named the **Cam**.

Meanwhile, down in Grantchester the river still keeps its old name. Perhaps the village was not important enough to have to fit Norman speech, and was able to keep its original first element. Our earliest records of it give us the Old English form *Granteseta*, 'settlers of the Granta'. this shows that the -chester has nothing to do with the ending indicating Roman settlement. However, Cambridge itself had the alternative Old English name *Grantaceaster*, 'Roman town on the Granta', which was used by some writers into the 12th century, and this may well have influenced Grantchester's name.

The Celtic Realms

M ost of the place names of Roman Britain were Celtic, and the invading Anglo-Saxons did not exterminate the native British. Groups of British speakers survived under Saxon rule, possibly as late as the 8th century. The Celtic Realms reveals the survival of British

names in English-speaking areas, and looks at those areas the Saxons did not reach, or only reached too late to dominate the place names – Cornwall, Wales, Ireland and Scotland.

The Celtic languages – minding your Ps & Qs

The Celtic languages spoken in the British Isles fall into two groups. One branch is the direct descendant of the language of Roman Britain, and is made up of Welsh, Cornish, the northern dialect of British known as Cumbric and to some extent Pictish, once the language of north-east Scotland. The other branch is made up of Irish Gaelic or Erse and its descendants the Gaelic of the Scottish Highlands and Islands, and in part, Manx. These languages are called British or Brythonic for the first branch, and Goidelic for the second. They are also known as P-Celtic and Q-Celtic for the Brythonic group has the sound 'p' where the Goidelic group has 'q' or 'c'. Thus the Old Welsh word for Britain, Priten, appears in Old Irish as Cruithni, their name for the Picts. The original Irish form of the British St Patrick's name would have been 'Cothric' and the Welsh word pen 'head, chief' appears in Goidelic names as ceann.

The Celtic languages spoken today share a common feature which can make them seem very difficult to outsiders. The first sound of a word can change or disappear depending on its relationship with the preceding word. If this seems unlikely, rest assured that it is even done to a minor extent in English, but we do not show it in our written word forms while the Celtic languages do. Try saying 'I have got to catch that train' as you would say it if you were running down a station platform. Even though there are five 't's, you only hear two of them: one in the middle of 'got to' and one at the end of 'that'. If you wrote it down exactly as you say it then it would look something like 'I (or I've) gotta cash that rain.' The origin of consonant mutation in the Celtic languages was similar, although more formalized than in English.

The changes had been caused by the grammatical endings of words which were later lost, just as they were in the change from Old to Modern English. However, and this is where life gets complicated, the mutations were not dropped. They were thought to have been caused by the grammar rather than the sounds of a sentence and have remained in use to the present day, not only in everyday speech, but also in place names. The rules which govern these changes are too complicated to be explained in a place-name book, but a chart (see pp. 99, 106, 110) is provided to show the different mutations as each language is dealt with.

of the country depopulated and were freer to chose their own names. That the people who moved to Brittany included a strong element from the south-west is certainly supported by the fact that the Breton language is closely connected with Cornish, which would presumably be similar to the British spoken in Devon. The British tribal names the *Cornovii*, the source of modern Cornwall, and the *Dumnonii*, the source of modern Devon, are also found in Brittany.

As well as many river names surviving from the British speech, the names of other prominent natural features have survived. Ranges of hills such as the **Malverns**, 'bare hill', the **Quantocks**, '?border' and the **Mendips**, 'mountain', are Celtic, while the **Cheviots** and **Chilterns** are also pre-English, and possibly pre-Celtic. The **Pennines** present a special problem. The name is not found until the 18th century, when it is used in a chronicle supposedly by a medieval monk called Richard of Cirencester, but actually a forgery by someone called Charles Bertram. No one feels inclined to trust the evidence of a forger, but the name looks as if it comes from the common British element *pen* used of hills, and it is inconceivable that these hills, which form such an important barrier to east-west communication even today, did not have some sort of a name before then. Some Celtic forest names such as **Arden**, 'high district', and **Wyre**, from a local 'winding river', have also survived. These three types of feature, hills, woods and rivers, have also been the main source of surviving Celtic names in England.

One British word for a hill was **bregh*, which can take the modern form Bre-, Bra-, Bri- or -ber (but does not include the Scottish *brae*, which comes from an Old Norse word meaning 'brow'). Thus we find **Bredon** (H&W), 'hill hill' (as we shall see, a common enough phenomenon, when an Old English element of the same meaning has been added to the British description of a prominent feature, found in an even more extreme form in **Breedon on the Hill**, Leics). Similarly there is the Devon **Bray** (but not that in Berkshire which probably comes from the French for marsh), and **Brill** in Buckinghamshire where the 'll' is the remains of yet another 'hill'.

As a second element it is found in names such as **Kinver** (Staffs) and reduced even further in **Mellor** (GMan and Lancs), found earlier as *Melver*, 'smooth hill'. **Brean** (Som)

The river names of this country tend to get older the further north or west you go, and the same applies as a general rule to the survival of early British names. There are, however, local fluctuations, depending, we must assume, on the history of relations between the two races. Even these fluctuations can help us reconstruct the past, and an interesting case is Devon. Cornish names are predominantly Celtic, and Celtic names are common in Dorset and Somerset, but are rather less common in Devon, although we might expect them to be more common.

One explanation for this is that the mass emigration of the British to what is now named Brittany (after them), which took place between the mid-5th and the early 7th centuries, had included a large proportion of the population of Devon. When the Anglo-Saxons had pushed west through the more densely populated Somerset and Dorset and reached Devon in the mid- to late 7th century they found parts probably comes from the same root, while a related word *barr 'hill-top' gives us **Great Barr** (WMid), the county of **Berkshire** and **Barrow in Furness** (Cumb). The latter case is a typical example of the area in that it is made up of a mixture of Celtic and Old Norse elements: the -ow part of Barrow comes from the old Norse *ey*, 'island', here used to indicate 'headland', while the -*ness* of the second part, originally the Old Norse *Fuththernessa*, also means 'headland'. The first part of *Fuththernessa* means 'island shaped like someone's backside'. A third Celtic hill term is *brinn, found in **Bryn** (Shrops), the second half of **Malvern**, and as *bryn*, a common modern Welsh word.

Celtic *croco* – which has developed into modern Welsh *crug* and has been discussed in the Roman source for Penkridge (p.26) – can also mean 'hill', but has a rather wider range of meanings, including 'ridge' and 'burial mound'. It is found in **Crich** (Derbs), **Crichel** (Dors), **Cricklade** (Wilts), **Cricklewood** (GLon), **Crewkerne** (Som), less obviously in **Christon** (Som), **Kirkley** (Nmbd) and many more places. It is not the source of Kirkley in Suffolk which is the more obvious 'clearing belonging to a church'. It is also the source of many of the **Churchill**s, the repetitive 'hill' having been added after the meaning of the first element has been lost, and the first element 'rationalized' to 'church' even if there had never been a church on that particular hill. The related word *creig, 'cliff, rock' gives us names such as **Crayke** (NYorks), **North** and **South Creake** (Nflk) and **Creaton** (Northants).

Our old friend Penkridge (see p. 26) re-appears again in the last hill element *penn, meaning 'end, head, headland, hill', and as an adjective 'chief'. This element is still found in Welsh, but needs to be carefully distinguished in place names from those which come from Old English *penn*, 'a pen for animals'. Two *penn names find their way into every book on place names to illustrate the way that the meaning of *penn must have been lost to the Anglo-Saxons, for they added elements of their own with the same meaning. These are **Penhill** (NYorks) and **Pendle Hill** (Lancs). The meaning of the first is obvious. The second one is actually 'hill' three times, Pendle being a reduced form of Pen-hill, with another 'hill' added later.

Names from this group are found throughout the areas where British was spoken. In Scotland we find names such as **Penicuik**

(Loth; 'cuckoo hill'), there is **Penrith** 'chief or hill ford' in Cumbria and a steady spread of names throughout the country down to **Penryn** 'headland' and **Penzance** 'holy headland' in Cornwall. Sometimes in Wales and elsewhere the 'Pen-' becomes changed to 'Pem-' so we find **Pembroke** in Dyfed which is in Welsh **Penfro** or 'Land's End'.

A group of three names – **Pencoyd** (H&W), **Penketh** (Ches) and **Penge** (GLon) – brings us on to our next element *ced (modern Welsh *coed*), for they are all forms of a name meaning 'chief wood' or 'wood's end'. In chapter one we have seen that Lichfield comes from the Roman names *Letocetum* 'grey wood', and **Lytchett Matravers** and **Lytchett Minster** in Dorset show us the form the name would probably have taken if it had not acquired its English second half, for they come from the same words. Other names using *ced (the 'c' would have started hard, but tended to become /ch/ in Old English) include the repetitive **Chute Forest** (Wilts), **Melchet Forest** and **Chetwode** (Bucks), **Culcheth** (Ches) and **Culgaith** (Cumb) both meaning 'narrow forest', **Cheadle** (Ches), **Chicklade** (Wilts) and **Chatham** (Kent).

The last three bring us to an interesting problem of interpretation. We know that the Anglo-Saxons were quite capable of inventing a founding hero for a place whose name they did not understand, for we have seen them do it with 'Hrof' of Rochester and 'Port' (see p. 25). A number of names such as **Chattenden** (Kent), **Chattisham** (Sflk), **Chatton** (Nmbd) and **Chetwynd Aston** (Shrops) are interpreted as referring to an Anglo-Saxon name such as Ceatta, Catta or *Ceatt. How many of these may actually come from *ced, but have had a founder invented for them? We can't

---

Black Waters

England, Ireland, Scotland and Wales all share Celtic place names meaning 'black water', which serve to illustrate the relationship between the two branches of the Celtic tongue. Those in England and Wales – The Rivers **Dalch** and **Dawlish** in Devon, the **Dowles**, **Dowlish** in Somerset, and the **Dowlas**, **Dulais** and **Dulas** in Wales can be traced back to the British words *dubo* 'black' and *glassio* 'water, stream', or the Welsh equivalents *du* and *(g)lais*. **Douglas** – found in England, Scotland, Ireland and the Isle of Man – comes from the Irish or Gaelic *dubh* and *glas* (earlier *dub glas*), words with the same root and meaning. While many name elements are much further apart than this, there are many other examples in this book of elements common to both branches which are sometimes divided more by the different spelling systems than by their sounds.

know the answer to that, but it is a possibility worth keeping in mind, for there is no doubt that there are a good number of names such as **York** (see p. 27), that we would never guess were Celtic in origin, if we did not have the evidence.

Our final group of names, those from rivers, includes a large group of places which are named from the river on which they stand. Obvious examples are **Nether** and **Upper Exe, Exebridge, Exeter, Exford, Exminster, Exmoor, Exmouth** and **Exton**, all named after the Celtic **River Exe**, meaning 'water'. We have already seen that Cambridge (see p. 93) is not named from the river Cam, but **Cam** and **Cambridge** in Gloucestershire are named from a **River Cam** which comes from a common Celtic element meaning 'crooked, winding' which is found in **Kirkcambeck** (Cumb), **Camelford** (Corn) and **Camerton** (Avon) among others. It is not always a stream that is crooked, for **Cambois** in Northumberland refers to the bay it is on, and **Camborne** in Cornwall is 'crooked hill'. We have already seen another element meaning 'water' in Dover (p. 27) and to this list can be added **Candover** 'pleasant waters' and the less attractive **Micheldever**, 'boggy waters', both in Hampshire. Finally, the word which is now the common Welsh element *lynn* 'lake, pool' is found in names such as **King's Lynn** in Norfolk, not to be confused with the similar **Lyme Regis** ('of the king') in Dorset, which gets its name from a Celtic word meaning 'stream'.

One good way of identifying Celtic names is if the stress of the word is on the second element of the names, which reflects the original stress, as opposed to the usual English stress on the first part of the word. This is found in names such as **Cardurnock** (Cumb) from *cair*, 'fort', and **durnog*, 'pebbly', **Tretire** (H&W; from *rhyd*, 'ford', and *hir*, 'long'), and our old friend **Pensax** (see p. 44). These names have the adjective following the noun, so that Tretire means 'ford-long' rather than 'long ford'. Celtic names of this form are later than those that are formed adjective + noun, and later still are some of the purely Welsh names found in parts of Shropshire and Hereford, which have been given by Welsh settlers in the area, some of them as recently as the last century. Examples are **Nant Mawr**, and **Maes-Coed**, both of which are made up of Welsh elements listed below.

This brief survey of some of the commoner elements has of course only covered a small proportion of the Celtic survivals, many of them important towns such as **Crewe** 'the weir or fishtrap' in Cheshire and **Leatherhead** 'grey ford' in Surrey. However, the place names of the heirs to the British speakers of Roman and Dark Age times, the Welsh and the Cornish, must be considered. For the sake of simplicity an attempt has been made to call all the places in Celtic areas by the name that they are most widely known, rather than by local names that supporters of local languages might prefer. Apologies are offered for any offence given.

Welsh place names

The place names of Wales fall into three main groups: English, Norse and Celtic. Many of the English names are transparent in their meaning. **Newtown, Newport, Holyhead, Holywell, Bridgend, Flint** and **Welshpool** all mean exactly what they appear to be. Others like **Chepstow**, 'market place', **Hay,** 'hedge', and **Knighton**, 'the young men's farm', should be easily interpreted by reference to earlier chapters.

However, the development of other names has sometimes been affected by the local accent

or spelling convention or they have used a mixture of English and Welsh, so they may not be instantly recognizable. For instance, **Prestatyn** in Clwyd would normally have become Preston in England. But in Wales the stress is usually put on the second to last syllable, so the 'e' found in the Domesday Book entry *Presteton*, the Old English inflection that showed that it was 'the farm *of* the Priest', has been preserved to become the 'a' in the middle of the name. The final *-ton* has become *-tyn* under Welsh influence in the same way as the name that is found in England as Moston, became **Mostyn** in Clwyd.

Another priest name is **Presteigne** in Powys, the second element being Old English *haemed*, 'household'. **Wrexham** in Clwyd means 'Wryhtel's pasture' and in England would have become something like *Wrightham. However, Welsh attempts to spell the name led to forms such as *Gwregsam* (found in 1291) and later *Gwrecsam*, and the name we have today comes from these. **Haverfordwest** in Dyfed, from Old English 'great ford', owes its 'west' to the local pronunciation which is 'Harford'. This led to possible confusion with the English Hereford, an important link in the Middle Ages between Wales and England, so the Welsh town, recorded as *Herefordwest* in 1471, acquired an extra part to its name to distinguish it from the English town.

Rhyl in Clwyd is an example of the hybrid names which mix two languages together. In England it would probably have become *Hill or *Hull, for its name comes from *hyll*, the Old English for 'hill'. However, the Welsh for 'the', *yr*, was put in front of it to make *yr hull* and Rhyl was born. Other hybrids are more simply understood, such as **Pontypool** in Gwent which is made up of Welsh *pont* 'bridge' + *y* 'the' and English 'pool'. **Glasbury** in Powys is made up of Welsh *clas* 'a monastic community' with Old English *burh* 'market town' on the end. **Portmadoc** and **Tremadoc**, even in their Welsh forms **Porthmadog** and **Tremadog**, should probably be counted among the hybrid names, although they look Welsh. They are both comparatively modern foundations, having been founded by William Alexander Madocks on land he had reclaimed from the sea. Tremadoc 'Madoc's town' was started about 1800, and Portmadoc 'Madock's port' in 1821. They are hybrid because if the names had been truly Welsh the initial sound of Madocks would have changed (see below) and the names become *Trefadog and *Porthfadog.

Before leaving the English names of Wales, it is worth issuing the usual warning that not everything is as it seems. **Chirk** in Clwyd looks very English, but is actually a heavily anglicized form of the name of the River Ceiriog. **Barmouth** in Gwynedd looks very simple. It is on a river mouth which had a prominent sand bank across part of it, and on maps of the area there is a river mouth marked as 'The Bar'. But all this is deceptive. The name is actually Welsh and means 'mouth of the River Mawddach'.

The river was earlier the *Mawdd*, the *-ach*, which is an ending meaning 'little' having been added later. The town was first found as *Abermau* in 1284. The first syllable of *aber* 'river mouth' was dropped and the river name rationalized as the English word 'mouth', giving us Barmouth. (The town has not fared much better in Welsh, where the same original name has ended up as **Y Bermo**.)

Welsh names

Before looking at the elements that make up names that come from Welsh, it is necessary to look at the Welsh language itself. As explained in the box on p. 96, Celtic languages undergo mutation or regular changes to the first sound of a word, under certain circumstances, depending on the preceding word. Welsh consonants can mutate in three different ways, shown in the table below.

sound		mutated forms	
b	f /v/	m	
c /k/	g	ngh /ngh/	ch /kh/
d	dd /th/	n	
g	sound dropped	ng /ng/	
ll/hl/	l		
m	f /v/		
p	b	mh	ph /f/
rh	r		
t	d	nh	th /dh/

Not all consonants mutate, and not all that do take all the mutations. As a guide to Welsh pronunciation the sound of the letters is indicated between // after the mutated form, if it differs from English.

The circumstances under which these changes take place are too complicated to explore here, and can be found in any introduction to Welsh, but it is worth noting that the mutations listed in the first column are the commonest, and that they occur in the second element in compound place names. They are also likely after feminine words (Welsh, like French, has masculine and feminine nouns and adjectives). Since mutations obviously make it difficult to look words up, some of the commonest elements have been listed in both their root and most frequent mutated forms.

Those feeling impossibly confused by this can take heart in the fact that the Welsh themselves can be fooled by the mutations in

Llanfairpwllgwyngyllgogerychwyrndrobwllllandysiliogogogoch

The artful construction of Llanfairpwllgwyngyllgo-gerychwyrndrobwllllandysiliogogogoch out of two adjoining par-ish names with all the trimmings added, but of no real antiquity, has been a source of considerable additional revenue to railway companies as well as proving to be a lucrative attraction to credulous but hard-headed business operatives. In this manner Gwynneth Pierce dismisses this now-discredited village name on Anglesey, now shortened to Llanfairpwllgwyngyll. But the name can still function as a useful introduction to analysing Welsh names.

The first two syllables are made up of *llan* = church and *fair*, the mutated form of *Mair*, 'Mary', and the original name was 'The

Church of St Mary at Pwllgwyngyll'. *Pwllgwyngyll* is a place name made up of *pwll* = pool, *gwyn* = white and *gyll* = hazel, i.e. 'The white hazel pool'. Sometime in the 19th century some joker – said to be the local tailor – decided to see if he could improve on this. The next section breaks down into *goger* = near, *y* = the, *chwyrn* = rapid, *drobwll* = mutated form of *trobwll* (*tro* + *pwll* again) meaning 'whirlpool', a reference to the Pwll Ceris in the nearby Menai Strait. To this was added the name of another parish, Llandysilio, 'St Tysilio's Church', but in the form that is found in the parish of the same name in Dyfed, with *Gogo(f)*, 'by the cave' as a distinguishing ending. The *-goch* at the end seems simply to have been added for the heck of it, to round the whole thing off.

place names. **Kidwelly** (Welsh **Cedweli**) comes from the Welsh personal name Cadwal + the ending 'i' meaning 'territory of', but popular etymology understands it as '*ced* + *(g)wely*'. *Gwely* is the Welsh for 'bed', and in a com-pound would lose its initial 'g'. In the past the name has been analysed as *cath* + *gwely*, 'cat's bed' or *cyd* + *gwely* 'common bed', thought to refer to the two rivers that reach the sea near Kidwelly. The Mid Glamorgan town of **Moun-tain Ash** – given its English name at the time of its expansion in the 19th century – has kept its old Welsh name of **Aberpennar**. This has the first element *aber* 'mouth' and then the name of the local stream, the Pennar. This probably comes from the word *pennardd* mean-ing 'height' referring to its source, but has also been interpreted as *pen* 'head' + *arth* 'bear' or *pen* + *garth* 'ridge', the source of **Penarth**.

We can now look at the different groups of elements that make up the commonest Welsh

place names. It is always dangerous to compare different languages and cultures unless you are equally familiar with both, but, nevertheless, the reader might like to speculate about the relevance to place names of Wales' long inde-pendence and its geography. Certainly, given the geography of Wales, it is understandable that the same word, *chwaen*, can come to mean both 'a piece of land' and 'windy place' or in a society largely dependent on farming, *cyfoeth*, a word with the basic meaning 'wealth', can come to mean 'territory, land' in place names. But the existence of *chwileiriog*, 'land infested with maggots or vipers', and *chwilog*, 'land infested with beetles', is a bit more puzzling. What will be clear is the status of Welsh as the heir of British, for many of the name elements will be familiar from chapter one and the first part of this chapter.

The best-known word connected with water is probably *aber*, meaning an estuary or the confluence of two bodies of water. This is

Mutation to mythology

On a visit to the town of **Beddgelert** a tale will be told of how Llywelyn, Prince of Wales, left his hound Gelert to guard the cradle of his baby son. When he returned Llywelyn found the cradle empty, Gelert's jaws dripping with blood and no sign of the baby. In grief and fury the prince pulled out his sword and killed the dog. Only then was the baby found alive and well by the body of a wolf (or snake) the condition of which showed that it had only been killed after a desperate battle with the faithful hound. There is even a stone raised to commemorate the noble beast.

Alas, Beddgelert does not mean 'grave of Gelert', but is from an Irish personal name Celert or Cilert, no doubt one of the many Irish settlers who came to Wales in the early Middle Ages, and the tale of Gelert is a folk tale found in different versions throughout the world. The earliest recorded form of the town's name is *Bekelert* (1258) and forms with a 'g' only occur from the 16th century, no doubt influenced both by the story of Gelert and by the fact that 'g' is a mutation of 'c'. As for the grave stone – this is said to have been put up by the landlord of the Royal Goat Hotel, at the

end of the 18th century, thereby encouraging both the story of Gelert and the local tourist trade.

In the same way Wales is full of legends of Helen or Elen – either stories of Helen, mother of the Emperor Constantine the Great, or of Elen Luyddog, in legend the wife of Magnus Maximus who led the Roman legions from Britain to seize the emperor's throne. Many of the Helen stories seem to come from a blending of these two women, and have given rise to many roads or tracks with the name 'Sarn Helen'. *Sarn* is an interesting word, often used of old Roman roads, and at one time it was believed that any *sarn* must be a Roman road. However, we now know that many of the 'sarns' have nothing to do with Roman roads, as the term could be used for any firm road surface, whether it be the remnants of a metalled Roman road or a firm causeway across a marsh. 'Sarn' is also used of a road along which a particular commodity is transported, and it is likely that many a romantic-sounding Sarn Helen is actually a corruption of *Sarn-yr-halen*, 'salt route' while others are *sarn hoelion* 'paved causeway'.

found in dozens of Welsh names; on its own in Dyfed and Gwynedd, in **Aberaeron** in Dyfed, where the second part comes from Aeron, the ancient goddess of battle, in **Aberavon** (*Aberafan*; WGlam), **Aberdare** (MidGlam), **Aberdovey** (*Aberdyfi*; Gwyn) and **Abergele** (Clwyd), which all take their names from the rivers on which they stand. *Aber* is of course also common in Scotland, in names such as **Aberdeen**, *aber* + River Don, named from Devona, another Celtic goddess, and **Aberdour**, *aber* + River Dour, a name that comes from the same root as Dover and means 'waters'. Here the element is a reminder of the way that British was once spoken throughout the island, before the Anglo-Saxons took over the bulk of the land.

The second element of Aberdour appears in Welsh as *dwfr* or *dŵr*, 'water'. *Afon*, 'river', is a common Welsh element, which in its British form was the source of the many River **Avon**s throughout the island. *Carrog, glas, glais* (frequently found in its mutated form *las, lais*), and *nant, nentydd* (pl) or *nannau* mean 'brook, stream', as does *ffrwd, ffrydiau* (pl), which is also used of a mountain torrent. This could start its life at a place containing the element *ffynnon*, 'a spring', and flow via a *rhaeadr, rhaiadr* or *rhayader* or a *pistyll* both meaning 'a waterfall', to a *ceunant*, 'ravine, gorge' although this is sometimes used just to mean 'a brook'. **Bala** (Gwyn) gets its name from the Welsh word for the point where a river flows out of a lake, words for lake being *llyn* or *llwch, llychau* (pl). *Pwll, pyllau* (pl) means 'pit, pool'.

A *ffos, ffosydd* (pl) means 'a ditch', as does *clawdd*, although this can also be used for a hedge. *Glan* means 'river-bank', although it can also be used of an ordinary bank or even a hillock. *Ystum* means 'bend in a river', as does *cemais* or *cemeas* although this can also mean a similar curve of the coast. *Cilfach*, often met in its mutated form *gilfach*, is made up of the words *cil* 'a corner' + the mutated form of *bach* 'little'. It means 'a little nook' hence 'cove, creek, corner'. To cross any body of water either a *rhyd* 'ford' or *pont* 'bridge' is needed. The latter often appears in its mutated form *bont*.

Down at the sea (*môr*) there are names with *trwyn*, 'point, cape' (literally 'nose'), *traeth*, 'shore', *porth*, 'harbour' (also 'gateway'), and *ynys, ynysoedd* (pl), 'island' (also used for 'water meadow').

Finally, various elements for wet land include *cors* (mutated *gors*), *mign, mignen, mignedd* (pl), or *morfa, trallwng* or *trallwm*, all meaning

Is Cowbridge Roman?

Cowbridge, South Glamorgan, is made up of two clearly English elements 'cow' and 'bridge', but it is just possible that its name goes back to Roman times or even earlier. It is thought that Roman Cowbridge was called *Bovium*, a name which in British would mean something like 'cow-place'. The similarity of meaning may be more than coincidence. When the town reappears in our records it is *Coubrugge* (1263) in English and *Pont y Fywch* (1657–60) in Welsh. The latter comes from *pont* 'bridge', *y* 'the' and *buwch* in its mutated form, 'cow'. Meanwhile, another bridge had been built, this time of stone, and an alternative name of *y Bont Faen* 'stone bridge' had grown up.

The issue was confused in the 18th century when an attempt was made to reconcile this alternative name with the English name and *Pont y Fôn* was invented which, it was claimed, meant 'cow bridge'. This led a lot of students of place names to think that there was no original connection between the Welsh and English names. There is no possibility of any antiquarian influence in the development of the name, for the Roman name of Cowbridge is nonsensical in the only ancient text it is recorded in, and its form has been reconstructed in modern times from the name stamped on some roof tiles found at an excavated Roman villa.

'bog, marsh, fen'. *Gwern* (mutated *wern*) originally meant 'place where alders grow' but has expanded its meaning to 'swamp'.

Some well-known places that contain some of these elements are **Amlwch** (Gwyn; 'near the pool'), **Llanymddyfri** (Dyfed; 'church near the waters'), **Nantyglo** (Gwent; 'coal brook'), the various places called **Pontnewydd** ('new bridge'), along with many other pont names such as **Pontardawe** 'bridge over the River Tawe' and **Pontardulais** 'bridge over the Dulais' (WGlam). **Pontllanfraith** in Gwent originally had *llyn* as its middle element and meant 'bridge by the varicoloured lake', but popular etymology changed *llyn* to the more common *llan*. **Pontypridd** (MidGlam) is 'bridge of the earth house' and **Talybont** in Powys means the same as **Bridgend** in Mid Glamorgan. **Porthcawl** in Mid Glamorgan is the 'port where sea-kale grows', while the meaning of **Aberporth** in Dyfed should be clear. **Pwllheli** in Gwynedd is 'salt pool'.

It will come as no surprise that the rugged land of Wales has led to a wide range of place-name elements for different aspects of hills and mountains. *Blaen, blaenau* (pl) is the term used for uplands in general, although it can also indicate 'head, end, source of a river'. *Bre*, which we have met before in its British form, and *bryn, bryniau* (pl) mean 'hill', while *allt, elltydd* (pl) is often a wooded hill or can mean a hillside or slope. *Gallt* shows the same range of hill shifting to slope and wood, reflecting a way of thinking that covers not just the shape of the country, but its ecology. Other words for slope are *llethr* and *rhiw*, while *bron* (mutated to *fron*), *bronydd* (pl) literally means 'breast', so is the swelling side of a hill, as is *llechwedd*. *Ael* is the brow of a hill or a headland. More ambiguous are *garth* (mutated to *arth*) which can signify hill, promontory or enclosure, and *banc, bencydd* (pl) meaning 'bank, hill or slope'. Smaller hills or knolls are found in names with *cnwc(h), twyn* and *crug, crugiau* (pl) which can also mean 'a heap'.

The standard Welsh word for 'a mountain' is *mynydd* although in place names this word can also signify 'moorland' (more often found as *rhos, rhosydd* (pl) or *gwaun, gweunydd* (pl). *Carn* mutated to *garn, carnau* (pl) can also mean mountain but is also 'cairn, tumulus, rock' and its variant *carnedd* (mutated to *garnedd*), *carneddau* or *carneddi* (pl) has the same range of meanings. *Moel* (mutated *foel*) is a bare hill on which nothing will grow. People who live in mountains learn to see them in more detail than lowlanders, so that their place names have a variety of terms for different rock formations. *Clogwyn, craig* (mutated *graig*), *creigiau* (pl), *diffwys, tarren* (mutated *darren*), *tarenni* (pl) all have different shades of a general sense 'crag, rocky height, precipice'.

Braich, literally 'an arm', is a ridge or spur, while *esgair*, literally 'a leg', indicated a long ridge, an ordinary ridge being *trum* (mutated *drum*) or *cefn, cefnydd* (pl). Gaps and passes are also important if one is to travel in the mountains, and often appear in place names as *adwy, bwlch, bylchau* (pl) or *drws*, literally 'a door'. Terrain of this sort may not be the most hospitable of places to live in, but at least it is easy to defend – a fact reflected in elements such as *cadair* or *cader*, 'seat, stronghold' (also used of mountain peaks), *dun* (or *din*) and *dinas* meaning 'hill fort', but also used of natural features, and *caer* (mutated *gaer*) 'fort, stronghold' although this last is by no means restricted to upland forts.

Examples of places using these elements are **Penarth** (SGlam) 'end of the hill' (mutated *garth*), **Blaennau Ffestiniog** (Gwyn) where the second element probably means 'fortified position', and **Blaenavon** (Gwent) 'headwater of the river'. **Bryn-mawr** (Gwyn) means 'great hill', **Rhayadar** (*Rhaeadr*) in Powys means 'waterfall', while **Rhos-llannerchrugog** in Clwyd is made up of *Rhos*

'moor, heath' + *llanerch* 'clearing' + *grugog* 'heathery'. As well as appearing in British names dealt with earlier in the chapter, *crug* is found in **Criccieth** (Gwyn) 'mound of the captives', **Crickadarn** (*Crucadarn*) in Powys 'secure mound', and **Crickhowell** (*Crucywel*) in Powys 'Howell's mound'. **Caerphilly** (*Caerfili*) means 'Ffili's fort', **Caerleon**, fort of the legions', from the big Roman fort there, **Caernarfon**, 'fort facing Môn' (Anglesey), and **Cardiff**, 'fort on the river Taff.'

The peak of **Cader Idris** 'The seat of Idris' is supposed to be the place where the giant Idris, magician and astrologer, had his observatory. **Dinas Emrys** 'the hill fort of Ambrosius' has an important role to play in Arthurian legend as the site of the conflict between Ambrosius and Vortigern, the man who is supposed to have invited the Saxons to Britain. In fact, important archaeological remains from the Arthurian period have been found both at Dinas Emrys and at **Dinas Powys** 'the hill fort of Powys', **Powys** coming from a Latin word meaning 'province, region'. The related *dun* is found in **Denbigh** in Clwyd (in Welsh *Dinbych*) meaning 'little fort' and also in **Tenby** in Dyfed which is the same name, the 'd' hardened to 't' under the influence of English or Scandinavian speakers. It is probably also in **Rhuthun** in Clwyd, which is more likely to be *rhudd* 'red' + *din* than *rhudd* + *hin* 'bank, edge'.

Forts, of course, are not the only buildings in Wales. The traditional social structure of medieval Wales was of a prince or chief with his court or *llys* as the administrative centre. Much of the land was divided into administrative units. A small unit was called a *maenol*, a large unit a *maenor* (mutated *faenor*), which in turn were grouped into *commotes* and *cantrefs*, 'hundreds'. These terms used in place names usually indicate the house of the local chief, or the rich land which surrounded it. The settlement that grew up around the big house was known as the *maerdref* or *maerdre* (mutated *faerdre* (f)) or 'steward's hamlet'.

The second part of the word *maerdref* is the very important element *tref* (nearly always reduced to *tre* in speech, *dre* in its mutated form). It is found in such names as **Tredegar** 'farm of Tegyr' in Gwent and **Trefriw** 'farm on the hill' in Gwynedd. This element has a range of meanings similar to the Old English element -*ton*, and indeed the two elements are sometimes interchangeable in the Welsh or English versions of place names so that **Laleston** (MidGlam) can also be **Trelales**, and **Bonvilston** (SGlam), named after Simon de Bonville, appears in Welsh as **Tresimwn**. *Tref* originally had the meaning 'homestead, farm'. As the farm developed, no doubt often via an extended family, it became 'a group of people cultivating an area of land' (these would be peasants or villeins owing service to a common lord, rather than wealthy landowners). This group could then expand into a 'hamlet or village', and finally, just as *-tun* developed the sense town, *tref* could come to mean 'town'.

Another important group of place-name elements comes from the farming habit in mountainous areas of moving the animals up to the mountain pastures for the rich summer grazing, and back down to the more sheltered home farm for the winter. The home farm was called the *hendref,* literally 'old tref', while the summer dwelling was *hafdre*, 'summer tref', with alternative forms *hafod, hafodol, hafodty,* the last introducing the important name element *ty, tai* 'house'. As the tref expanded it could develop an offshoot on the further part of its land, which would be called a *pentre* (f). Another farm term is *tyddyn*, shortened to *ty'n,* meaning 'a small farm'. Humbler still is a *llety* or *lluest* both meaning 'a hut, shelter or cottage', while *bod* is simply 'an abode, dwelling'.

If we return to the ruling classes, they could live in a *cas* or *castell* meaning 'castle, fortified house' (also used of a similar natural feature and of ancient fortified sites), or a *plas*, 'hall, mansion'. The craftsmen are also represented in place names, with elements such as *efail, gefail* meaning 'smithy' and *melin (felin)* meaning 'mill'. A settlement with a mill is a *melindre,* and is found in Dyfed and Powys in a re-spelling of its mutated form **Velindre**. Industry is represented by *odyn*, 'a kiln' and *pandy* 'a fulling mill'. The latter is a common element, found for example in **Tonypandy**, 'meadow with a fulling mill', in Mid Glamorgan, which reminds us of the importance of the woollen industry in Wales.

Christian worship in Wales stretches back in an unbroken line to Roman times, and not surprisingly has had a great influence on place names. **Bangor** in Gwynedd acquired its name from the word for a monastery, originally a humble one built of wattle. *Mynachlog* is another term for monastery, and *diserth* a hermitage. *Betws* or *bettws*, as in **Betws-y-coed** (Gwyn), means 'prayer house in the wood'.

Betws is a term for a chapel of ease – a chapel built for the use of those who live too far from the church (*eglwys*) to reach it conveniently (*betws* must be approached with care, as there is an identical word meaning 'place where birches grow'). *Merthyr* can also mean church, as a development from its primary sense of 'burial place', so that **Merthyr Tydfil** (MidGlam) is 'The grave of St Tudful'. Another word for grave is *bedd, beddau* (pl), although this is also used for ancient burial mounds.

The Welsh church abounds in early and obscure saints, many of whom appear in place names, their sanctity shown by *sain, san* or *sant, saint* (pl). The most common word of all for a church or monastery is *llan*. Because it is so common, popular etymology has sometimes been at work and it has absorbed other elements. **Llancarfan** (SGlam) and **Llanthony** (*Llantoni*; Gwent) were originally *Nantcarfan* and *Llanddewi Nant Hoddni*, containing the element *nant* which originally meant 'valley' but later 'stream'. They are by no means alone in converting *nant* to *llan*.

Similarly we have already seen in **Pontllanfraith** (see p.101) one of the names where *lynn* becomes *llan*. Other elements that can shift to *llan* are *glan* 'bank' which becomes *lan* in its mutated form, *llwyn* 'bush, copse', and *llain* 'strip of land'. However, the majority of *llan* names are churches, many of them with very early foundations. **Lampeter** in Dyfed is

---

Chapel names

As Nonconformity spread through Wales in the early 19th century the Chapel rapidly became the centre of religious life for many of the ordinary people, although the Anglicized gentry tended to stick to the Church of England. The Chapels that were built could become so central to the lives of the people that the name of the Chapel, taken from a place name in the Bible, could actually replace the original name of the village. Similarly in some cases a settlement would grow up around an isolated chapel.

The best-known example of this is **Bethesda** (Gwyn), which was originally called *Y Wern Uchaf*, 'The upper marshland'. Bethesda, the name of a healing pool in Jerusalem where Jesus performed one of his miracles, is found elsewhere in Wales. Other biblical names include **Berea**, a town where St Paul preached, **Bethel** 'House of God' where Jacob had his dream of the stairway to heaven, and **Bethlehem**. **Beaulah** was a sort of promised land also found in *Pilgrim's Progress*. **Carmel** was prominent in the stories of Elijah and Elisha, and **Cesarea** was where the Holy Spirit first descended on a Gentile. **Hebron** was a city of refuge and once King David's capital, and **Nebo** was the mountain where Moses died. More puzzling are **Sodom** and **Babel** in Clwyd. Sodom may have been chosen to indicate the sinfulness of the penitent worshippers there, but it has also been suggested that it was originally Salem and corrupted by malicious neighbours, and Babel, alas, is probably from Welsh *pabell*, 'a tent, tabernacle'.

the English form of *Llanbedr Pont Steffan*, 'The church of St Peter at Stephen's Bridge'; Stephen was probably the name of a Norman charged with the upkeep of the bridge. **Llandaf(f)** (SGlam) is 'the church on the Taff', and **Llandeilo** (Dyfed), 'the church of St Teilo', is *Llandeilo Fawr* in Welsh. It is derived from *mawr* 'great' since it was the See of St Teilo, an early bishop (compare **Llanfairfechan** 'Little St Mary's' from *bechan* 'little'). **Llandudno** (Gwyn) is dedicated to St Tudno, **Llanelli** (Dyfed) to St Elli (said to have been the daughter of the Brychan who gave his name to the district of **Brecon**), **Llangollen** (Clwyd) to Collen, an early saint who reputedly resisted temptation by fairies, and **Llanrwst** (Gwyn) to St Gwrwst.

    Llandrindod Wells in Powys takes its name from *trindod*, the Welsh for 'trinity'. The 'wells' part was added in the 19th century when the town was being promoted as a spa. **Llantrisant** (MidGlam) is 'the church of the three saints' – Saints Illtud, Gwynno and Dyfodwg. St Illtud, one of the greatest scholars of his day, reappears in the name of **Llantwit Major** (*Llanilltyd Fawr*, SGlam). In the 6th century it was a centre of learning where St Illtud taught some of the most outstanding men of the day, including Gildas and St David of Wales himself. The common name **Llanfi(n)hangel** or **Llanvihangel** records a dedication to St Michael.

    Finally, we will list some other elements which are useful for interpreting Welsh names. Little words that show the relationship between other parts of the name include:

am = around, about
ar = on, upon, over, by
dan = under, below
fry = above
is = below, under
tan = under, below
tros = over
uchaf = upper, higher, highest
uwch = above, over
y, yr, 'r = the
yn = in

Words that describe or give more information on the basic meaning of the name include:

bach = small, little, lesser (as noun: corner, nook)
brych, brech = speckled

cam = crooked, bent
canol = middle
coch = red
dau or *dwy* = two
deg see *teg* (also means 10)
du, ddu = black, dark
dwy see *dau*
fach see *bach*
ganol see *canol*
garw = rough, coarse
glas = green, blue
goch see *coch*
gwyn, gwen = white
gwyrdd, gwerdd = green
hen = old
hir = long
isaf = low, lowest
isel = low
las see *glas*
lwyd see *llwyd*
llwyd = grey, brown
mawr = great, big, greater
melyn, melen = yellow
newydd = new
sych = dry
tair see *tri*
teg = fair
tri, tair = three
uchel = high
wen see *gwyn*

Other common elements include:

bro = region, vale, lowland, plain
cae, caerau = field, enclosure
cil, ciliau = corner, retreat, nook
clun = meadow, moor
cors = bog
croes = cross, crossroads (as adj: overhanging)
croesffordd, croeshoel or *croeslon* = crossroads
cwm, cymau or *cymoedd* = valley, dale
dol, dolau or *dolydd* = meadow
dyffryn = valley
ffin = boundary
fforch = fork
ffordd = way, road
garth = hill, promontory
glyn = glen, deep valley
gors see *cors*
groes see *croes*
heol or *hewl* = road
llawr = flat valley bottom
llech, llechau = slab, stone, rock
maen, meini or *main* = stone

maes, meysydd = field, plain
meini see maen
mign or mignen, mignedd = bog
morfa = marsh, fen
mwyn = ore, mine
pant = hollow, valley
parc = park, field
pen = head, top, end, edge
penrhyn = promontory

tâl = end
tir = land, territory
tomen or tom = mound
ton or tonnen, tonnau = grassland
trallwng or trallwm = marshy land
traws = direction, district
troed = foot, bottom
waun see gwaun
ystrad = valley, river-meadow

Cornish names

By the 10th century the Anglo-Saxons had pushed their way so far west that the River Tamar had become the boundary between them and the last remnant of the British peoples of the south-west. At this point Cornish started its life as an independent language, for the speakers of the south-western dialect of British no longer had land contact with their fellow British speakers of Wales. Gradually, over the centuries, Cornish speakers were confined to a smaller and smaller area and the language boundary inexorably moved westward. By the middle of the 16th century English was the dominant language east of Bodmin, and Cornish had died out by the end of the 18th century, although there has been an enthusiastic revival of the language in modern times.

From the 9th century onwards real power in Cornwall had increasingly been in the hands of the Anglo-Saxons, and part of the reason for the death of Cornish was its demise at the centres of power. It became the language of the countryside only. As a consequence it comes as no surprise to find that many of the older town names of Cornwall are English. **Wadebridge**, for instance, which was originally just Wade (the Old English for 'ford') until the bridge was built in the 15th century, is pure English, as is **Newquay**, also built in the 15th century. **Newlyn**, however, is not English. It is a corruption of Cornish *lulyn* 'fleet-pool' or, in the case of the Parish of Newlyn East, from the name of St Newlyn, princess and martyr. **Camelford** 'ford on the River Camel' (pos-sibly from British *camm*, crooked), **Falmouth** 'Mouth of the Fal' (unknown meaning) and **Padstow** 'Holy place of St Petroc' all combine local proper names with English endings. **Launceston** is slightly more complicated, containing Cornish

lann given an English spelling + St Stephen + English *ton*.

The spelling of Cornish was never fixed, and as the roots of the language became weaker, spelling became even more erratic, with the result that the 20th-century revivalists had to adopt a whole new spelling system. The forms of the names were corrupted as the language died, often to the extent of identifying Cornish elements with totally unconnected English

Brychan

As Wales and Cornwall share so much in the way of language and culture, it comes as no surprise that they also share the same legends. One legend concerns King Brychan or Broccan who gave his name to the Welsh region of **Breconshire** – *Brycheiniog* in Welsh – and whose name also lies behind Scotland's **Brechin**. His children are an important source of names in Cornwall. According to legend Brychan decided to leave his throne and his Queen, Gladwys, in order to lead a holy life in Ireland. He stayed in Ireland for 24 years before returning to his wife. They then managed somehow to produce 24 sons and daughters.

All 24 of these are supposed to have become saints in Wales, Cornwall or Devon. In Cornwall **St Endellion** is named from Brychan's daughter St Endilient who was King Arthur's god-daughter. **St Minver** is named from another daughter, St Menfre, who rejected the devil's advances by throwing her comb at him. **St Teath** and **St Wenn** acquired their names from other daughters called Tedda and Wenna, along with **Egloskerry** 'church of St Keri', and **St Keyne** from Kayn, two more daughters. Another daughter, St Morwenna, is supposed to have carried stones herself to help build the church at **Morwenstow**. **St Clether** comes from a son, St Cleder, and another son, Iti or Yse gave his name to **St Issey** and **St Jidgy**, **Landulph** 'church-place of Dylyk or Delek' comes from another son, but the sex of St Mabon, after whom **St Mabyn** is named, is not clear. Finally **Gwennap** may come from another daughter, St Gwenep or Wynup.

It may well be that this group of names and the stories round them contain a memory of actual events. We know that Irish immigrants settled in the areas where the names are found in the 5th and 6th centuries, for they left their gravestones behind. If Brychan represents the Irish settlers in Brycheiniog, then the stories of his many descendants can be interpreted as evidence that some of the Irish settlers in Cornwall came not directly from Ireland, but from Wales.

Tintagel, 'fort on the isthmus', is the traditional birth-place of King Arthur. Although archaeologists have found many remains from the right period, the ruins in the picture date from the 13th to the 15th century. (ANTHONY JANJIC/HORIZON/IMAGES)

words. The corrupted forms have made it more difficult to identify the name elements with dictionary words than in Wales. In Wales an understanding of the meaning of many of the elements has been a check on the tendency of place names to drift from their original forms. As a consequence we find 'Englished' Cornish names such as **Cheesewarne** from *chy* 'house' and *sarn* 'nook' or the wonderful **Halldrunkard**, an alternative name for Hallworthy, which comes from Cornish *hal* + *troen-goes* 'marsh of the promontory-wood'.

As a Celtic language, Cornish shares the habit of mutation of the first sound, most notably after *an*, 'the', and after feminine nouns. The mutations are:

	becomes
b	v
c/k	g
d	dh (spelt 'th')
g	w (or is lost as in Welsh)
m	v
p	b
t	d

In place names only, f can become v, and s become z. In addition certain sounds tend to change in place names so that places that were originally spelt with a c or k now appear with a t. Letters r and n can become an l, particularly at the beginning of a name. In the middle of a name not much distinction is made between r

and s, and yr or er in the first syllable of a name can become ar. In addition just as the common welsh *llan* (see p.103) absorbs the elements, so does the Cornish equivalent *lan*. The other two famous Cornish elements *tre* 'farm, village' (which also appears as *trev, tor* or *tr-*), and *pol(l)* 'pool' can also replace the original form. Thus *nans*, the Cornish equivalent of Welsh *nant*, has become *Lan* in **Lanteglos** from *nans* + *eglos* 'church valley', as it has in **Lantewey**, originally 'valley of the River Dewy'. Similarly *lan* has taken over *lyn* 'lake, pool' in **Lanyon** 'cold pool'. (*Nans* also appears as *La-, le-, lans* or *lant* as well as the more obvious *nan, nam, nance* and *nant*, and *lyn* as *lidden* or *lin*.)

Pol has taken over *porth* 'cove, harbour' in **Polperro** and **Polruan**, both from *porth* + a personal name. *Pen* has taken over *porth* 'end, head' in **Polmennor**, the second part meaning 'hill' (*porth* also appears as *par(n), port, per* or just *pr-*, and *pen* as *pend, pe,* or *pr-*). *Tre* names may well contain the Old English form of 'at the', as in **Treheath** and **Trehill**. Names beginning with *Tres-* may also contain a form of *ros* 'heath or promontory' as in **Treslay** 'heath of the flat stones' and **Tresmarrow** 'heath of Mark'. (*Tre* names also appear with *trev, tor* or *tr-, -dra, -drea*, while *tre* + *an* 'farm of the' give *trem* and *tren*.) Despite all the difficulties and changes listed above, the relationship between the Welsh and Cornish elements is often quite clear and a simple listing should be sufficient.

Elements dealing with water, this time reflecting the long coastline of Cornwall, include:

> dowr, dower = water
> enys, ennis, ince, innis, ninnes = island, the last of these having an, 'the' in front
> gover = stream
> logh, looe, loe = creek, inlet, estuary
> mor = sea
> treth, treth, -dreath = beach
> -vose, voose = ditch

Examples of the above elements are illustrated in **Looe**, **Ince**, **Ninnes**, **Pentreath**, 'end of the beach', and **Parnvoose**, where the first element comes from porth, giving 'cove of the ditch'.

Highland features give us:

> ard, ardh, ayr = height
> bar = top
> bray, brea, -vrea, -vra = hill
> brenn, burn = hill
> carn, can = rock pile, tor
> carrack, carrag, carrik = rock
> creeg, creek, crig, creet = mound, barrow
> goon, gon, gun, -woon = downs
> -van = height

Examples of the use of these elements are: **Talvan(s)** 'next to the height'; **Canworthy** 'tor' + the English for 'farm'; **Goonhilly** '?hunting downs'; **Goonvrea** 'hill downs'; and **Carrick Roads**, the second part being English 'anchorage' and the first the islands called **The Carrocks** (Carrick is a widespread Celtic name, found in Cornwall, Strathclyde and Donegal).

Other geographical features are:

> cos, coose, coys, cus, cut, -gett, -gus, -goose, -quite = wood
> gelly, gilly, kelly, killy = grove
> hal, hale, hall, haul, hole, -hallow = moor
> kernick = corner
> main, mayne, mean, men, min = stone
> re, red, res, ris, ros, -rice from res 'ford' but these are often confused with ros 'promontory or heath' which also gives rose
> scawen, scow, -scoe = eldertree(s)

Cos is a form of our old friend the British ced (see p. 98) reflecting a Cornish tendency to turn British t/d into 's'. Thus **Penquite** and **Pencoose** show different stages of the same name 'end of the wood'. **Withielgoose** is a repetitive name containing an element meaning 'wooded area' + cos. The romantic sounding **Lostwithiel** has a first element meaning 'tail, end of' so has the same basic meaning as Pencoose. **Quethiock** is from the related cuidoc 'wooded place'. **Penhale** and **Penhallow** are both 'head or end of the moor', while **Tremaine** is 'farm of the stone' and **Tresco** in the Isles of Scilly is 'tref of the elder trees'.

Man-made landmarks, some reflecting Cornwall's tin-mining history, are found in:

> bal = mine
> bod, dos, bo, be, bis, bus = house, dwelling
> car, caer = hill fort or walled village
> chi, chy, che, ch-, -gey, ty = house
> crows, grows = cross
> din, dun, deen = fort
> dennis, dinas = fort
> eglos, -iglas = church
> gof = smith
> hels, helles = old court
> mellan, molin, bolin, vellan, vellyn, valley = mill
> pons, ponds, pols, pont = bridge
> les, lis = court
> -stain = tin
> wheal = mine

These elements give us names such as **Bodmin**, from bod meneich 'house of the church land', **Liskeard**, 'court of Kerwyd', **Lizard**, 'court on a height', **Treneglos**, 'farm of the church', **Egloshayle**, 'church on the estuary', and **Tintagel** from din 'fort' + an element which probably means 'neck of land', reflecting the castle's position. The quite common name **Chipponds** or **Chyponds** is 'bridge house' and the wonderfully evocative mine name **Wheal 'Tis Gentle** is a corruption of Cornish an dus jentyl, 'of the Gentleman'. **Lamellion**, **Lamellyn** and **Lamellyon** were all originally nans + the word for mill.

Some of the many descriptive elements are:

> braze, brawze = big
> coath, coth, goth = old
> craze, -graze = middle
> -dew, -due = black
> dow, do, du = two
> -drizzick, -drisack = brambly
> gwen, -gwin, gidden, -quin, -quidden, -wen, -widden, -win, -wyn = white
> har, her, -heer, -hyr = long
> hen = old
> -laze = blue, green

mul = bare
-newth, nouth, noweth, nowth = new
-pean = little
ruth = red
vear, veor = great
-zance = holy

Gwendra is 'white beach' and **Rosewin** and **Tredwin** are both formed from *rid* 'ford' and the word for white. The common name **Hendra** 'old house' is the same word as the Welsh *hendref* 'home farm'. **Marazion** comes from *marghas bichan* 'little market'; the final element of this is usually reduced to *-pean*, but in this case has been influenced by the preceding 's'. **Redruth** is an interesting case. It looks at first glance like one of the English town names, but is undoubtedly Cornish. Its derivation has been questioned, but it is most probably from *rid* or *rys* 'ford' and *rudh, ruth* 'red'. It

is interesting to speculate whether the meaning of the second element has influenced the development of the first.

Finally, personal names are always an important influence on place names. The Cornish were fiercely proud of their own saints, and their names have survived in many places. Some are obvious as in **St Austell**, **St Ive(s)**, **St Breoc**, **St Neot** and **St Constantine**. Others are less obvious, as in **Luxulyan** from *loc Sulian*, 'Sulian's monastery', and **Mevagissey**, dedicated to Mewa and *(ag)* Ida (it shows the common change of 'd' to 's'). St Perran has given his name to **Perranporth**, **Perranarworthal** and **Parran Uthnoe**. The second halves of these place names are of rather obscure meaning, possibly 'in the marshland' and 'St Judno'. **Perranzabuloe** is Perran + a corruption of the Latin *in sabulo*, 'in the sand'.

Irish and Gaelic names

Irish and Gaelic are something of a nightmare for the writer on place names. To start with, few of us are experts in all the many languages that go to make up the stock of British place names, and Irish is the language we are least likely to be familiar with. It is difficult to write clearly and concisely about a language that has little apparent connection between the spelling and pronunciation of a word. Irish has eight different forms of the word for 'the' and has a sound system so different from English that it has four different ways of pronouncing the sound that in English is simply /n/. Luckily, when it comes to place names the problems are not quite as severe as they seem at first, although the reader will have to take rather more on trust than in other sections.

Irish and Gaelic are very closely related, Gaelic being a Scottish development of the dialect spoken in the northern part of Ireland, particularly Ulster. Place names such as **Elgin** 'little Ireland', **Glenelg** in the Highlands, which has the same element, and **Banff**, which is claimed to mean 'young pig', apparently an old poetic term for Ireland, commemorate this connection. Irish and Scottish legend have many stories about how Gaelic speakers came to Scotland, including the story of Deirdre of the

Sorrows who fled to Alba (Scotland) with her lover Naoise to avoid an unwanted marriage.

More prosaically the history books tell us that the first Irish settlers arrived in the northern part of Strathclyde some time after 450 (not that long after the Anglo-Saxons had started taking over England). They settled successfully and started to expand their territory. At first their ties were close to the homeland, and the language did not start to take its own course until after a few centuries, when greater independence came with greater power. By 846 Kenneth MacAlpin was king of the Gaelic Scots of Galloway, and of the Scots of Dal Riada. Dal Riada was the main Gaelic kingdom and stretched over the west of Scotland from Lochaber to the Mull of Kintyre. It was named after the Irish kingdom of the same name (the northern part of Antrim), meaning 'descendants of Riada'.

MacAlpin had seen off a Danish invasion of his territory by 846 and conquered the Picts to become king of Alban, a territory which covered the bulk of modern Scotland. By the 11th century Gaelic was spoken throughout Scotland except in small areas of the south-east where Old English was spoken, and in the far north where Old Norse was dominant. Not

The Isle of Man

The Manx language is basically Gaelic, related to Scots and Irish but differing from both, and with signs of Scandinavian influence. It was spoken in the island until the 19th century and is kept alive by the Manx Gaelic Society, but not as a first language. The place names of Man reflect its history. The name of the island itself is obscure. Some say it is linked with an Irish god called *Manannan mac Lir*, others that the name *Manannan* itself means 'little Manxman'. The Roman name was *Mona* or *Monapia*, which may be related to Welsh *mynydd* 'mountain', referring to the area around **Snaefell** (Scandinavian for snowy mountain). The adject-ive, Manx, is from Norse. Most place names are either Gaelic (Manx or Irish) or Norse, with some later English ones. While the majority of crofts and minor landmarks have Gaelic names, a larger proportion of major settlements have Scandinavian names.

Andreas or **Kirk Andreas**: St. Andrew's church: Norse *kirk* with Celtic word order.

The Ayres: gravelly banks, from Norse *eyrr*.

Ballacarnane Beg: little farm of the cairn; Gaelic *balla* 'farm' (related to Irish *baile*), carnane 'cairn', beg 'little'.

Ballasalla: Gaelic *balla* 'farm'; *salla* may be from Gaelic and mean sallow tree, but the Manx name assumes that the adjective is *sallagh* 'dirty'. This is probably a modern corruption.

Castletown: an anglicized name, first recorded in 1511. It is a translation of its Manx name, *Balley Cashtal*.

Cregneish: crow's nest or crow's headland, from Norse *krakuness*, but popularly supposed to be from Gaelic *Creg n' Eash* 'Rock of Ages'. Creg (rock) is common in island place names.

The Cronk: the hill (Gaelic). Cronk is a common place-name element on the island.

Dhoor: black ford; Manx *doo aah*.

Douglas: black stream; Irish *Dubhglais*.

Jurby: certainly Norse, but the meaning is not certain. It may be Ingvar or Ivar's *by* (farm or homestead) or the first element may be *dyrr* meaning beast or wild animal.

Knockaloe Moar: Knockaloe is from Gaelic *knock* 'hill', with the Scandinavian personal name Olaf; *mooar*, meaning 'greater', is Gaelic (there is also a **Knockaloe Beg** 'little Knockaloe').

Laxey: salmon river.

Lhingague: the yard or enclosed land. It was first recorded in 1511 as *Le Garre*, from French *le* and Norse *garthr*. The later form is probably a mistake, possibly based on Gaelic *lhing* 'pool'.

The Isle of Man

Niarbyl: the tail, referring to a long reef jutting out from the land; Manx *Yn Arbyl*.

Onchan: from the parish name, Kirk Conchan. *Conchenn* was the Irish name for St. Christopher. It means dog's or wolf's head. In the Greek church the saint is sometimes shown with a dog's head but no one seems to know why. The parish church, now rededicated to St. Peter, contains some old slabs with carvings of dog-headed 'monsters'.

Peel: from Manx *peeley* 'castle', built here in the 17th century. The earlier name of the settlement, *Holmtowne*, was from Norse *holmtun* 'island town'.

Port Erin: Manx *Purt Chiarn* or *Yiarn*, Lord's Port or Iron Port, with some confusion with *Erin*, the archaic or poetic term for Ireland.

Ramsey: wild garlic river, with the river name transferred to the town at its mouth; Norse *ramsa a*.

Ronaldsway: Ronald or Reginald's ford; Norse *vath*. Reginald is from the Latin form of the name Reynold, which is from the Germanic name *Reginwald*, meaning roughly 'mighty ruler'. Ronald is from the Scandinavian form *Rognvald*.

Smeale: farm of the smiths or craftsmen; Norse *smithabol*. Another settlement nearby is called *Ballaseyr*, a Gaelic name with the same meaning.

long after, however, the Anglo-Normans came to power, and Gaelic began its gradual retreat. Today it is only spoken on the western sea-board and the Western Isles. During all this time Gaelic had developed its own features, but the place-name elements which are found throughout the country are more often than not recognizably the same as those of Ireland, except where they have been influenced by English or Norse.

Irish has also long been in retreat. At one time the first language of the island, Irish began to lose ground as early as the 12th century with

the invasion of the Norman Fitzgeralds. How-ever, it was not until the 19th century that its real decline set in. Officially, Irish is still the first language of the Republic of Ireland, and all laws have to be written in both Irish and English. However, it is actually only spoken as a first language in isolated pockets mainly on the south and west coasts, as well as by bands of enthusiasts in some of the cities who make a conscious effort to learn Irish and use it as a first language.

Ireland has a long history of fine writing, and by the 13th century had developed a standard form of the language called Classical Gaelic. This was the language of the lettered classes in both Ireland and Scotland, and was in use until the break up of traditional Gaelic society in the 17th century. After this speakers in both Scotland and Ireland came under severe political pressure from the Government, which attempted to break the strength and thus the opposition of the clans in both countries. It led to the loss of Classical Gaelic and the development of more marked regional dialects.

Today there are distinct differences in pronunciation between, say, the Irish of the north and south of the island, and between the Gaelic of the different islands, which can lead to name elements taking different forms, both in the original language and in anglicized forms. However, while the language has changed in modern times, unfortunately for the outsider the spellings have not changed as much. The spelling of Classical Gaelic was based on that of Old Irish, which had taken its spelling from the pronunciation of Latin in Britain in the 4th and 5th centuries. Pronunciation had changed, and in particular many sounds had been dropped, but the words continued to be written as if this had not happened. Thus the place named

Amhalghaidh in Gaelic has an English form, reflecting its pronunciation, of **Awlay**.

The spelling has been simplified in this century, but it is still something of a challenge, and the old forms are still encountered. At first it can all seem hopelessly confusing, but luckily the English, as opposed to Irish, forms of Irish names are usually at least a rough guide to the Irish pronunciation. As has been said, Irish has many sounds that are not found in English and no attempt will be made to guide the reader in the many complexities of the different regional pronunciations, but a list of the mutated forms with a guide to how they are usually pronounced *in place names* follows (root letters are pronounced as in English).

	becomes	pronounced	or	pronounced
b	bh	/v/	mb	/m/
c	ch	/kh/	gc	/g/
d	dh	/kh/ or silent	nd	/n/
f	fh	/kh/ or silent	bhf	/v/
g	gh	/gh/ or silent	ng	/ng/
m	mh	/v/		
p	ph	/f/	bp	/b/
s	sh	/h/ or silent	(s + e or i gives /sh/)	
t	th	/h/ or silent	bp	/b/

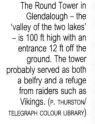

The Round Tower in Glendalough – the 'valley of the two lakes' – is 100 ft high with an entrance 12 ft off the ground. The tower probably served as both a belfry and a refuge from raiders such as Vikings. (P. THURSTON/ TELEGRAPH COLOUR LIBRARY)

In the majority of place names, those sounds marked 'or silent' will not be pronounced, the exceptions being where the place name retains the pronunciation from earlier times. In addition under certain circumstances a word beginning with a vowel takes an 'h' or an 'n' in front of it, so that, for instance the official Irish name for the Republic of Ireland is **Poblacht na hÉireann**.

It should be noted at this point that the term 'Ireland' is being used for the geographical unit rather than for any political unit. The political division of the island is too recent, in place-name terms, to have had a significant effect on the development of names in the Irish language.

Some of the most common elements found in Irish and Gaelic place names are listed on pp. 112–13. Under 'Irish elements' the form that most commonly appears in places is shown. (Most Irish places have at least two names – the ordinary everyday name that is usually an anglicized form of an Irish name, and one or more names in the Irish language, not necessarily the same as the name that gave the anglicized form. The dead hand of the map-maker was felt at a later date in Ireland, and names have never been as fixed as in England, so alternatives have not been lost.) In the second column is the proper Gaelic form of the word, in the third the anglicized form of the Gaelic, and in the fourth the English meaning. The proper Irish forms have not been given, partly because they are so near to the Gaelic, and partly because they will usually be illustrated in the text. To avoid repetition, and because we will have more to say about Scots names elsewhere, Scottish names from Gaelic sources will be dealt with alongside the Irish.

Ireland is famous as the land of Saints and legends, and this is readily illustrated in its place names. Monasteries, often founded by princely families and treated as family possessions, were an important feature of the early Irish church. One of the important differences between the Celtic Church and the ideas brought to Canterbury by St Augustine was the relative importance of Abbots and Bishops. Anyone who looks at the history of the early church in Ireland will find that the names of the monasteries founded by the most prominent saints became nearly as famous as their founders.

St Ciaran's monastery of **Clonmacnoise** (*Cluain Mhic Nois*) 'meadow of the sons of Noas', founded in 545, was famous for its scholarship and the beauty of the metalwork produced there. Its fame led to repeated raids by the Vikings and just about anyone else in a position to follow their example. St Kevin's foundation of about half a century later at **Glendalough** (*Gleann Dá Loch*) 'valley of the two lakes' is equally famous, and was as famous for its natural beauty in the Middle Ages as it is today. In the same century St Brendan the Navigator founded the monastery at **Clonfert** (*Cluain Fearta*) 'meadow of the grave'.

Place names in 'Kil(l)-' from *cill* 'a church or monk's cell' are one of the most common forms of place names in Ireland. Naturally these famous saints had churches dedicated to them, and sometimes the place would take its name from the church. Thus there are several **Kilkiaran**s (*Cill Chiaráin*) from dedications to St Ciaran, and a **Kilcavan** (*Cill Caomhán*) 'St Kevin's Church' in Wexford, and Scotland has a **Kilbirnie** in Strathclyde dedicated to St Brendan. However, the church may not be dedicated to the saint you first think it is. There are vast numbers of Irish saints, many of them with the same name. There are said, for instance to be over 30 saints called Columb, and 22 called Mo-Ernoc, one of whom gave his name to **Kilmarnock** (Strath). (The 'Mo' part of this name actually means 'my' and is commonly found in front of saints' names to indicate affection and devotion, so the name Malcolm, for example, is Mo added to the front of Columb.)

To add to the complications, while 'Kil(l)' usually indicates either a monastery built before the 12th century, or a church or graveyard after this date, it can also absorb other elements such as *coill* 'wood, grove' or more rarely *cuil* 'nook, corner', *cul* 'back, ridge' or even *caol* 'narrows', the source of 'kyle'. Some Kil- names are from saints as in **Kilkenny** (*Cill Chainnigh*) 'St Kenneth's church', and **Kilmallock** in Limerick (*Cill Mocheallóg*), and **Kilmakilloge** in Kerry, both 'St Mocheallóg's church'. Others describe the people associated with the church or its situation: **Kilkeel** (*Cill Chaoil*; Down) means 'church of the narrows', **Killarney** (*Cill Airne*; Kerry) means 'church of the sloe trees', **Killybegs** (*Na Cealla Beaga*; Don) means 'the little churches', and Dublin's **Killiney** (*Cill Iníon Léinín*) means 'church of the daughters of Leinin'.

Other Kil- names have nothing to do with churches at all, those starting with 'Killy-' being particularly untrustworthy. There are many

Common Irish and Gaelic Place-Name Elements

Irish	Gaelic	Anglicized	Meaning	Irish	Gaelic	Anglicized	Meaning
Agh(a), augh	achadh	ach, auch	field, land, plain	Derg	dearg, dheirge, deirge	derg	red
Aglish	eaglais	egles, eglis	church	Derry, der, derri	doire, darach	der(ry), darroch	oak grove
Aile, aill, aul	ail, aileach		rock, stony place	Desert	diseart	dysart	hermitage
Alt	allt	ald, alt, auld, ault	gully, stream, Irish: also wooded glen, mountain	Donagh			church
Anna(gh)	aber(s), abor		marsh or ath na 'ford of the'	Doo, duff, duv	dubh, dhu(i)bh, duibhe, dubha	dow, du, dove	black
Ard	ard, aird		height, promontory	Doon, dun, don	dun, duin		fort, Gaelic: also mound
Ath, ah	àth		ford	Drohid, droit	drochaid		bridge
Ballagh, vally	bealach, b(h)ealaich	balloch	road, inlet, pass	Drom, drum	druim	drem, drim, drom, drum	a back, ridge
Ballin(a)	baile an		either 'town of the' or 'ford mouth of the' depending on source*	Glan, glen	gleann, g(h)linne	glen	glen, narrow valley
Bally, vally	baile, b(h)aile, bally	bal, balla, bally	homestead, town, hamlet, Irish: townland*	Gort	gort, gart, goitean		field
Ban, ben, bin	beinne(e), beann	ben	mountain, Irish: peak, headland	Green	grianan		sunny hillock
Bane	bàn, bàin(e), bhàin, bàna	bane, vane	fair, white	Inch, inis, ennis	inis, in(n)se	inch, insh	island, place set apart
Batter, boher, voher			road, path		Inbhir	inver	confluence or mouth of a river
Beg	b(h)eag, bhig, bige, beaga	beg	small	Keel, kill	caol, caolas	kil, kyle(s)	firth, narrow
				Kil(l)	cill, cille, ceall	kil	church, grave
Bel(la)	beul, b(h)eoil		mouth*	Kin	ceann, c(h)inn	ken, kin	head(land)
Blar	Blàr, b(h)làir	blair	cleared space, plain	Knock	cnoc, c(h)nuic	(k)nock	hill
Bool, boley, voley, vooly	buaile, buaOiltean		cattle-fold, Irish: also summer pasture	Lack	leac, lice	leck	flat stone, slab
				Letter	leitir, leitre leitreach	letter	slope, hillside
Boy	buidhe	bowie, buie, vuie	yellow	Lis	lios, leas	lis	Irish: ring fort, court, Gaelic: garden
Bun(n), bon	bun or bonn	bon	base, foot, river-mouth				
Caher	cathair, cathrach		circular stone fort	Lough, loch, low	loch, locha		lake
Carn	carn, c(h)uirn, c(h)airn	cairn	heap of stones, Irish: burial	Maghera	machair, m(h)achaire, mach(a)rach		plain
			mound, Gaelic: round, stony hill	Maul	Meall, m(h)ill		lump, round hill,
Carrick	carraig	carrick	rock	Monaster			monastery
Cashel	caiseal		ring-fort, Gaelic: stone wall	Money	monadh/muine		1) thicket, 2) moor, bog
Castle	caisteal		castle, Irish: mansion	More	m(h)or, mhoir, moire, mora	more	great
Clare	clàr, chlair		plain	Moy	magh, moighe, muighe	moy	plain
Clon	cluain		meadow, pasture				
Cool, cul	cuil		nook, corner	Mulla(gh)	mullach, m(h)ullaich		top, summit
Cor			hill or weir	Mullin, vullen	muileann, m(h)uilinn, muilne		mill
Crag, craig	creag, creige	craig	rock, fell				
Crogh, croag	cruach		lit. 'heap' so mountain				
Croghan	cruachan		a little 'crogh/cruach'	Oughter	uachter	auchter, ochter	top, upper
Cross	crois		cross, crossroads	Owen, aw	abhainn, aibhne		river, water
Cull, kil, kyle	coille		wood				
Dangan			stronghold	Port	port, p(h)uirt		port, refuge

Irish	Gaelic	Anglicized	Meaning	Irish	Gaelic	Anglicized	Meaning
Rath	ràth	ra	ring-fort	Srah, (s)tra	srath	strath	valley
Rin(g)	rinn, roinn reanna	rhin	point, promontory		stob		peak
				Temple	teampull, teampuill		church
Roe	ruadh		red, rusty-brown				
Ros	ros, rois	ross	wood, promontory	Tober, tubber	t(i)obar, t(i)obair(t)	tiber, tibber, tipper, chipper	well, spring
Sgorr, sgurr	sgor		rocky peak				
Shan	sean	shan	old	Tulla(gh), tully	tulach, tulaich tullagh	tilloch, tilly, tullich, tulloch, tully	hillock, knoll
Shee	sídh, síth, sídhean	schie, shee	fairy hill				
Slieve, sle, tlieve	sliabh, sléibhe		mountain(s)	Villa, ville, villy			old tree used as a point of assembly

* indicates a fuller explanation in the text.

examples from Ireland. **Kilmacthomas** (*Coil Mhic Thomáisín*; Wat) means 'wood of the sons of little Thomas', the common name **Kilclare** (*Coill an Cláir*) means 'wood of the plain', **Killaloo** (*Coill an Lao*; Kerry) means 'wood of the calf', **Killyclogher** (*Coillidh Chlochair*; Ty) means 'wood of the stony place', and its plural form **Kiltyclogher** (*Coillte Clochair*; Lei) means 'woods of the stony place'. Scotland has **Killiecrankie** (Tay) from *coille creitheannich* 'wood of aspens', **Kilchurn** (Strath) from *caol + carn* 'Kyle of the cairn', and **Kilcoy** (High) from *cul + coille* 'back of the wood'. Even **Kildrummy** (Grmp), once known as Kindrummie from *ceann* 'head' and *druim* 'ridge', has changed its name under the pressure from Kil-.

In Ireland *coil* also appears in forms such as **Cullybackey** (*Coill na Baice*; Ant) 'wood of the hollow' and **Cullahill** (*An Chúlcoill*) 'the back wood'. It also appears as **Kyle** or **Kylemore**, common names which sometimes mean 'the wood' and 'the big wood' and sometimes come from *cill* again. Cul- names can also be from *cuil* as in **Culmullin** (*Cul Múilín*; Meath) 'the mill corner', and **Culmore** (*An Chúil Mhór*; Derry) 'the big nook'. But *cui* is more likely to be 'cool' as in **Castlecoole** (Fer) 'secluded castle', **Coolroe** (*An Chúil Ruadh*) 'red nook', the various places called **Coole** (*An Chúil*) 'the nook' and places called variously **Coleraine**, **Cooleraine** or **Coolrainy** 'nook of the ferns'.

As common, if not more common, than Kil- in Ireland is Bally-, which also has a mixed ancestry. Usually Bally is from Irish *baile*, one of those words like English -ton and Welsh tre- which can mean a unit from any size from a single farm to a town. In addition it is the technical term for a townland – an administrative unit that can vary between a smallish field

and 7000 acres. *Baile* is often combined with *na* to give 'town of the . . .' and this is usually anglicized as Ballin(a)-.

Once again such a common term has tended to absorb other similar-sounding terms. The most important of these is *béal* which literally means 'mouth, estuary'. It is often combined with the word *áth na* 'ford of the' to give 'ford-mouth' indicating 'approach to the ford of' which can also appear in place names as Ballin(a)-. When *béal atha* appears without the *na* it can be another source of Bally-, and when *béal* appears by itself it becomes Bel(la)-, which can also come from *baile*. Just to make life even more complicated there is a third element *bealach*. It usually means 'road' in Ireland, but also 'pass, inlet' in Scotland. This often appears as Ballagh- (which can also come from *béal atha*) but can also become Bel(la)-.

This is all hopelessly confusing in English, and the only solution is to go back to the Irish form of the name, which luckily for the curious traveller in the Republic of Ireland is usually given on signposts along with the commoner name, while in Scotland signposts are also bilingual in Gaelic-speaking areas. A few examples will probably help to throw light on the problem and also serve to illustrate some of the other elements listed on p.112.

Ballynahaglish (*Baile na hEaglaise*) in Mayo and Kerry is 'townland of the church' (**Belleheiglash** in Grampian has the same meaning), and **Ballinard** (*Baile an Aird*) in Limerick is 'townland of the height'. The common name **Ballagh** and the two **Balloch**s in Scotland are quite simply from *bealach* 'the road' (the 'v' form is illustrated in **Corvalley** (*Cor an Bhealaigh*) in Monaghan 'bend in the road' and **Belvelly** (*Béal an Bhealaigh*) in Cork 'mouth, entrance to the road'). Similarly the

The Giant's Causeway in Antrim is an extraordinary formation of 37 426 distinct and perfect basalt columns. According to legend it was built as a causeway to Scotland either by Formorian giants, or by the folk-hero Finn Mac Cool. (SLIDE FILE)

common name **Ballina** (*Béal an Átha*) is usually just 'mouth of the ford'. **Ballycrovane** (*Beál an Churraigh Bháin*) in Cork 'mouth of the white marsh' shows the 'v' form of the word for 'white' (compare Strathclyde's **Ben Vane** 'white mountain'). **Ballybane** (*Baile Bán*) in the same county is 'the white townland'. **Ballinvoher** (*Baile an Bhóthair*) 'townland of the road' shows the 'v' form of an alternative word for 'path, road'. It appears more obviously in **Boher** (*An Bóthar*) in Offaly, **Batterjohn** (*Bóthar Sheáin*) in Meath 'John's road', and **Stonybatter** (*An Botar Clochach*) in Dublin 'the stony road'.

Ballybeg (*An Baile Beag*) is found in several places and comes from *Baile Beag* 'small homestead'. It should be compared with **Balbeg** in the Highlands. **Ballinaboy** (*béal an Ath Buidhe*), another common name, is 'mouth of the yellow ford' (compare **Ben Buie** 'yellow mountain' on Mull). **Ballycastle** is another common name, but one that has to be treated with care. The Ballycastle in Antrim is *Baile an Chaistil* 'farmstead of the castle', but Ballycastle in Mayo is *Baile an Chaisil* 'homestead by the stone fort'. It contains an element that more commonly appears as **Cashel**. Similarly **Ballyclare** in Antrim is *Bealach Cláir* 'road of the plain', but Ballyclare in Roscommon is *Baile an Chláir* 'townland of the plain'. One has to distinguish in the same way between the sources of **Ballymoney**: the one in Antrim is *Baile Muine* 'homestead of the thicket', but *Baile Monaidh* 'homestead on the moor' is also found. Most important of the Bel- names is that of **Belfast** which comes from *béal Feirste* 'mouth of the sandbank'.

W.F.H. Nicolaisen has looked at a number of Gaelic place-name elements in southern Scotland in an attempt to see if their use can be dated, and if they throw any light on the history of the area. One of the most telling bits of research he did was on the element *sliabh* 'a mountain', usually written in English slieve or slew. He showed that while names with this element are common throughout Ireland, they have a very limited distribution in Scotland. Their distribution matches very well with the area of the earliest settlement from Ireland, in the Kingdom of Dal Riada. They are notably present in Islay and Jura and adjoining areas of Strathclyde, and also found in the upper reaches of the valleys of the Tay and Spey, an area of early expansion. But he also found an area where they were even more common, in the Rhinns of Galloway, a peninsula facing the Ulster coast.

This area had not been recognized before as one of the earliest areas settled, although common sense would make it a likely spot. Work by archaeologists later showed Nicolaisen's conclusions to have been correct. (Elsewhere in Scotland *slieve* is still used by Gaelic speakers as a word, but in place names *beinn* – in English Ben – is the usual term for mountains.)

Nicolaisen has also examined the terms Kil- 'church', *achadh* 'field, cultivated area', and our old friend *baile*. The element *achadh* has become attached to settlements and given rise to such names as **Affleck**, **Achleck** and **Auchinleck**, all meaning 'place of the flat stone'. (In Ireland it appears in a slightly different form as in **Aughnacloy** (*Achadh na Cloiche*; Ty) 'field of the stones' and **Agha** 'the field'.) When he examined the place-name evidence for Scotland south of the Forth-Clyde line he came to some very interesting conclusions. Kil- names were often associated with early saints and concentrated again in areas of early settlement and he concluded that they were most actively used between the 7th and the middle of the 9th century. *Baile* and *achadh* have a rather different distribution. They were found over a much wider area and must have remained in use much longer.

However, the elements represent very different types of settlement: *baile* represents a permanent settlement, sometimes a town, and *achadh* the presence of Gaelic-speaking farmers. Since the distributions of these two terms do not match each other, it was concluded that those areas where *baile* is found and not *achadh* (and *baile* is found over a much wider area) represent areas where Gaelic-speaking landowners were the most powerful people in the settlements. However, as the surrounding fields did not have Gaelic names it would suggest that the peasants working their fields were not Gaelic-speaking. This would reflect, for example, the period between the second half of the 10th century and the beginning of the 12th when Gaelic-speaking overlords ruled the area then known as Lothian, but the peasantry was English-speaking. Hence we have place names such as **Gilchriston** and **Gilmerton** in Lothian where the first part is a Gaelic personal name (meaning 'servant of Christ' and 'servant of Mary'), presumably that of the local lord, but the second element is English *tun*.

Forts and churches

We have talked of Ireland as a country of ancient saints, and religion is an important element in place names. We find **Aglish** (*An Eaglais*) 'the church' as a common name, as well

---

The remains of pagan Ireland

A visitor to Ireland is struck by the magnificent remains of the pagan past found throughout the island. Museums contain the wonderful gold work and jewellery made in the distant past, and the land is full of the vast grave-mounds and standing stones put up by believers in a long lost religion. A few traces of the old religion are still to be found in folk traditions of the fairies and the healing wells, and the lost gods can also be found in place names.

Rivers and gods had a special connection for the ancient Celts, and the names of gods are preserved in some Irish rivers – both the rivers **Bann** and **Bandon** are thought to get their names from a word meaning 'goddess'. The **Boyne** is said to come from the name of the river-goddess Boand, whose name is connected with the words *bo bhán* 'white cow', an ancient symbol of prosperity and fertility. The **Shannon** probably means 'the old one' which would have been the title of a god, while the **Avonmore** 'great river' was once called the Dea, which like the English Dee, means 'the goddess'.

Other divinities are recalled in the hills called the **Paps of Anu** in Kerry; they are named after Anu, a form of the Irish mother-goddess. **Pallas Green** in Limerick, which has nothing to do with the Greek goddess Pallas Athene, refers to the sun goddess Grian, for the name is a corruption of *Pailís Ghréine* 'Grian's palisade'. The goddess had her 'throne' nearby at *Cnoc Greine*. The goddess Macha, both a fertility goddess and a warrior goddess whose worship may go back to pre-Celtic times, appears in two important place names: **Emain Macha**, the ancient capital of the former kingdom of Ulster, and **Armagh** (*Ard Mhacha*) 'Macha's height'. Another ancient royal site, **Tara**, probably also contains the name of a goddess, that of the earth-goddess Temair whose name means 'the dark one'.

Minor goddesses are found at **Teltown** (*Tailtean*) in Meath, translated as 'Taillte's place'. It acquired its name from Taillte or Tailltu whose name may mean 'the beautiful one' and is described by some as a goddess and by others as a queen. **Knockainy** (*Cnoc Aine*) in Limerick means 'Aine's hill', Aine being the ruler of the local fairy hill on whom the great king of Munster Oilill Olum thrust his unwanted attentions.

Names such as the common **Kilbride** 'St Brigid's Church' present a special problem. In the pagan past one of the most important and popular goddesses was Brid (Brigid or Briget), the goddess of poetry, learning and the crafts. The most popular Irish female saint is also called Brigid, and it is no coincidence that she too is patron of the same fields. It is not always possible to distinguish which Brigid is referred to in such place names, or in stories associated with the name. For example **Kildare** (*Cill Dara*) 'church of the oak' is said to get its name from the church that St Brigid founded in a pagan sacred oak grove.

Finally, there are some names that reflect ancient practices. **Tempo** (Fer) comes from the Irish *An tIompu Deiseal*, 'the right-hand turn'. It reflects the view, found in early literature, that turning clockwise, the way of the sun, was propitious, but that circling to the left brought bad luck. **Beltany**, found in various places, and **Bedlam** in Donegal both get their name from the pagan festival of Beltane, held at the beginning of May when bonfires were lighted in the hills (the name probably means 'bright fire') and the coming of summer celebrated. **Knocksouna** (*Cnoc Samhna*) in Limerick, meaning 'Samhain's hill', refers to the festival held in November that marked the end of summer and the harvest.

---

as **Donagh** (*Domhnach*) which means the same. The latter, however, is usually only used of very early sites, often associated with the early missionaries, up to the 6th century. *Desert* 'monastery, a hermitage', which is the same word as our 'desert' for it implied a place that was deliberately set up away from other habitation, gives us such names as **Desertmartin** (*Déseart Mhártain,*) in Derry 'St Martin's hermitage', and **Dysert**, which is found in both Ireland and Scotland. More welcoming monasteries have the element *monaster* – as in **Monasterboice** (*Mainistir Bhuithe*) in Louth 'St Buite's monastery'. It is thought to have been founded by this obscure saint on a pagan sacred site in the 6th century. Later churches (13th century onwards) can be indicated by *temple-* as in the common name **Templemore** (*An Teampall Mór*) 'the big church', or the intriguing **Templeshanbo** (*Teampal Seanbhoth*) in Wexford 'church of the old hut'.

Curiously enough words that on the surface mean 'fort' often refer to churches or monasteries. The joining of war and the Church may seem surprising to us, but Ireland has a history of conflict, and it made sense to build places of devotion behind protective walls. In other cases the religious foundation may have been attached to a chief's court, and taken its name from the fortified place in which he lived. There are a number of terms used in Irish place names which have the basic meaning of 'fort' but in which the meaning has rather drifted into other areas.

Dun is found as Dun- or Doon- or Down as in **County Down**, which takes its name from **Downpatrick** (*Dun Pádraig*) 'St Patrick's fort'. It is also visible in the common name **Dundrum** (*Dún Droma*) 'fort of the ridge', **Dungannon** (*Dún Geanainn*; Ty) 'Geanann's fort'; and **Dungarvan** in Waterford 'Garbhain's fort'. It was usually used to describe a large fort, a king or chief's main residence, and a number of these became the sites of early churches. It is the source of a number of names of towns in Scotland as in **Dumfries** 'fort of the copses', **Dundee**, probably the fort of someone called Daig, **Dunfermline**, a fort of unknown meaning, and **Dunoon**, from *Dun Obhainn* 'fort of the river'.

Ráth was a similar term, strictly meaning a 'ring-fort' but often indicating a church as in the case of a number of places called **Rathaspick** (*Ráth Easpuig*) 'fort of the bishop'. The name was probably given to a foundation, under the control of a bishop, built in an old rath. It appears in **Ray** (*An Ráith*) 'the ring-fort' where there was once a monastery called **Moyra** 'plain of the fort', and **Killashandra** (*Cill na Seanrátha*) in Cavan 'church of the old rath'.

Inside the ring-fort was a court known as the *lios* (in British *(l)lis*), a term which came to be used of the fort as a whole and in Scotland was used of an enclosed area in general, such as a garden. This is found in names such as **Lisdoonvarna** (*Lios Dúin Bhearna*) in Clare 'court of the broken fort' which suggests a period in which the inner part of the dun was in use after the fortifications had become dilapidated. It is also found in **Lisbane** (*An Lios Bán*) in Down 'the white ring-fort', and **Lisburn** in Antrim, which is difficult to explain. The Irish name is *Lios na gCearrbhach* 'fort of the gamblers', and according to legend refers to old forts on the outskirts where outlaws would meet to play cards and dice.

Lis is not often used of old ecclesiastical sites, although the 'big enclosure' at **Lismore** (*Lios Mór*) in Waterford was built round the monastery founded in the 7th century by St Carthach and the **Lismore** in the Inner Hebrides is associated with the monastery set up in the 6th century by St Maluag.

Another term, *cathair*, related to Welsh *caer* and pronounced similarly, originally meant a stone ring fort. It later developed the senses monastery and even city or court. It is found as **Cahir** (*An Chathair*) in Tipperary 'the stone fort' and **Caher** from the same source and found in several places. *Cashel*, famous as the name of the Tipperary town where the fort was the centre of the kingdom of Munster for hundreds of years, is usually restricted to its basic sense of 'stone fort'.

Dangan, found by itself in **Dangan** and **Daingean** and in a corrupted form in **Dingle** (all *An Daingean*), can also mean 'stone fort'. It appears as a second element in such names as **Ballydangan** (*Baile Daingean*) in Roscommon, but is restricted to its basic sense of 'fortress, secure place'. Despite their ecclesiastical associations these strongholds really belong to the heroes of old, either legendary or real, and are referred to in names such as **Donegore** (*Dun na gCaradh*) in Antrim 'fort of the heroes'.

Legendary names

The place names of Ireland abound in references and stories of Ireland's ancient past. Innumerable places refer to people's names, most of them ordinary mortals now lost to history, some known and a good many out of legend. Most of these are now lost to us or only

---

Sprites and fairies

Ireland is, of course, the home of the little folk. In Irish they are the *sí*, pronounced 'shee'. Their name appears in a good number of place names. **Sheean** (*An Sidheán*) in Mayo means 'the fairy mound', **Lough Sheelin** (*Loch Sithleann*) means 'lake of the fairies', **Sheeroe** (*Sidh Ruadh*) in Longford means 'russet fairy hill', **Shehy Mountain** (*Cnoc Seithe*) means 'hill of the fairies' and the **Sheffry Hills**, 'mountains of the fairy mansion'. Their name is found less obviously in **Sion Mills** (*Muileann an tSiEain*) in Tyrone 'mill of the fairy hill' and **Cheekpoint** (*Pointe na Síge*) in Waterford 'point of the fairies'. In addition there is **Fairyhouse** (*Bru Sí*) in Meath and **Fairymount** in Roscommon. The Gaels took the *sí* with them to Scotland, giving us names such as the Campsie (Crooked Fairy) Fells, which gives its name to **Milton Campsie** (officially **Milton of Campsie**).

The *sí* are not the only spirits to be found in Ireland. The Puca (also called pooka or Puck as in England) is a mischievous hobgoblin, with a liking for playing tricks on those walking home late at night, particularly if they have been drinking. His tricks can be cruel, but he is on the whole benign. The Puca is found in names such as **Ahaphuca** (*Ath an Phuca*) in Cork, 'ford of the Puca', **Boheraphuca** (*Bóthar an Phuca*) in Offaly 'road of the hobgoblin', **Carrigaphooca** (*Carraig an Phuca*) in Cork 'rock of the Puca', and **Poulaphouca** (*Poll an Phuca*) in Wicklow 'Puca's pool'.

Lough Nafooey in Galway is 'the lake of the phantom'. Witches are found at **Castle Kirke** (*Caisleán na Circe*) in Galway meaning 'castle of the hen'. Legend says a witch and her hen built the castle in a single night, and – but only by mistake – at **Carrigogunnell** in Limerick. The Irish form of the name is *Carraig O gConaill* 'rock of the son of Connell', but folk etymology understood it as *Carraig na gCoinneall* 'rock of the candle'. There was a legend about a witch who lit a candle there every night, until St Patrick banished her. Even worse than witches is the Devil, found in **Devil's Glen**, Wicklow, **The Devil's Punch Bowl** in Kerry and the Galway mountain known as **The Devil's Mother**. One of the Irish names for this peak was the ironic *Machaire an Deamhain* 'the demon's plain'. The first word of this seems to have been anglicized, somehow, as 'Mother'.

St Patrick names

St Patrick, as Ireland's patron saint, is commemorated in a number of place names, and stories about him found in many more. **Croaghpatrick** in Mayo, also known as the Holy Mountain, is the mountain where St Patrick made a forty-day retreat which started a tradition of pilgrimage to the mountain which still flourishes. **Downpatrick** had its name extended from Down in the 12th century, when relics, said to be of the saint, were discovered there. The name of **St Patrick's Island** off Skerries near Dublin marks a stay that the saint is said to have made there. **St Patrick's Purgatory**, a cave on Station Island in Lough Derg, is said to be a gateway to Hell. St Patrick vanquished the devils which infested it.

St Patrick's first experience of Ireland was as a boy, when he was captured by Irish pirates raiding Britain. He is then supposed to have been a herdsman at **Slemish** 'Mis's mountain' in Antrim, before escaping and training as a priest in Gaul. On his return to Ireland as a missionary he started his ministry at **Saul** (*Sabhall*) in Down, whose name, 'the barn', refers to the wooden barn given to him to use as a church by the local chief Dichu, one of his first converts. **Dun Laoghaire** (formerly Dunleary) in Dublin refers to Laoghaire, a 5th-century high king of Ireland with whom Patrick soon came into conflict. Easter coincided with an important pagan festival at Tara, the seat of the high kings, during which no fire might be lit until the royal fire had been relit. Patrick defied this by lighting the Easter fire on the hill of Slane on Easter Eve. This was followed by a confrontation with the Druids from which Patrick emerged victorious, and although Laoghaire did not convert, he was forced to allow Patrick to continue preaching. **Duleek** (*Damhliag*) in Meath means 'stone church' and refers to one St Patrick founded. **Dunshaughlin** (*Dun Seachlainn*) in Meath 'Seachnal's fort' commemorates one founded by Seachnal or Secundinus, a co-missionary of Patrick's. Patrick is also supposed to have founded the church at **Glenavy**, Antrim (*Lann Abhaigh*), the Irish name meaning 'church of the dwarf'. It is an interesting example of Lann being absorbed by the common 'Glen', as opposed to the examples in Wales and Cornwall where other elements have been absorbed by (l)lann. 'The dwarf' is said to refer to a disciple of Patrick, who was called Daniel, but being rather short had this nickname. The Irish name for **Newry** in Down is *An tiur*, 'the yew' which refers to a tree that St Patrick planted at the monastery he founded there.

People associated with Patrick are found at **Inchagoill** (*Inis an Ghoill Cráibhthigh*) in Galway 'island of the devout foreigner' who was Lugnat or Lugnaed, the saint's pilot. **Kilcock** (*Cill Choca*) in Kildare 'St Coca's church' is supposed to have been the church of Patrick's aunt. St Conall was made bishop by Patrick and gives his name to **Kilconnell** in Galway. **Killaspugbrone** (*Cill Easpog Bróin*) in Sligo means 'the church of Bishop Bron', who was a follower of Patrick, and **Mahee Island** in Down is named after St Mochaoi, another disciple of his.

known locally. **Limavady** in Derry for instance comes from *Léim an Mhadaidh* 'leap of the dog' but no one seems to know the story behind this. But in some place names we can recognize figures from Ireland's great legendary literature. These are preserved in medieval manuscripts, but some undoubtedly go back to much earlier times. *The Táin Bó Cualnge* ('The Cattle Raid of Cooley') tells of how Queen Maeve instigated a raid to secure the great Brown Bull of Cuailgne, and of the great hero Cuchulainn's defence of the land. There are later stories of Finn MacCoole or Finn mac Cumaill (in Scotland often called Fingal, as in **Fingal's Cave**), his father Cumal or Comhal and his son Ossian.

The stories of Cuchulainn are commemorated at **Ardee** (Louth) which gets its name from the Irish *Baile Atha Fhirdia* 'town of Ferdia's ford', a reference to the single combat at the ford between the two warriors. According to the story a curse on the warriors of Ulster meant Cuchulainn alone was able to fight, and his defeat of Ferdia prevented the men of Connacht entering the territory. **Dundalk** (*Dun Dealgan*) in Louth is named after Dealga, supposedly the name of a chieftain of the Fir Bolg, traditionally one of the early peoples to have inhabited Ireland. Some have linked the name, the first part of which means 'people', with the Celtic Belgae found in France and England. It is also known as the birth place of Cuchulainn, and in some versions of his story also the place he died.

At **Loophead** in Clare Cuchulainn is said to have leapt from the cliff on to a rock in the sea to avoid the attentions of an importunate woman who perished in the attempt to follow him. (Loophead has a mixed history in that it comes from *An lúb* 'the leap' which became Norse *hlaup* of the same meaning.) Loophead also has a rock off the coast named from the great legendary lovers Grainne and Diarmaid. Grainne is also commemorated at **Tomgraney** (*Tuaim Gréine*) in Clare 'the burial mound of Grainne' where she is supposed to have been buried after drowning in Lough Graney to which she also gave her name. Grainne was going to be the wife of Finn, but instead fell in love with Diarmaid and eloped with him. Other places associated with Finn are **Seefin** (*Suidhe Finn*) in Limerick 'seat of Finn'. **Glenosheen** in Limerick is named after the great poet Ossian who was Finn's son.

A surprising number of women are commemorated in these legendary names. **Bear Haven** (*Béarra*) in Cork has nothing to do with furry animals, but is supposed to have been named after the Spanish princess brought back as the bride of Owenmore, the 2nd-century king of Munster. He named their landing-place after her. **Enniskillin** (*Innis Ceithleann*) in Fermanagh is traditionally said to have been named after Cethlenn, wife of the Fomorian Balor of the Great Blows (the Fomorians were a race of demonic pirates based on Tory Island who were constantly at war with the various races that make up legendary Ireland). Despite its meaning of 'clear lake', **Lough Finn** (*Lough Finne*) in Donegal is associated with Finna who is said to have died in the lake while trying to save her brother.

Many other loughs also have legends associated with them. **Lough Derg** (*Logh Deirgeirt*) on the Shannon is supposed to have acquired its name – 'lake of the red eye' – from a king who, having lost his eye, washed his bloody face until its water ran red. **Lough Erne** in Fermanagh is said to be named from the Erni, a tribe of the Fir Bolg who once lived on the plain where the lough now is. According to a legend that goes back to at least the 12th century **Lough Neagh** (*Loch nEathach*) in Antrim, the largest lake in the British Isles, was formed when a spring suddenly overflowed in the 1st century AD, and

buried many cities. Among the victims was Eochaid, king of Munster, who gave his name to the new lake.

It is not always possible to be sure if the people commemorated in these names were real or purely fictional. We can have our doubts about Ciar who is remembered in **Kerry** (*Ciarraí*) 'territory of Ciar's descendants'. He is said to have been the son of Maeve, Cuchulainn's opponent, and she is generally thought of as a remnant of one of the old goddesses. But what about Cairbre after whom **Carbury** Kild is named? He is said to be a son of Niall of the Nine Hostages. The existence of Niall is accepted as he reigned 379–405. **Carrickfergus** (Antrim) is named after a king of Dal Riada who brought the Irish settlements of Scotland to heel. **Athy** (*Baile Atha I*) 'town of the ford of Ae' gained its name from a Munster chieftain killed in battle there as recently as the 11th century.

Historical names

The early heroes were not the only ones to have towns named after them. There are a large number of names containing recognizably English, Scottish and Welsh surnames such as **Newtown Forbes**, Longford, **Newtown Hamilton**, Armagh and **Newtownmount-kennedy**, Wicklow. These are usually associated with the English and Scottish settlements of the 16th and 17th centuries. Known as 'The Plantations', the date of the settlements in fact cover a period from the Norman invasion of 1170 led by Richard de Clare, known as Strongbow, to the 20th century.

However, not all English-sounding names are necessarily English. **Mornington** (*Baile Uí Mhomáin*) in Meath means 'farm of the descendants of Mornáin' and was the source of the title Earl of Mornington held by the Duke of Wellington's elder brother. **Mornington Crescent** in London is named after him, and thus after the Irish village.

From the Middle Ages come **Mansfieldtown** in Louth, a corruption of the Norman family name Mandeville. **Thomastown** in Kildare is named after the seneschal of Leinster, Thomas Fitzantony, and **Rathmines** in Dublin is named after the de Moenes family who owned the rath in the 14th century. **Mitchelstown** in Cork gained its name from a 13th-century Welshman, Mitchel

Condon, and **Joyce's County** in Galway is named after another 13th-century Welsh family. **Buttevant** in Cork is popularly, but dubiously, said to come from the war-cry of the local Norman family the de Barrys '*Boutez en avant*'.

The events of 1577 gave their name to the **Rath of Mullaghmast** (*Mullach Maistean*) in Clare 'hilltop of Maiste', once the place where the rulers of South Leinster met for debate. An unscrupulous English adventurer called Maiste is supposed to have invited 400 of the chiefs of Leinster here for a New Year's banquet before murdering them. The Spaniards who gave their name to **Spanish Point** (Clare) were also killed, after their ship, escaping from the debacle of the Armada, was wrecked there. **Poyntzpass** in Armagh is equally bloody, commemorating a battle in 1598 between the troops of Sir Toby Poynts and those of 'the arch rebel' Hugh O'Neill, Earl of Tyrone. Although the village of **Tyrrellspass** in Westmeath only dates from the late 18th century, it commemorates a successful ambush laid against the English by Captain Richard Tyrrell in 1597.

Hamiltonsbawn (*Bábhun Hamaltun*) in Armagh 'Hamilton's enclosure' refers to a fortification built by John Hamilton in 1619 but destroyed in the Rebellion of 1641. **Jamestown**

in Leitrim refers to James I who gave the village a charter in 1621. (James was also responsible for turning one of the many places called Derry 'the oak grove' into **Londonderry** when he granted a charter for London merchants to settle there in 1607. Similarly **Virginia** (Cavan) was founded under his auspices and named after his predecessor Elizabeth I, the Virgin Queen.) **Bloodybridge** in Wicklow gained its name from the massacre of Planters that took place in 1641. In **Burntcourt**, Tipperary, a house built in the same year got its name nine years later when it was burnt by Oliver Cromwell. More peaceful were towns like **Cookstown** (Tyrone) built by Alan Cook at the beginning of the 17th century, and **Coothill** (Cavan) named after the Coote family who had land there in the same century.

In the next century came **Humewood** (Wicklow) named after William Hume who obtained the land in 1708. It kept in its Irish name *Coill an Bhuitléaraigh* 'Butler's wood' the name of earlier, Norman owners. **Stratford-on-Slaney** (Wicklow) was founded by Edward Stratford, second earl of Aldborough, to encourage industry in the area, and **Ballyjamesduff** (*Baile Shéamais Dhuibh*) in Cavan was named from an English officer who fought in the 1798 rising. Slightly later, in 1818, came **Draperstown** in Derry named after the London Drapers Company which had commercial interests there. Not every name is associated with bloodshed or with the ruling classes. In the late 19th century **Flannery Bridge** (Galway) was named after a local parish priest the Rev. T.J. Flannery, a friend of A.J. Balfour, then secretary for Ireland. One of the most recent of this group of names must be **Craigavon** in Armagh, a new town of 1965, which took its name from the first prime minister of Northern Ireland, James Craig, Viscount Craigavon.

A similar situation exists in Scotland. A number of historical names are quite old. **Grahamstown** in Central is said to be named after Sir John de Graham killed nearby in 1298, and **Athelstaneford** is named from the defeat suffered by the invading Athelstan, King of Mercia in the early 10th century. But a significant number of place names date from the late 17th to 19th centuries, some founded to control what the English saw as the rebellious and unruly inhabitants of Scotland and to break the power of the clans. Others were founded by those in power to provide accommodation for

some of those displaced by the Highland clearances and to introduce industry to their lands. One of the best-known examples of the first class is **Fort William**, a key site for controlling the Highlands, named by General Mackay in 1690 after King William. In fact both William and Mary are honoured in the name, for the civilian settlement was named **Maryburgh**. **Fort Augustus** was built in 1716, but given its present name in 1730 when it was recaptured from the Jacobites after their defeat at Culloden. It is named after William Augustus, Duke of Cumberland, more generally known as Butcher Cumberland. A third Highland fort, **Fort George**, is slightly later, being named after George II in 1751.

Other, more peaceful, 18th-century foundations include **Gardenstown** set up in 1720 by Alexander Garden of Troup. A large number of foundations date from the 1760s including **Alexandria** (Strathclyde) named after the local MP Alexander Smollett, and **Charlestown** (Fife) named after Charles Bruce, Earl of Elgin, who built it for the coal miners on his estate (**Charlestown of Aberlour** in Grampian, often now just called **Aberlour**, is later, being a model village founded c. 1812 by Charles Grant). **Cuminestown** in Grampian is another model village built by Joseph Cumine but should not be confused with **Cummingstown** in the same region built c. 1810 by Sir William Cumming. **Garliestown** (D&G) was built by Lord Garlies, **Gavintown** (Borders) was built by the local landowner David Gavin and **Grantown-on-Spey** (High) was developed by the local Grant family.

Invergordon (High) was founded by Sir Alexander Gordon and is an interesting illustration of how the Gaelic *inver* 'river mouth' had lost its true sense and was felt simply to be a suitable Scottish place-name element. **Gordonstown** (Grampian) was named by a landowner called Gordon in the 1770s, but **Gordonstoun** (also in Grampian) is much earlier. Sir Robert Gordon changed the unromantic name of his estate, until then called the Bog of Plewlands, in 1638. (Even earlier is **John o'Groats**, said to be named after a Dutchman called Jan de Groot who was Bailie to the earl of Caithness c. 1500.)

There was another flurry of building in the early 18th century giving us places such as the Edinburgh suburb of **Murrayfield**, named after a certain Archibald Murray, **Dufftown** (Grmp), and **Gasstown** (D&G) named after the local landowner Joseph Gass. **Armadale** in Lothian is a trick name. It belonged originally to the Highlands, and is a Norse name meaning something like 'arm valley'. It was transferred south, not in a deliberate plot to confuse students of place names, but when the then Lord Armadale bought some land in Lothian and founded a new town.

A surprising number of these towns were named after women so we find **Janetstown** and **Jeantown** in the Highlands (although **Janet's Brea** is said to be a corruption of Danes' Brae), and **Helensburgh** in Strathclyde, which took its name from Lady Helen Colquhoun, the wife of the landowner, soon after its foundation in 1776. **Bettyhill** (High) was set up by a younger relative of Lady Helen, Elizabeth Countess of Sutherland, to provide shelter for some of those evicted in the clearances. **Maryhill** (Strath) was actually founded in 1760 by someone called Mary Hill. Less obviously **Renton** (Strath) was founded by Jean Telfer-Smollet, sister of the writer Tobias Smollett in 1782 but named after her daughter-in-law Cecilia Renton. Sir George Munro named **Jemimaville** (High) after his wife in the 1820s. **Port Charlotte** and **Port Ellen**, both on Islay, were both named in the 1820s by the Gaelic scholar W.F. Campbell, the first after his mother, Lady Charlotte Campbell, the second after his wife, Lady Ellenor. It would be

difficult to find a similar group of names from this period in England, but not so in Ireland. **Helen's Bay** (Down) was named after Helen Sheridan, Countess of Dufferin, who lived nearby in the first half of the 19th century. **Bessbrook** in Armagh was named after Elizabeth Pollock, wife of the owner of the local great house, and **Maryville** (Tipperary) and **Katesbridge** (Down) were named after unknown women.

However, the island is full of false friends. **Bettytown** in Meath is in Irish *Baile an Bhaitaigh* 'Betagh's homestead', **Dollymount** in Dublin is a corruption of *Cnocán* (mount, little hill) *Doirinne*, **Mount Juliet** in Kilkenny is a corruption of the local abbey name Jerpoint, and **Sally Gap** in Wicklow is a corruption of 'saddle gap'. Names like **Clara** (Offaly) contain the Irish *Clóirtheach* 'level place', while **Clare** and those containing the element come from the Irish *An Clar* 'the plain'. As for all those names with Anna in them, they have two sources. Some of the names are from *eanach*, a marsh, as in **Annaduff** (Leitrim) 'black marsh', **Annaghaskin** in Dublin (*Eanach Sheascan*) 'marsh of the eels', and **Anny** (Mon). *Ath na* has given rise to **Annalong** in Down (*Ath na Long*) 'ford of the ships', **Annacotty** in Limerick (*Ath na Coite*) 'ford of the little boat', and **Annamoe** in Wicklow (*Ath na mBó*) 'ford of the cows'.

Scotland

There is one way in which the Gaelic names of Scotland differ significantly from those in Ireland, and that is in the way in which a good number of Old Norse elements have been absorbed. We find elements such as *acairseid* or *acarsaid* from Old Norse *akkarsaeti* 'place where you set your anchor' so 'anchorage'. *Cleit* from *klettr* 'rock, cliff' is found by itself as place names **Clett** and **Clatt** and **Cleat** and in combination elsewhere. There are also *cuidhe* from *kvi* 'cattle pen', *eilean* from *eyland* 'island', a very common element, and *fadhail* from *vathill* 'ford in a sea channel' to name but a few. This reflects the long co-existence of Norse and Gaelic-speaking peoples in the northern and western parts of the island. Their co-existence is brought out more clearly by names such as **Acharacle** (High) 'Torquil's ford'. It is made up of the Gaelic *ath* 'ford' and a Norse

personal name, originally the pagan Thorkettil 'cauldron of the god Thor' which was natural-

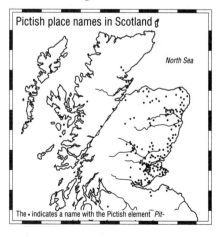

Pictish place names in Scotland

North Sea

The • indicates a name with the Pictish element *Pit-*

The distribution of *pit*-names can give us some idea of the area in which the Celtic form of the Pictish language was spoken. Based on a map in W.F.H. Nicolaisen's *Scottish Place-Names*, Batsford 1976.

ized as Torquil. We have concentrated on the Irish names at the expense of Gaelic because Scotland has one of the richest place-name heritages, of all of the countries that make up the British Isles and there is so much else to look at.

The problem of the Picts

Much of the confusion and mystery over the Picts comes from the romantic images of later ages of little dark painted men, living in burrows and guarding the secrets of the heather ale with their lives. In fact there is very little to support any of this. There are enormous gaps in our knowledge of the Picts, but what we do know is that often when early writers used the term 'Pict' they were only using it vaguely to indicate people living in the northern region, thus confusing things even more. We are probably dealing with two groups of people, for the few fragmentary Pictish inscriptions we have are in two different languages: one a form of Celtic, the other a language that we can read but not understand. It is impossible to say anything definite at all about this language, although this has not stopped people trying to prove their own theories.

Nearly all our reliable historical information about the Picts comes after their conquest by Kenneth MacAlpin in 846, by which time their culture was heavily influenced by the Gaels. There are many remnants of their wonderful art, in particular the magnificent metalwork and the fine carved stones.

In addition archaeologists are now increasing our knowledge of the life and times of the Picts. One of the problems in studying them is that despite the artwork of the elite, the ordinary person living under the Picts has left very little behind. Fragments of pottery, that standby of the archaeologist, are rare from this period and the people must have depended on utensils made from things such as wood and leather which do not survive. However, in the last few years archaeologists in the Northern Isles have been turning their attention to what lies underneath the Norse settlements and have been finding peculiarly-shaped buildings with curved walls unlike anything else we know. The buildings must have belonged to the people who lived there before the Norse settlers took over, and very recently archaeologists in the east of Scotland have also begun to be able to identify Pictish sites.

There is some hope that as a result it will be possible in the future to link the world of excavators and place-name students together and say more about the place names and the language of the Picts. Two of the important archaeological sites, **Pitcarmick** and **Pitroddie**, contain one of only two place-name elements we can be sure are Pictish. There are over 300 names in Scotland beginning Pit- and they can be used to define not the area ruled by the Picts, but the core area in which the Celtic-speaking Picts lived (see map). There are many problems attached to using the information, not least of which is the lack of records from the Picts themselves. All the evidence dates from after the conquest of their land by Gaelic speakers, but the general conclusions are reasonably safe.

Pit- names have developed from earlier spellings with Pet-. They come from a word *pet* or *pett*, which is found as *peth* 'thing' in Welsh or Cornish, but not used as a place-name element. However, if we look at the related language of ancient France, Gaulish, we do find a similar term. Late Latin had a word *petia* meaning 'a piece (of land)', adopted from Gaulish. It passed into French as *pièce*, and then came into English as our *piece*. The Pictish term is thought to have the same meaning as the Gaulish, and many scholars think that Pictish was most closely related to Gaulish. This would not present a very great problem. We have written evidence of tribes moving from Gaul to southern Britain (see p. 19), and archaeological evidence suggests some close connections between tribes in Yorkshire and Gaul. The only cause for speculation is why they settled so far north. The theory is reinforced by the fact that the French place names **Poitou** and **Poitiers** come from a Gaulish tribal name, the *Pictavi* or *Pictones*, almost identical with that of the Picts.

Unfortunately, we cannot use these Pit-names to find out other words in Pictish, as the second element in the name is nearly always Gaelic, showing that the names came into use after MacAlpin's conquest. Some of the names may well be translations of earlier Pictish names, some may be new creations. The use of Pit- as a name element had obviously passed into the vocabulary of the Gaelic speakers. Since a term meaning 'a share, portion' is likely to have legal associations, it may well be evidence that the conquerors adopted local land laws. This certainly happened in England where parish boundaries may sometimes go back to Roman times or even earlier, and where the Norman overlords changed much in the country, but were forced to accept the traditional local laws in much to do with everyday farming life.

The Pictish-Gaelic hybrid names include **Pitcaple** (Grmp) 'horse-share', **Pitcarmick** (Tays) 'Cormac's share', **Pitcorthie** (Fife) 'share of the pillar-stone', **Pitcox** (Loth) 'share of the fifth part', and **Pitliver** (Fife) 'share of the book' (i.e. the Bible and perhaps land given for some religious purpose). Other hybrid names are **Pitlochry** (Tays) 'stony share', **Pitmedded** (Grmp) 'middle share', **Pitsligo** (Grmp) 'shelly share', and **Pittenweem** (Fife) 'share of the cave'.

The other element that we can be pretty sure is Pictish is *carden*, which comes from the same root and most probably has the same meaning as the Welsh *cardden*, a 'thicket'. With the exception of **Cardross** in Strathclyde, these names all lie in the same region as the Pit-names. They include the common name **Kincardine** 'head of the thicket' from Gaelic *cinn* + *carden*, **Fettercairn** (Grmp), Gaelic *faithir*

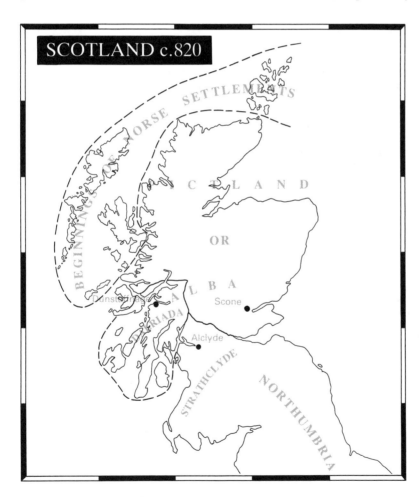

SCOTLAND c.820

'slope' + *carden*, **Cardenden** (Fife) from *carden* + the Old English for valley *denn*, and **Cardno**, **Cardny**, **Cairney** and **Cairnie**, all formed from *carden* + Gaelic *ach* 'field, place'.

There are other possible Pictish elements. *Pert* meaning 'bush' is the source of **Perth**, *lanerc* 'glade' the source of **Lanark**, *pevr* 'radiant, beautiful' is found in the two **Peffer**s in Lothian, and our old friend *aber* 'river mouth' is found in **Aberdeen** 'mouth of the Don' and **Arbroath** 'mouth of the Brothock'. These may be Pictish elements, but in that case their form was so close to the other British forms of the elements that we cannot really distinguish which language was being used to form the name.

It is worth noting that some of the traditional divisions of Scotland probably come from the Picts. A 12th-century manuscript, that is one written 300 years after the Picts had become Scots and therefore not wholly reliable, tells us that the seven provinces of the Picts were *Enegus cum Moerne* (**Angus** with **The Mearns**), *Adtheodle et Goverin* (**Atholl** and **Gowrie**), *Stradeern cum Meneted* (**Strathearn** with **Menteith**), *Fife cum Fothreve* (now **Kinross**), *Mar cum* **Buchan**, *Muref et Ros* (**Moray** and **Ross**) and *Cathanesia* (**Caithness**). The Picts are also remembered in the name **Pentland**, from the Old Norse *Pettaland* 'land of the Picts'.

Cumbric

The late, great Kenneth Jackson, whose work on the early languages of the British Isles has never been equalled, defined Cumbric as the Brittonic dialect of Cumbria, northern Lancashire and the south-west of Scotland. In the 7th century the northern part of this region was the kingdom of Strathclyde, with its centre at **Dumbarton** 'fort of the Britons'. South of that, reaching into England as far as the Eden valley was the great kingdom of Rheged, celebrated in the Welsh poetry which forms our earliest native literature. (The survival of this poetry in Welsh shows how close the two dialects of British were.)

During the 7th century the Northumbrians conquered most of Rheged and the early Welsh stories tell us of the constant fighting between the Strathclyde Britons and the Northumbrians. For some of the period between the 7th century and 1092, when the border was fixed, the Britons managed to regain possession of much of Rheged, down into northern Cumberland. Therefore it is not surprising that British names appear in this area, and even over the border into Northumberland as in the case of **Glendue** 'dark valley' which appears to have been borrowed from Cumbric speakers as late as the 11th century, although this was probably near the end of the dialect's life.

Just as there are key words for distinguishing the Pictish sphere of influence, so there are with Cumbric names. One in particular, *caer*, stands out. It is of course familiar from Welsh names, but probably has a slightly different meaning in the north. *Caer* is much less grand than in Wales, rarely meaning a fort, but more often an area with some kind of secure fence or ditch round it such as a farm with a stockade, or even just a hamlet. It is found almost exclusively south of the Forth-Clyde line, and hardly overlaps at all with *pit* names. In fact, its distribution is very close to what we know of the British kingdoms of Strathclyde and Rheged. It was probably a more common name-element in southern Scotland than we have sure evidence for, as it is difficult to distinguish between names from *caer* and those from or influenced by Gaelic *cathair*, 'fort'.

Places with *caer* include **Cramond** (Loth) 'fort on the (River) Almond' (fort here, because it is the site of a Roman station), and **Caerlanrig** (Borders) from *caer* + *lanerc*, here a Cumbric rather than Pictish element. Similarly it featured in the two **Carfrae**s from *caer* + *bre* 'hill', and **Cathcart** (Strath) 'hamlet on the (River) Cart'. An exception just north of the Forth, **Kirkcaldy** (Fife), is found in early forms as *Kircalthyn*, which comes from *caer* + *caled* 'hard' + *dun*.

South of the modern border, but still within the old Cumbric area of Cumbria are **Carlisle**, **Cardrew**, from *caer* and *du* 'black', **Cardurnock** from *caer* + *durnog* 'pebbly', and **Castle Carrock**. There is a Northumbrian addition to this group in **Carrick**, which unlike other places of this name does not come from the British for 'rock' but is Cumbric *caer* + Old English *wic*. The second element was added to the Cumbric when the Angles took over the area. What makes *caer* so distinctively Cumbric is that the element is not found south of Rheged until Welsh names are reached, unlike other British elements which are spread thinly over the country.

There are three other elements which are particularly associated with the Cumbric area, although they are also found outside the area of *caer*. *Penn*, 'end, head', which we have already found as *pen* in Wales is found in southern Scotland in the names **Pencaitland**, **Penicuik**, **Penmanshile**, **Pennygant** and **Penvalla**. *Pren* 'tree' is found both north and south of the Forth-Clyde line, twice as the place name **Pirn**, and combined with an unknown element in the names **Pirnie**, **Pirny Braes**, **Pirniehall** and **Kinpunie**. In **Prinlaws** (Fife), from **pren las*, we have a green tree, and **Primside** (Borders) is a white tree as an early form is *Prenwensete*, *pren* + *wen* 'white' + Old English *sete*. However, **Primrose** has nothing to do with colour or the spring flower, but is **pren ros* 'tree on the moor'.

Many of these names centre round the area controlled in Roman times by the tribe known as the Votadini and later as the Gododdin, one of whose major centres was on the volcanic plug crowned by a hill fort known as **Traprain Law**. The final part is Old English *hlaw*, but the first word, rationalized by English speakers, is *tref* 'homestead, settlement', again familiar from Welsh, + *pren*.

While *tref* is indicative of Cumbric speakers the situation is rather different from those elements we have already looked at. As a second element *tref* is a widely-spread element, occurring south of Hadrian's Wall, in the old British kingdoms, and notably in Pictish areas, but as a first element it is again restricted to south of the Forth-Clyde line. It is found in the English Cumbric area in **Triermain** in Cumbria, **tref yr maen* 'homestead on the rock', and in **Troughend** in Northumberland, of obscure meaning. The same name is found in Scotland as **Torquhan** and twice as **Troquhain**. Further south *tref* is only found in **Treales**, Lancashire (*tref* + *llys* 'court') until Wales is reached. In Scotland it is found in names such as **Tranent** (Loth) 'homestead on the streams', **Traquair** (Bord) 'village on the Quair', and **Terregles** (D&G), **tref yr eglwys* 'homestead of the church'.

There are other important place names from Cumbric, many with elements familiar from other Celtic place names. **Bathgate** in Lothian has an earlier name, *Batket* (1153–65) meaning 'boar-wood'. The second element is the same as Welsh *coed*. **Dalkeith** in Lothian (*Dochet* 1144) comes from *dol* 'meadow, valley'

Arthur's Seat, Edinburgh. Arthurian names are found in the areas where British languages survived: the south-west of England, Wales and lowland Scotland. The many archaeological remains on the hill suggest that this may be the original Eidyn. (POPPERFOTO)

+ *coed* again, and **Glasgow** comes, via a Gaelic form, from *glas cau* 'green hollow'. **Kirkintilloch** in Strathclyde in the 10th century was *Caerpentaloch*, but has had *Caer* changed to Kirk, Cumbric *pen* 'head' translated into Gaelic *cenn*, and has a Gaelic final element meaning 'eminences' which was probably originally the Cumbric word of the same meaning,

bryn. **Linthigow** (Loth) 'lake in the damp hollow' comes from *llyn* 'lake', *lliath* 'damp' and *cau* 'hollow'. **Melrose** (Borders) comes from *moel* 'bare' and *ros* 'moor', and in **Peebles** (Strath) the Welsh word *pebyll* 'tent' can be recognized, probably originally a place of only temporary dwellings. **Renfrew** (Strath) comes from **rhyn frwd*, 'point of the current'.

English Scottish place names

Many of the place names of Scotland are English. As they follow in general the same rules and history as English names, earlier chapters would have more details on the elements that formed these Scottish names. While English names are found throughout Scotland, the oldest ones are naturally found in the areas of Scotland which have been English-speaking the longest, starting with the south-eastern area occupied by the Northumbrians from the 7th century. This gives us Old English names such as **Haddington** (Loth) 'farm associated with Hadda', one of those -*ing* names so fascinating to place-name students, **Hawick** (Borders) 'village surrounded by a hedge', and **Jedburgh** (Borders) 'enclosed homestead on the river

Jed'. Other Old English names are **Livingston** (Loth) 'Leving's farm', **Prestwick** (Strath) 'priest's dwelling', and **Whitburn** (Loth) 'white stream'.

In the Middle Ages Scottish villages tended to remain small, preferring, even as early as the 12th century, to split into smaller groupings. Often each kept its original name with some distinguishing term. This can be seen on maps as frequent groupings of village names distinguished by terms such as Upper, Nether, East(er) or West(er). There were also the big feudal estates, the home or main farm of which gave rise to the distinctively Scottish place-name phrase 'The Mains of . . .'. The widely scattered population can also be seen reflected in the number of names that refer to only one dwelling. **Easthouses** may be an example of this, as its earliest form is the singular *Esthus* (1241) (compare Glasgow's **Easterhouse** estate).

Sometimes names from English reflect the local Scots dialect. **Fauldhouse** (Loth) (again singular) means 'house on unploughed land' from Old English *fealh*. But early on the name was confused with the Scots *fauld* '(sheep) fold'. **Loanhead** (Loth) is a northern development of the Old English *lane* and *heafod*, 'head or end of the lane'. **Stenhousemuir** (Cent), meaning 'moor of the stone-house' (singular again), was originally just 'stonehouse' until the 18th century when the 'muir', the Scottish spelling of 'moor', was added. Many of these English names are, of course, translations of earlier names in other languages, although this earlier history is often lost. **Broxburn** in Lothian meaning 'badger's stream' is not recorded until 1638. The earlier name was *Easter Strathbrock*, the Gaelic for 'badger's valley'. **Falkirk** (Central) is first recorded in 1080 as *egglesbrec*, Gaelic for 'the speckled church', and the modern name is a Scots translation of this.

Foreign names in Scotland

Scotland is rich in names from abroad. Many of them are the sort of biblical names found elsewhere. Edinburgh has a **Joppa** and **Jordan** and there is another Joppa in Strathclyde. Tayside has a **Zoar**, from a small village once near Sodom and Gomorrah, a **Jericho** and a **Padanaram**, an unusual biblical name which means 'plain of the Aramaeans' in Hebrew. More unusual are the large number of names commemorating battles. There are **Balaclava**s in Highland and Strathclyde after the Crimean War battle of 1854 and at least three **Waterloo**s and a **Portobello** in Lothian. (These are also found in England.) More unusual is **Omoa** in Strathclyde named by someone who had fought in the Battle of Omoa in Honduras in 1779, and **Patna**, renamed c. 1800 by someone who had been born in the Indian city.

Admiral Sir A. Cochrane is responsible for the importation of the Spanish name Lamancha to the Borders c. 1736 because he had lived there, and another retired warrior, a certain General Johnstone who had fought in Egypt around 1800, is responsible for a whole rash of names – **Egypt**, **Grand Cairo**, **Rosetta** and **Valenciennes** – in a single parish in Dumfries and Galloway. One of the most remarkable of these names is **Friokheim** (Tays), which looks as if it is from Germany. In fact it is only half German. The first part is the old name of the village, but in 1824 John Andson, who had lived a long time in Germany, officially added the typically German second element, meaning 'home', to the old name, thereby tricking at least one German scholar to write of possible Swabian settlement in the area.

One name that has been conspicuous by its absence in this section on Scottish names is that of **Edinburgh**. It is an embarrassing fact that we do not know the meaning of this great city's name, any more than we do of London. We have ample evidence of early forms as it is mentioned repeatedly in the earliest Scottish (Cumbric) poem *The Gododdin* of about 600 as *Eidyn* or *Din Eidyn* ('the fort of Eidyn'), but this takes us no nearer the meaning. We do know that the popular story that it was named after Edwin King of Northumbria (617–33) cannot be true as our earliest records of the name are from before Edwin came to the throne. One small comfort for the experts is that the Gaelic name *Dun Eideann* and the English Edinburgh only translate the sense 'fort', which suggests that the meaning of *Eidyn* may have been as obscure in the distant past as it is today.

From pub to place name

Places which acquire their names from pubs are found throughout the British Isles and a number of English ones are mentioned elsewhere in this book. However, they stand out particularly clearly in those areas where the first language of place names is not necessarily English, as in Scotland, Cornwall and Ireland. On the outskirts of Dublin alone you can find **Buckandhounds**, **Fox and Geese**, **Redcow** and **Pass-if-you-can**. Elsewhere we find **Royal Oak** in Carlow, **Horse and Jockey** in Tipperary, and **Blue Ball** in Offaly. **Enfield** in Meath was originally 'Innfield' but 'corrected' or refined to the less obvious name.

Scotland has its fair share of such names too, such as **Grantshouse** in Borders and **Finstown** in Orkney, reputedly named after David Phin, an Irishman who retired from soldiering to build a pub there at the beginning of the 19th century. A certain Tammy Grant had been a local figure in the 18th century, and gave his name to a pub, Tammy Grant's Inn. In the following century a railway station was built on the new line passing through the area, and the railway company named it after the inn. This is rather unusual, for although only the locals would recognize it as a pub name, companies looking for new names usually try to be cleaner than clean and to stay away from anything like the demon drink.

Scotland also has one of the most attractive pub place names: **Beeswing** in Dumfries and Galloway. There are a number of pubs in Britain of this name, all named after a highly successful racehorse which won 51 of the 64 races it entered between 1835 and 1842. In this particular case the pub was built by the horse's owner, which may explain how it was transferred to the town. In Cornwall **Jamaica Inn** on Bodmin has become famous from Daphne du Maurier's book, but is still little more than an isolated inn. More significant are **Bugle**, from a pub built in 1840, **London Apprentice** named after a popular 18th-century ballad, **Indian Queens** from another 18th-century song, **Victoria**, obviously 19th-century, and **Cripplesease** from a 19th-century pub built at the top of a long hill. There are three places named simply **Taphouse** from the old name for a pub, one of which dates back to at least 1533 and **Wainhouse Corner** was founded as early as 1417 and whose name goes back to the Old English *winhus*, 'wine house'.

Modern Names

Most books about British place names concentrate on the early names, given by the colourful Anglo-Saxons, Celts, Scandinavians and Normans. There are good reasons for this. Most town and village names fall into these categories, and most scholars come to place names through studying the languages of this period. From the historian's point of view later

place names are less important because there is more written evidence of other kinds. Thus many books give the impression that by about 1500 the process of naming places was all over.

However, place-naming does not stop, any more than history does. Just as early place names tell us about waves of migration, conquest and settlement, so later place names tell us about the development of the country once the last of the invaders had become natives.

New town names

Until the Industrial Revolution, and much later in some parts, the majority of people lived in the country and gained their living, at least in part, through farming. Industry tended to be small-scale and localized. Many craftsmen, miners, saltworkers, etc. also kept livestock on the common and perhaps cultivated an acre or two. Various factors combined to change all this. An overall increase in the population, the introduction of enclosures, the development of steam power, improvements in transport, the emergence of the factory system all encouraged people to leave the countryside for the town. Towns and cities spread rapidly, swallowing up surrounding villages and hamlets. Many ill-defined districts of modern towns carry names which show they were once independent settlements.

New industries and the need to ease the pressure on existing towns (a 20th-century phenomenon) gave rise to new settlements. In some cases the new place has an old name, as in **Milton Keynes** which took the name of one of the villages swallowed up by the new development. Others added 'New' to the name of a neighbouring settlement, as in **New Earswick** (NYorks) and **New Ash Green** (Kent), or to the name of a place which the new town resembled or wished to be associated with. In **New Holland** (Humb) the terrain was similar to the district of Holland to the south, and several resorts optimistically called themselves **New Brighton**.

'New' can also refer to some new feature of an existing place. The name of **Newchapel**, a district of Kidsgrove in Staffordshire, came into use in the late 19th century after a chapel there was rebuilt, and **Newquay** in Cornwall was named after the quay was repaired in the 15th century. **Newhaven** (ESx) was once called *Meeching*. The name changed after the mouth of the Ouse at nearby Seaford became blocked by shingle in the late 16th century, forcing the river to find a new outlet and so create a new harbour. 'New' settlements can be surprisingly old. Several places called **Newbald** or **Newbold**, **Newbegin** or **Newbiggin** (all meaning 'new house or building') and various **Newcastle**s and **Newmarket**s date back to the 12th or 13th centuries.

But there are some new towns with new names, and these often reflect the reason for the town's existence, although sometimes in a roundabout way. Those set up to serve a new factory or industry may carry the name of the

Canary Wharf (see previous page) is one of the many modern developments that takes its name from the trade formerly carried on there; in this case the importing of fruit from the Canary Islands. It is already known locally as 'the Budgie's Cage', an example of how quickly nicknames can arise.
(ADINA ANSEL TOVY/HORIZON)

Casualties of war

After World War I a centre was set up in the village of Knight's Enham (Hants) to provide care, sheltered housing and workshops for disabled ex-servicemen. After World War II the Egyptians started a fund to support the village as a way of expressing their thanks to the British servicemen who won the Battle of Alamein, and the name of the village was then changed to **Enham Alamein**.

Before the days of ejector seats military aircrew often suffered horrific burns before escaping from their stricken aircraft. The Royal Victoria Hospital at East Grinstead (WSx) became famous during World War II for treating such burns and for reconstructing the faces and limbs of the injured by plastic surgery. The chief surgeon, Sir Archibald MacIndoe, pioneered new treatments and techniques and his (literally) long-suffering patients called themselves the *Guinea Pig Club*, and a local pub is still called the **Guinea Pig**.

company. **Corytown** in Essex comes from an oil refinery opened in 1922 by Cory Brothers and Co. Nearby **Shellhaven** also has the name of an oil company. **Vulcan Village** on Merseyside housed workers at the Vulcan Works, a 19th-century iron foundry, and the workers of Vickers' shipyard at Barrow lodged at **Vickerstown**.

Sometimes the product gave its name to the town. **Ironville** (Derbs) grew up around the Butterley Iron Company's works, and **Port Sunlight** (Merseyside) housed the workers at Lever's Sunlight soap factory. In other names the connection with industry is less clear. **Dresden** and **Etruria** in The Potteries, Staffordshire are both named for other famous centres of china and pottery manufacture. **Coalville** (Leics) grew up around a house of that name built by a 19th-century colliery owner. **Peterlee**, a 20th-century new town in Durham, was named after a much-respected miners' union leader, and **Silver End** in Essex was built by the firm of F.H. Crittall who

produced shiny metal window frames. There are many other examples of such new names, and most have a distinctly 'new' flavour, with elements like -**town**, -**ville** and **village** instead of the old -**ton** and -**ham**.

The oldest new village?

Nuneham Courtenay (Oxon) can claim to have been a new village twice in its life. The second time was when it was moved to its present site.

The village took its name from the *Curtenay* family, probably from Courtenai in France, who owned the manor of Nuneham in the 13th century. In 1710 it was acquired by the Harcourt family, and in the 1760s the first Earl Harcourt moved the family seat from Stanton Harcourt and created a new house with landscaped grounds, now Nuneham Park. The old village spoilt the view and the family demolished it and had a new one built well out of sight of the house. The Earl did not change its name – the days of the Norman manorial affix were long over – but he did follow a later fashion of the squirearchy and gave his name to the new village inn, the **Harcourt Arms**.

And the first time? We don't know exactly, but **Nuneham** comes from Old English *aet the niwan ham*, 'at the new village'. It was first recorded in the 10th century.

Ironbridge Gorge is named after the first cast-iron bridge to be erected. The gorge is surrounded by industrial names: the 18th-century new town of Coalport and the 20th-century new town of Telford. The old name of the valley, Coalbrookdale, despite appearances, is not one of these. It was first recorded in 1250 as *Caldebrok*, 'cold brook', and became known as Coalbrook because of the many small mines driven horizontally into the hillside. (POPPERFOTO)

Streets, fields and buildings

The 'new town' names are a tiny fraction of the later names. The main focus of place-name study in this period changes from settlements to what the experts call the 'minor' names; those of fields, streets and even individual buildings. These are the province of the local historian. Many of these names are in a language we can all understand, and local knowledge is more important in studying them than linguistic expertise. Many of the examples in this chapter come from London and Oxfordshire as we are using our own local knowledge of the places where we live or spent our childhoods. There are plenty of similar examples around most people's home town.

These 'minor' places fall into categories such as fields and farms, streets, estates, pubs and other buildings. But the categories overlap. A street can be named after a pub or contain an old field name, and can in turn give its name to a trading estate, swimming pool, railway station, etc. Many field names have been given to farms, districts or estates. Developers are quite fond of using old field names for new housing estates, sometimes with a cosmetic change. *Blackford Leys* in Oxford, named from its dark soil, became **Blackbird Leys**, with wild flower and bird names for its roads. Names can even go full circle: the **Angel and Greyhound** pub in Oxford is named after **Angel and Greyhound Meadow**. The meadow itself gained its name from two pubs, the Angel and the Greyhound, which used it for grazing.

Field names

Some field-name elements date from the early medieval period and have Anglo-Saxon or Scandinavian roots. Some Anglo-Saxon and Scandinavian elements remained in use during and after the later medieval period. Some arose in Middle English, others are modern.

The division of old large fields into smaller units and the cultivation of new land demanded an increasing number of new names. The division of land continued into the 19th century in some places as landowners tried to add to their income and the population gradually increased. The developer seeking an 'old' field name for his new estate may not have to go back very far.

Middle English *innam* 'a piece of land taken in or enclosed', appears in various guises: **Inham(s)**, **Inholm(s)**, **Innome**, **Innims** and **Ingham(s)** are examples. A related word gives rise to **Inning(s)**. The corresponding Scandinavian word *intek*, appearing as **Intake** or **Intack**, usually referred to land reclaimed from a moor or wetland. Middle English *inheche* – 'land newly hedged or fenced' – gives rise to **Inhedge** and the obscure **Image**, as well as **Innage**, **Innidge**, and **Ennige**. *Inhoke* (land 'hooked in' to cultivation) appears as **Inhooks**, **Innox**, **Innicks** and **Enocks**, among others. Any of these words can take an *n* from a Middle

English inflectional ending on the word *the*, as **Nineham(s)**, **Ninnings**, and **Ninnicks**.

Many field names refer to the size of the field or the appearance or quality of the land. Some are humorous, even if we suspect that the owner was 'laughing to keep from crying'. So while **Handkerchief Piece** and **Mouse Park** were obviously names for small fields, 'Hundred Acre' might refer to a very large field, or to a tiny one. There are a few names referring to good soil, often containing words such as **Excellent**, **Butter**, **Fat**, **Good** or **Lucky**, or names such as **Golden Valley**, **Providence**, **Milk and Honey**, **God's Garden** or **God's Plot** (which may have given its name to the Cardiff suburb of **Splott**). However, these are far outnumbered by the **Barebones**, **Breakhearts**, **Hungerhills** and **Labour-in-Vains**.

Lousy in field names can mean just that, but if the name is recorded very early it may contain Old English *hlose* 'pig sty'. This can also appear as **Loose**, **Lose-** or **Lucy**. These uncomplimentary names are seldom transferred to streets or estates (quite the wrong image) but many have become farm names. A roadside sign outside Abingdon (Oxon) proudly advertizes 'Starveall Farm Bed & Breakfast'. Prospective visitors should not be put off, but be glad that the owners have found a way to make a living out of the place.

A common type of field name is called rather grandly by scholars 'nicknames of remoteness'. These are the fields that lay some distance from the farm they belonged to, and were given the names of faraway places. **Nineveh, Dunkirk, China, Gibraltar** and many North American states and cities appear in field names. Some have negative overtones. **Van Diemen's Land, Botany Bay**, and **Isle of Elba** suggest transportation and exile. **Moscow** and **Siberia** may have been cold as well as distant. The new **North Pole** railway freight depot near Paddington may ultimately take its name from just such a remote and chilly site, although there has been a **North Pole Road** and pub called the North Pole here for many years.

On the other hand, **Egypt** probably produced a good corn crop, and **California** and **Klondike** may have been exceptionally profitable, where the farmer could 'strike it rich'. Strangers visiting Chelsea are sometimes surprised to hear bus passengers asking for 'the stop past the **World's End**'. The local story is that the area was beyond the fashionable part of town, but this is not an uncommon name for a remote field.

A few field names refer to ancient customs and practices. Names containing **Bell, Rope** and **Lamp** often indicate that the income from the field was dedicated for the maintenance of the church bells, bellropes or lights. **Gospel, Amen** and **Paternoster** often refer to the old custom of beating the bounds, when the village worthies walked the parish boundary to make sure that all the boundary markers were intact.

Heaven, Hell and Purgatory

Early in the 19th century the south London suburb then known as *Little Hell* was renamed **Belmont** 'beautiful hill'. Its old name may have been a corruption of *Little Hill*, or may have come from an uncomplimentary field name. Belmont was a popular name in the 19th century, and appears in many street and district names. A similar name, **Mount Pleasant**, was often ironic. One was the site of the workhouse, later a cottage hospital from which the locals claimed you never came out, and Mount Pleasant in central London once led to a huge mound of rubbish by the Grays Inn Road.

Purgatory is found quite often in field names, the unfortunate farmers perhaps hoping that their hardships would be rewarded at harvest time and maybe even in the afterlife. It was also occasionally applied to a particularly nasty stretch of road. (For **St. Patrick's Purgatory** in Donegal see p. 118.)

Heaven is occasionally found in field names. Much more common, however, is **Paradise**, which is often found in street names. The word comes via Greek and Latin from a Persian word meaning 'garden'. It was once a common name for a public park, and was sometimes given to houses built on the site of a garden, orchard, or burial ground. Surrounding names may provide clues. It could just mean a pleasant place to live. Applied to a row of 'model' workmen's houses it may have represented the benefactor's inflated opinion, but may indeed have been paradise compared to the stinking slums where so many were forced to exist. In Castleton on the Isle of Man it has yet another derivation. The street stands on the site of **Paradise Farm**, said to have been worked by the Saint family.

At each stop a prayer would be said or a passage of Scripture read. **Gospel Oak** is one such name, now belonging to a district in north London. There is another in **Wednesbury** (WMid; 'Woden's stronghold' overcome), and no doubt others elsewhere. **Lot** indicates that the land in question was shared out by drawing lots: **Lots Road** in Chelsea was built on such a patch. **Lammas**, quite common in street names, refers to land which was given over for common grazing after a crop had been harvested, traditionally on Lammas Day, 1 August.

Street names

Street names are the most diverse group of names, and perhaps the most interesting from the point of view of local and social history. However, the sheer number of street names means that it is possible only to deal with a fraction of them here.

The street and urban names which appear on the *Monopoly* board are familiar to most people, whether or not they have ever visited London. They are a mixed bag, but by chance they include most types of urban name. A study of them, and of names associated with them, will give a good idea of the diversity of names and naming processes.

As a broad generalization the oldest names in a town will be in the centre. But town-centre redevelopment, infill building and the fact that many towns have incorporated surrounding small villages and hamlets give many exceptions to this rule.

Whitechapel, formerly a village outside the city wall, means what it says. 'White' probably indicates that the chapel was built of stone.

Naming names

Local councils have a statutory duty to make sure that streets and buildings are named and numbered. They must consult the Emergency Services and the Post Office about proposed names, and must give local residents the opportunity to object. Most names are suggested by councillors or developers, and some councils will approach local groups or residents' associations for ideas (although they may not use them). There is nothing to stop anyone putting a name forward for consideration.

Most councils issue guidelines concerning the sort of names they will accept. Many dislike long names, those likely to be (deliberately) misinterpreted, such as *Typple Road* or *Hoare Street*, and those which give a bad image. *Slagheap Lane*, *Pigsty House* and *Sewage Farm Road* are unlikely to get past the committee, however appropriate they may be. Some limit the generic terms (*street*, *road*, *close*, *avenue*, etc.) which may be used, or restrict some of these terms to residential roads. Many discourage new names which differ from existing names only in the generic term: for example *Guinness Road* would be rejected if there was already a *Guinness Street* or *Guinness Way* in the town. (Edinburgh, however, has a collection of names with **Swanston**: **Swanston Avenue**, **Crescent**, **Drive**, **Gardens**, **Green**, **Grove**, **Loan**, **Place**, **Terrace**, **View** and **Way,** and the locals call the estate **The Swanstons**.)

Changing an existing name can lead to confusion and inconvenience, and most councils will only do so if there is a very good reason for it. Again, they must consult the Emergency Services, the Post Office and local residents. Sometimes a request for a new name comes from the residents: *Rillington Place* in Kensington was renamed after the remains of several murder victims were found in one of the houses. But a request by the proud congregation of a new Sikh temple that the road be renamed after their spiritual leader was blocked by objections from local residents from another congregation following a different guru. You can't please everybody!

Old Kent Road is the old road into Kent. **Becket Street** and **Pilgrimage Street** lie at its northern end. The name of Thomas Becket is adopted by several institutions along the route including a primary school and a petrol station. The names reveal the use of this road by medieval pilgrims to Becket's shrine at Canterbury. At its northern end the road used to be called *Kent Street* but was renamed **Tabard Street** by a worthy and literary-minded council. Tabard refers to the Tabard Inn from which the pilgrims in Chaucer's *Canterbury Tales* set out. **Manciple Street**, **Prioress Street** and **Pardoner Street** nearby refer to members of the same company. Chaucer's name also appears on a pub and a primary school in the area. (Fictional characters do not often appear in street and other 'official' names, but the same council named a group of streets around the site of the old Marshalsea prison after Dickensian characters, including Little Dorrit, whose father was imprisoned there.)

Pentonville Road is the road to **Pentonville**. The district of London is named after Henry Penton, Member of Parliament for Winchester, who owned and developed the land. The **-ville** marks it as a modern name, in this case from the late 18th century, although occasionally **-ville** can represent Old English *feld* (see p. 52). The ending became fashionable in the 18th century and persisted throughout the 19th century.

Euston Road runs past Euston station but actually predates it. It represents a type of name common in London but also occurring in other cities. It arises from large and interconnected aristocratic families developing their lands in the 18th and 19th centuries. To cut a long and complex story short **Fitzroy Square** and **Street** contain the family name. **Arlington Road**, **Stanhope Gardens**, **Drummond Crescent** and **Street**, **Ferdinand Place** and **Street** and **Warren Street** were named after members of the extended family. **Cleveland Street** and **Row**, **Grafton Crescent**, **Place**, **Road**, **Terrace**, **Way** and **Yard**, **Harrington Square**, **Conway Street**, **Hertford Place**, **Southampton Road**, and **Mornington Crescent** are from titles that they held. **Euston Road** and **Malden Crescent**, **Place** and **Road** are named after estates they owned, in Suffolk and Surrey respectively. The names represent piecemeal development by different generations of the family, and a comparison of the street names with the family tree would give a rough chronology. It is quite common for the name of a county, town or village in a street name to represent a title or estate of the landowner.

The Angel is a common pub name, often denoting a hostel once owned by a religious house. This one was an old coaching inn on the corner of Pentonville Road and Islington High Street. There has been an inn on this site since the 17th century but in recent years the pub here has been closed. The Angel is one of those vague districts which most towns have, usually centred on a local landmark which may no longer exist. Everyone knows where it is, most local people will define its boundaries, but no two versions would agree. Many such districts do not appear on maps. The Angel in London does because it has an Underground station.

Northumberland Avenue marks the site of **Northumberland House**, owned since 1642 by the Dukes of Northumberland. The **Avenue**, related to modern French *avenir* meaning 'to come to', originally referred to a tree-lined approach to a country house but came to mean any broad or spacious street, especially

134

one with trees. In this case the 'approach' is to the Victoria Embankment, and the house was compulsorily purchased and demolished in 1874 as part of the Embankment development scheme.

Whitehall is named for the former **Whitehall Palace**, of which only the Banqueting Hall survived a fire in 1698. It was the London residence of the Archbishops of York, including Cardinal Wolsey. After his death Henry VIII took it. *White Hall* was often used in the 16th century for a hall set aside for festivities, but 'white' may also refer to stone, as in Whitechapel (see above). The naming of a street after a prominent building is very common, and the street name usually remains when the building is destroyed or demolished.

Pall Mall is named after a game similar to croquet which was played here in the 17th century. Charles II laid out a new pall-mall alley in St. James's Park, and this is now **The Mall** (a street name also found in many other towns). **Mall** came to refer to a sheltered walk, and later to a shopping precinct.

Other names referring to sports and pastimes include **The Butts** (in many towns, sometimes in a district, estate or pub name) used for archery practice. Archery was a 'sport' that all citizens were encouraged and sometimes obliged to practise. Pub names such as the **Archers Arms** or the **Arrow** may also be significant. **Artillery Row** in Westminster led to an area used for archery and handgun practice. More than one person has claimed that **Shotover** in Oxford was a practice ground which the archers 'shot over'. Another theory is that the name comes from French *chateau vert*, meaning 'green castle', referring to the prominent wooded hill there. It actually comes from Old English *sceot* (a steep or slippery slope) and *ofer* (hill). The **Bullring** in Birmingham refers to bull-baiting and in **Bearward Street**, Northampton, a man kept bears, either for baiting or as dancing bears.

Other 'bull' and 'bear' names may have similar backgrounds, but need treating with caution as they may come from pub names. Bulls and bears appear quite often in heraldry and there is sometimes a connection with the heraldic symbol of a family or organization (see Leicester Square below).

Vauxhall in south London and **Ranelagh Grove** in Chelsea stand on the site of 17th-century pleasure gardens. Some Vauxhall and Ranelagh names in other parts of the country

---

Names in the wrong place

A transplanted or displaced name is always worth following up. We have already met places named after a battle, or the title or estate of the landowner, the Biblical names in the Welsh chapels, the twin towns and the 'nicknames of remoteness' in field names (see p. 133). **Pennsylvania** is common as such a nickname, but the village of that name near Bath was once owned by members of William Penn's family. As a devout Quaker Penn deplored naming places after people. It is rumoured that his name was attached to the state he founded only at the mischievous insistence of Charles II. He would have been horrified to know just how many places now bear his name.

In the Fylde area of Lancashire there are two farms called **Kentucky** and **Louisiana**. In the late 18th century these territories in America were attracting colonists. A local story has it that two brothers from the Fylde went across and made enough money to come home and buy some land, which they named after the source of their 'wealth'. It has to be said that the land was swampy and poor so they probably did not make all that much. There seems to be no documentary evidence for these two brothers, but the 'returning colonists' theory is quite plausible and no doubt many farms and estates did acquire their names in this way.

---

have been influenced by the London names (sometimes a 'Vauxhall' is really a 'foxhole' with pretensions).

In this century many sports grounds have been built over, and a collection of sporting terms or athletes' names on an estate could well indicate a former sports ground. In Greenford (GLon) an estate built on part of a recreation ground includes the names of cricketers **Bedser** and **Larwood** and athletes **Mary Peters**, **Lilian Board** and **Roger Bannister**. In Acton a group of streets including **The Fairway**, **Long Drive** and **Brassie Avenue** were built on the site of a golf course, and a few miles away in Southall three tower blocks overlooking a golf course are themselves named **Sheringham**, **Gleneagles**, and **St. Andrews**.

Trafalgar Square, commemorating the Battle of Trafalgar in 1805, was not in fact started until 1829 and was finished in the 1840s. There are thousands of such commemorative place names, usually with little or no connec-

---

When is a gate not a gate?

When it's a way. In the Danelaw old street names containing **gate** may come from Norse *gata*, meaning a street or way. London has **Aldgate** (old gate), **Newgate**, **Moorgate** (which led onto the moor or wasteland) and **Notting Hill Gate** (not a town gate in this case but a toll gate). But York has streets called **Coppergate** (where the joiners – Norse *koppari* – worked), **Skeldergate** (*skjaldari*; shieldmakers), **Petergate** (leading to the Minster, dedicated to St. Peter), **Micklegate** (the great or wide street), and **Whip-ma Whop-ma Gate** (possibly named for the whipping post and pillory that stood at one end).

tion between the place and the event, but they do convey the intensity of public feeling at the time. This is perhaps more true of the many small local names. Fields, pubs, streets, rows of terraced houses, etc. were usually given their names while the event was still fresh in the memory. Many towns have a pub called the **Lord** or **Admiral Nelson**, the **Trafalgar**, or the **Victory** (after his ship), and most of these will date from the early 19th century. In at least two cases – the Nelsons in Lancashire and Mid Glamorgan – the Admiral's name has been given to a village which grew up around the pub.

Other 'famous victories' are **Balaclava**, **Alma** (which also became a girl's name) and **Sebastopol** from the Crimean War, **Waterloo**, and **Porto Bello**, a port on the Gulf of Mexico captured from the Spanish in 1739. These have given their names to everything from a pub or small field upwards. Only Alma does not seem to have a town named after it. Sometimes the battle is not identified in the name. The village of **Battle** (ESx) is near the site of the Battle of Hastings, and the **Battledown** pub in Cheltenham commemorates a skirmish during the Civil War.

Not only battles were commemorated, of course; witness all the **Coronation Street**s and **Jubilee Street**s (and of course the **Jubilee Line** on the London Underground). When investigating these names remember there may be several possible coronations and jubilees.

In the 19th century, a desperate need to house a growing urban population forced some local authorities into agreements with breweries. The brewery was given permission to build a pub only if it also undertook to build a certain number of houses. It often resulted in a combination such as **Waterloo Terrace** with a pub called the **Duke of Wellington**. Pubs in any case are particularly likely to have commemorative names, and often refer simply to something that was in the news at the time. It is unwise to rely entirely on a pub name for dating. For one thing the name may just reflect the landlord's interests. A pub called the **Rocket** may have been built around the time when Stephenson's locomotive was in the news, but the name could have been given at any time if the landlord was a railway enthusiast. Similarly while street names are fairly durable, needing official action to change them, pub names can be changed more or less at the landlord or brewery's will.

Fleet Street led to the Fleet river (see p. 36). Usually a street named after a river will lead to it, probably to a convenient crossing place, but in some cases the street will run beside the river, or even on top of a culverted stream. London has several 'lost' rivers, and many towns have at least one, often traceable by **brook**, **burn** or some other 'watery' element in a field or street name.

The Strand was once the main road between the two separate cities of London and Westminster, and marks the old shoreline of the Thames. It may also mark a shoreline in other 'strand' names. **Strand on the Green** runs beside the Thames by Kew Bridge and used to flood quite regularly. **Strand Street** in Liverpool runs parallel to the Mersey behind the docks, and some seaside towns have strands rather than promenades. However, The Strand was once a fashionable street and some names are simply copies with no relationship to a river. **Strand Close** in Hull is named after the Strand cinema which stood nearby, this no doubt named after London's Strand Theatre.

Piccadilly is named after *Pickadel Hall*, the nickname of a grand mansion built by Robert Baker. Baker was a man of humble origins who earned his money by making *piccadills*, a kind of fancy border for collars and ruffs, fashionable in the 17th century. **Piccadilly** in Manchester is named after this street. In the 18th and 19th centuries the names of many well-known London streets were adopted by up-and-coming provincial towns. Liverpool, Manchester and Birmingham all have several such 'transplants'. Because of its large railway station, **Snow Hill** in Birmingham is now much better known than its London original.

Coventry Street is named after Henry Coventry, who bought a mansion known as *Shavers Hall* in 1673 and renamed it *Coventry House*. Shavers Hall had been built for Simon Osbaldeston, the Earl of Pembroke's barber. It became a fashionable gambling saloon, and its nickname referred both to Osbaldeston's occupation and to the gamblers who were 'shorn'. The mansion was demolished in 1685. **Shavers Place** and Coventry Street enclose the site.

Leicester Square stands on the site of *Leicester Fields*, owned by the Earl of Leicester, who built a mansion there in 1631. Nearby **Lisle Street** contains the title of his son, Viscount Lisle. **Bear Street** and the **Bear and Staff** pub probably refer to the Bear and

Ragged Staff which appeared on the family coat of arms.

Vine Street marks the site of the vineyard tended by the Minoresses (*Sorores Minores* 'little sisters') of St. Clare, who gave their name to **The Minories**. In the Middle Ages most noble or religious houses had their own vineyard, and vineyards are shown on maps of Clerkenwell in the late 18th century. Before the age of rapid transport and refrigeration country and town were more closely related and it is not uncommon to find a market garden, orchard or dairy farm name quite close to a town centre.

Field and street names referring to vines or vineyards are usually quite straightforward. **Grape Lane** in York and **Grape Passage** in Reading are not. These are politely altered versions of *Grope* or *Gropecunte Lane*, once quite a common name for a narrow or secluded lane, usually but not always used by prostitutes and their clients. A few have become **Love** or **Lovers Lane**s, some have strayed even further from the truth and become **Maiden Lane**s but most have changed their names completely.

Marlborough Street, originally **Great Marlborough Street**, was the first of many streets to be named after John Churchill, 1st Duke of Marlborough. It was begun in 1704, the year of his victory at the Battle of Blenheim. It commemorates a person, another common type of name. A distinction must be drawn here between those places which contain the name of their owner or founder, and those which are named by a third party to honour someone or to borrow some of their status or glamour. There can be an overlap, as when a developer names a new town or the streets in a new estate after family members.

The golden rule about commemorative names – if there can ever be a 'golden rule' in place-name study – is that, except in the case of the great aristocratic family estates such as the Fitzroys, the more eminent or popular the person the less chance there is of any personal connection with the place. Local worthies and celebrities may be commemorated in their home town by a single street, pub, council building, community centre, health centre or school, but national heroes turn up everywhere. It is always worth looking for a personal connection – everyone has to be born, live and die somewhere – but in most cases there will not be one.

Recognition in a place or street name can be a long time coming. While the **Giles** pub in

Islington has been named during the cartoonist's lifetime, **Mozart Street** in Westminster was renamed in 1991 to mark the bicentenary of the composer's death (Giles was born nearby, Mozart lived in the street for a short time). **Charlie Butler**, head horsekeeper of Young's Brewery and winner of many prizes with their black shire horses, had to wait until he retired after 45 years' service to have a pub near the brewery named after him.

Many developers and councils like to give streets on an estate connected or thematic names. They give names of flowers or trees to give a pleasant rural image, or names which reflect some aspect of the town, such as the cathedral names in the cathedral city of Exeter, for example. It is easy to disregard a group of poets', artists', or generals' names, but the theme may have been suggested by the fact that one of them was born in the town.

When there is no personal connection it is worth asking why this eminent person has been chosen. We have already mentioned sportsmen's names perhaps marking the site of a sports ground. Sometimes an event is being commemorated by using the names of the people concerned. In Southall (GLon) **Hunt Road** and **Hilary Road** are unremarkable. **Tensing Road**, however, pinpoints the event – the first ascent of Everest by Edmund Hilary and Tensing Norgay (popularly known as Sherpa Tensing), in an expedition led by John Hunt.

In other cases an image or an intention dictates the choice. The Victorians seem to have chosen achievers such as artists, explorers, scientists and engineers while actors, politicians, philanthropists and social reformers went

---

'Ghosts' in Fleet Street

The journalists and printers have left London's Fleet Street, but the local pubs are still, metaphorically, full of them. A **Printer's Devil** was an apprentice or errand boy in a printing house. **Printer's Pie** goes back to the days when type was hand-set, the tiny metal characters being kept in huge flat segmented cases. A 'printer's pie' was the result of dropping a case of type. No one who has done so could ever forget the feeling of horror and despair as it slips from the hands, and it was often considered cheaper to buy another case than to spend time sweeping it up and sorting it out.

The humorous magazine *Punch* was born in 1841 and closed shortly after celebrating its 150th anniversary. The **Punch Tavern**, where the idea for it was born, has outlived it. The tavern was probably named from Punch and Judy shows once held nearby. The **Wig and Pen**, a restaurant and club for lawyers and journalists opposite the Law Courts, has lost many of the 'pen' half of its clientele. The writers remembered in the **Hand and Pen** nearby were not Fleet Street scribblers but scriveners, who made fair copies of legal documents.

largely unremarked. The new town of **Telford** (Shrops) is both commemorative and expresses a hope for a bright industrial future. Thomas Telford was an 18th-century Scottish civil engineer who became county surveyor for Shropshire and worked on canal projects in the area. **Brunel University**, near Uxbridge (GLon), bears the name of the great engineer, Isambard Kingdom Brunel. It now teaches many subjects but was originally planned as a university of engineering and technology. Its former site in Acton is marked by **Brunel Way**. Another site marked by a person's name is the once world-famous department store Derry and Toms, in Kensington High Street. **Derry Street** separates it from its equally famous neighbour Barkers. Both stores closed in the 1970s.

In our own day commemorative naming can be fiercely political, to the extent that some local authorities now avoid such names altogether, seeking safety in old field names and local landmarks. Often the political bent of the local council is reflected in the names chosen. Hayes in West London has **Attlee Road**, **Bevin Road**, **Keir Hardie Way**, **Morrison Road** and **Webbs Road**, all named after Labour leaders, while neighbouring Ealing – traditionally Conservative – favours Tory Prime Ministers, although it does have a **Gladstone Close**. It will be interesting to see whether, and where, *Kinnock Road* appears – with Neil Kinnock's predecessors in Hayes or in Ealing, where he lives.

Some black political activists are also beginning to appear on the map. There is a street and a small industrial estate in London named after Mahatma Gandhi, and two streets in London and one in Liverpool named after Steve Biko, the black South African leader who died in police custody. Most popular is Nelson Mandela, who has at least seven streets and two municipal buildings to his name in London (no doubt there are others elsewhere). As new names these reflect the concerns of a multiracial society and most people have heard of Gandhi, Biko and Mandela and accept them as distinguished figures. As new names these seldom cause more than a few raised eyebrows. Attempts to change existing names, or to use the names of less eminent figures, are liable to meet with opposition. A plan by Lambeth council to rename several municipal buildings and parks after less well-known black activists was withdrawn (the opposition claimed that they had no local significance, while the names being replaced had, and that some so-called activists were involved in terrorism). Henry **Havelock**, James **Outran** and Colin **Campbell** are commemorated in many street names. They were Victorian heroes who helped to quell the Indian Mutiny in 1858. It was a particularly nasty struggle (on both sides) and it is very unlikely that they would have been so honoured today. None of the roads named after them have been changed, although some Asians would like them to be.

Bow Street is a simple descriptive name, from its slightly curved shape. It is similar to all the **Long Lane**s, **Broad Street**s, **Crescent**s, and **Circus**es, etc. Other descriptive terms are **Turnagain** and **Blind** for a cul-de-sac, and **Cross** and **Union** for a street which links two others. **Carfax** (related to modern French *carrefour* 'crossroads') refers to a place where four roads meet, as opposed to a crossroads, where one road crosses another. A few need treating with caution. **The Straight** in Southall (GLon) runs in a dead straight line beside the railway, but **The Strait** in Lincoln means 'narrow', as it was originally a narrow alley.

Bond Street was part of a late 17th-century development by Sir Thomas Bond, a wealthy financier. The name was officially changed to **Old Bond Street** when a continuation of it, **New Bond Street**, was built some forty years later. An 'Old' name usually means a 'New' name nearby. If none exists 'Old' may mean 'former', as in the case of the **Old Bailey**, which marks the site of a mud-built rampart which once stood outside the city wall. On the other hand it may be an integral part of the whole name, as in **Old Parr Road** in Banbury, which is named after a murderer called Old Parr who was hanged there in 1747. A 'New' name does not necessarily indicate a corresponding 'Old', although it is worth looking for one. It can just mean something newly built. Once it becomes part of a name it usually sticks and there are some 'New' names dating from the 13th century or even earlier.

Oxford Street is marked as the 'road to Oxford' on some early maps. Followed for long enough the road would still lead to Oxford. It was usually called *Tyburn Way* after its more immediate destination, the Tyburn gallows which stood at the western end near Marble Arch. Edward Harley, 2nd Earl of Oxford, acquired land on the northern side of the street in 1713. The street soon began to be known as

Oxford Street; no doubt the residents of the fashionable Harley estate, of which Oxford Street is the southern limit, were happy to shake off the association with Tyburn.

Regent Street was designed by John Nash as a carriage drive from Carlton House, the Prince Regent's mansion, to **Regents Park**. Regents Park had been enclosed as a hunting ground by Henry VIII, became a farm under Cromwell, and was restored as a Royal Park by the Prince Regent in 1811. This is one of many places of all kinds throughout the British Isles named after members of the Royal family. Apart from the **King**, **Queen**, **Prince**, **Duke**, etc. names may simply use the royal personage's first name. **Victoria** and **Albert** are probably the most popular, followed by **George**, if only because there were so many of them. It is worth remembering that other memorable people also have first names. A name may come from the dedication of a church nearby, and George can also be a surname or a saint. **Mary** is more likely to be from the Blessed Virgin or some other saint than a queen or princess.

Streets and pubs with 'royal' names seldom have any personal connection. They are usually named from a gesture of affection and esteem or an attempt to borrow status. Most have been given during the person's lifetime or shortly after their death, so can be an aid to dating (with all the usual cautions, especially about pubs). Hospitals, schools, bridges and other great public works often do have some connection, if only that the person laid the foundation stone or declared them open. Sometimes the 'royal' was a patron of the institution and took an interest in its work. **Royal** attached to a name implies a connection which may range from a single visit to patronage over several generations. Often the 'Royal' belongs to the name of an institution: **Royal College Street** in Camden Town and **Royal Hospital Road**, Chelsea, are two such names.

Pubs called the **Crown** are common and often no more than a convenient symbol. When the crown is joined to something that would have made a distinctive inn sign by itself then there may well be a royal connection. The **Crown and Horns** in East Isley (Berks) commemorates the royal charter granted to the village in the 17th century as well as the sheep fair held nearby. The **Crown and Sugarloaf** in the City of London draws attention to the fact that one of the sugar refineries

---

Is there a 'Ghost and Gumboil'?

Many pub names consist of a combination, sometimes a very unlikely one, of two creatures or objects: the *George and Dragon*, *Pig and Whistle*, etc. These are so common that a phrase like this is instantly identifiable as a pub name (unless of course it's Cockney rhyming slang). In his long-running radio series *Ray's a Laugh* the comedian Ted Ray often spoke about going 'down the frog and toad to the Frog and Nightgown' – down the road to the local. The landlord of a pub in south London adopted the name **Frog and Nightgown**, which remains as a small reminder of a much-loved performer.

We seem to remember that Ted Ray used to mention another pub, the *Ghost and Gumboil*, but as yet no one has taken up this name.

---

here in the early 19th century supplied the court. The **Crown and Arrows** in Shilton Lock near Derby borrows the emblem of King Edmund (see p. 79) as the pub stands next to St. Edmunds church. There will usually be something in the local records to explain the reference.

Mayfair marks the site of the annual fair held during the first two weeks of May from 1688. It became notorious for all kinds of wickedness, was banned in 1708 but continued in some form until the site was built over in the mid-18th century. **Cloth Fair** in the City has a similar origin. Although St. Bartholomew's Fair held there specialized in the sale of cloth and was much older it suffered the same decline and eventual fate. There are also streets called **Horse Fair** in several towns.

Weekly markets are held throughout the land, some of them very old and some referred to in urban names (see p. 60 for names based on Old English *ceap*). The **Saturday Market** and the later **Tuesday Market** in King's Lynn have become names for the two main districts of the town. Beverley in Humberside has a **Saturday Market** and a **Wednesday Market**, Nottingham has a **Weekday Cross** (Old **Market Square** was formerly *Saturday Market*), and Penzance has the heavily disguised **Market Jew Street**. 'Jew' comes from the Cornish word for Thursday, *yow*, and the name shows the characteristic Celtic word order.

In York, **Bootham**, **Bootham Row** and **Bootham Terrace** derive from Norse *buthum* 'at the booths' and refer to the weekly market held here in the Middle Ages. '**The Shambles**' comes from Old English *sceamol* 'bench', referring to the benches from which meat was sold. Many towns contain names such as **Cornmarket**, **Haymarket**, **Poultry Cross**, **Butter Cross** etc. denoting a place where these commodities were sold, and as a rule these are quite straightforward. (The Old English words for many crops and commodities are given in the second section of the Anglo-Saxon Chapter. They may appear again in street names.) We have yet to see a *Sunday Market Street* or a *Boot Fair Green*, but it is surely only a matter of time.

Park Lane runs alongside Hyde Park, although it is now a busy dual carriageway rather than a lane. It is an example of what some place-name scholars call a 'locative', a name that indicates where it is or where it leads. There are thousands of them and usually of

interest to the historian only when the place referred to no longer exists or has changed its character. Many 'wall', 'bury' and 'bailey' names refer to old town fortifications. **The Barbican** and **London Wall** are two well-known examples in the capital. In Abingdon (Oxon) there is a short road called **The Motte**, referring to a motte and bailey castle which once stood here. A name containing '**Mound**' often commemorates such a castle, a perishable structure of wood and earth. Rather more prosaically, **Sainsbury Way** in Hull leads to a Sainsbury's supermarket.

The Stations

Liverpool Street itself was named after Lord Liverpool, Prime Minister from 1812 to 1827. He died in 1828 and the street was built shortly afterwards. The station name is typical of a London station in that it does not have 'London' in its name. The main purpose of the name is to distinguish this mainline terminus from the dozen or so others in the capital. It was originally a locative name (the station at Liverpool Street), but a station immediately becomes a landmark in itself. A case in point is **Victoria** which has given its name to the area and to an Underground line which used to end there. This pattern is repeated in every city with more than one station, and in most cases the fact that these are station names is not significant, although the landmarks they are named for may be interesting in themselves.

There are two theories about the name **Fenchurch Street**, both plausible and with evidence in other place names to back them up. **Fenchurch** refers to the old church of St Gabriel that stood on the south side of the street. One theory suggests that this was simply the church by the fen. The street runs through the **Langbourne** ward of the City, traditionally named after a stream, now lost, which might account for the fen. However, **Gracechurch Street**, which crosses Fenchurch Street, refers to the old St. Benet's church which was once known as the 'grass church'. It is believed that a fodder market was held here, and it has been suggested that Fenchurch is a similar name, from French *foin* 'hay'.

King's Cross took its name from a memorial to King George IV erected in the middle of the crossroads there in 1830. By most accounts

it was a pretty hideous building, and it was demolished in 1845.

The 'bone' of **Marylebone** comes from Old English *burna* 'stream', and in 1490 the name was recorded as '*Tyborne otherwise called Maryborne*'. The stream has long since been culverted. The original name of the stream was *Teoburnan*, meaning 'boundary stream', and it formed part of the ancient boundary of the city of Westminster. As the **Tyburn** it became associated with the gallows. No doubt the locals were just as pleased as their later neighbours in Oxford Street to rid themselves of such an unpleasant name. There was a church by the stream dedicated to St Mary and it is quite possible that the change of name might have happened in any case. The **le** probably comes from Old French *lez* 'next to, associated with', but was mistaken for the definite article, giving rise to the idea that the name means 'Mary-the-Good' (*Mary-la-Bonne*). To railway buffs, of course, Marylebone will always mean the terminus of the Great Central Railway, the last main line to come into London. It is, alas, no more, and only suburban services now run from here, but it is commemorated by the **Great Central Hotel** nearby.

The stories behind the names in this group give a picture of London at various stages in its past. They reveal the history of markets, fairs and vineyards in the heart of the city, the town houses of the aristocracy and a rising middle class, some of quite humble birth, investing in property. The notorious gallows casts a shadow over fashionable new residential streets in the 17th and 18th centuries. The building of the Victoria and Albert Embankments revealed a shift in power as it was completed despite the opposition of the powerful Northumberlands. The private companies brought railways into London, thus encouraging the development of the suburbs which changed the face of the Home Counties and the lives of thousands of their inhabitants. We have also seen that similar events took place in other towns and cities, and that these cities sometimes 'borrowed' names from the capital.

Landmarks of the trade

In medieval towns tradesmen and sellers of particular commodities tended to congregate in certain streets. Most of these are obvious. It is easy to guess what was sold in the various **Milk**, **Bread**, **Fish**, **Silver** and **Pepper** Streets and Lanes. Similarly it is not impossible to work out what went on in the various **Butcher**, **Smith**, **Hosier**, and **Tanner** Streets and in **Brick Lane**, **Ironmonger Lane** (GLon) and **Woolmonger Street** in Northampton. **Cable**, **Rope**, **Roper**, **Ropewalk** and **Ropemaker** are straightforward enough. In theory such streets should be long and straight. **Cable Street** in Stepney runs dead straight for over a mile. A very short street may once have led to the ropewalk rather than forming part of it, and an enclave of relatively new buildings may mark out the site.

Less obvious elements in street names that refer to the world of trade are:

baxter =	baker
barker =	tanner
crocker =	potter
pilcher =	a maker of *pilches*, outer garments made of skins
fletcher	usually means a maker of arrows, but can refer to a 'flesher' or butcher
spicer =	a grocer rather than someone who dealt only in spices
souter =	a shoemaker (compare with Sutterby, p. 60)
spurrier =	a maker of spurs
lorimer =	a person who made the metal parts of harnesses
tenter =	a rack on which cloth was stretched, or the person who stretched it. Similar to the 'rope' names in that you are looking for traces of a piece of open ground where the racks stood
blake =	may sometimes be from Norse *bleikja* 'bleach' and refer to a field where linen was bleached and laid out to dry
lister =	a dyer
tucker =	a cloth-finisher
fuller =	a cloth-finisher, particularly one who made the cloth thicker by shrinking and pounding it; also known as a *walker* and, less commonly, a *scutcher*

However, many words for tradesmen have also become surnames. The older the street name the more likely it is to be from a trade rather than a surname. Look also at the surrounding street and pub names which may refer to related trades.

In more modern times trades and industries are less likely to be celebrated quite so openly in street names, although some streets were named after prominent factories. **Rockware Gardens** in Ealing comes from the Rockware Glass Works. **Scotts Road** in Southall got its name from the factory making Scotts Emulsion, a remedy based, as far as we remember, on cod liver oil, and Firework Lane in Mitcham is named after Pain's firework factory. These factories have all now gone. Firework Lane has also disappeared and the factory is commemorated by **Pains Close**.

There are numerous **Gas** and **Gasworks Streets**, **Foundry** and **Steelhouse Roads** etc., mostly dating from the 19th century. **Electric Avenue** in Brixton (GLon), however, does not get its name from a power station or even from the electric railway nearby, but because it was one of the first streets to be lit by electricity. The so-called **Electric Brae** in Strathclyde seems to owe more to magic than electricity. When a driver stops his car facing up the hill, and takes off the handbrake, the car will happily continue on its way. The layout of the surrounding hills confuses the eye and appears to reverse the direction of the slope.

Pubs are a rich source of industrial names. The textile trades are remembered in the **Spindlemakers Arms** in Preston, the **Cap and Stocking** in Kegworth, and many names containing **shuttle** and **bobbin**. Shipbuilding is commemorated in the **Jolly Caulkers** in Chatham and the **Tall Cranes** on Clydeside, as well as various **Shipwrights**, **Carpenters**, **Welders**, and **Sailmakers Arms**. Steelmaking was carried out near the **Smelters Arms** in Consett, the **Fiery Holes** in Bilston, and the **Open Hearth** in Corby and Scunthorpe.

Sadly many of these industries have now gone or are in decline. The British Rail works in Swindon, from which the **Rolling Mill** and the **Carriage** were named, closed in the late 1980s. A new trading estate on the site is named after George Churchward, chief mechanical engineer of the Great Western Railway for nearly 20 years. He designed some of its finest locomotives. However, they still make hats in Luton and drink at the **Strawplaiters**, the **Boater** or the **Panama**, and the catalytic cracking plants which gave their names to the **Catcracker** near Stanford-le-Hope, Essex and the **Cat and Cracker** on the Isle of Grain, Kent still exist.

Many pubs are named after a product manufactured nearby, such as the **Canopus** (flying boat) in Rochester, the **Buccaneer** (fighter plane) in Brough on Humberside and the **Silver Ghost** (car) in Alvaston near Derby. The **Flying Lady** in Crewe is also named for Rolls Royce, after the emblem which adorns their cars. The **Small Arms** in Birmingham was named from the British Small Arms company, which originally made firearms but is best remembered for BSA bicycles and motorbikes. The **Flying Bedstead** and the **Harrier** pubs at Hucknall (Notts) commemorate the fact that the experimental vertical takeoff aircraft and its grandchild the jump-jet were tested at Hucknall aerodrome. **Cody's Tree** at Farnborough (Hants) recalls trials made there by Colonel S.F. Cody in the early days of aviation. To measure the thrust of his engines he attached the plane to a measuring device which in turn was tied to a tree. The pub was opened in 1970.

Except for buildings bearing the name of the company (or perhaps the chairman of the company) trading from them, modern names are more likely to commemorate trades that had already disappeared when the place was built. Roads on new trading or housing estates often take their names from the former use of the site. The estate roads on the old Heston Aerodrome (GLon) are named after pioneers of aviation, including **Blériot**, **Sopwith**, **Wright** and **Cobham**. **Shearling Way**, **Yoke**, **Ewe** and **Lambs Close** and **Manger Road** in Holloway sound idyllic but replace an old slaughterhouse. On a brighter note a pub in Kent called the **Stork at Rest** stands on the site of a maternity hospital.

Docklands developments are full of such commemorative names, in which a sincere desire to preserve the history of the area has to be balanced with the need to present a pleasant image to prospective buyers. So there is more likely to be a *Lightermans Close*, a *Watermans Row* and a *Sailmaker Street* than a *Dockers Street* or *Porter Alley*. *Clipper Row* or *Galleon Quay* will be preferred to *Dredger Lane*, and a *Spice*, *Madeira* or *Tobacco Wharf* will be chosen as names rather than a *Pig Iron* or *Anthracite Dock*.

In such areas new names can commemorate old names that were once significant. At one time timber was imported into the Surrey Docks, with individual basins named after the places they traded with: *Canada*, *Quebec*, *Russia*, and *Norway* Docks. These have now been filled in, but the street names include **Canada Street**, **Quebec Way**, **Wolfe Crescent** (after General Wolfe who captured Quebec from the French), **Russia Walk**, **Archangel Street**, **Finland Street** and (a good Norse name) **Norway Gate**, as well as **Timber Pond Road**, **Fir Trees Close** and **Mahogany Close**. In this kind of development it is essential to separate the old from the new before a guess at the significance (or authenticity) of any name can be made. In the same group of docks there is a **Ropemaker Road**, a short road leading out onto a long, narrow open space; just the place for a ropewalk. A 1950s map reveals that they would have got their feet wet, as most of the open space was once the Russia Dock. Probably rope was made in the vicinity, but not precisely where the street name would lead us to believe.

Stops along the way

In the 18th century various Road Acts allowed turnpike companies to improve and maintain roads and to charge for their use. There are various names – mainly of pubs – relating to this in different parts of the country; for example many **Turnpike** and **Toll Gate** pubs. **Five Mile Drive** in Oxford is said to represent the length of a detour which enabled those in the know to bypass the toll gate.

The turnpikes led to an increase in road traffic, the introduction of stagecoaches, and the setting up of coaching inns to supply the needs of travellers and their horses (stagecoaches required a change of horses every ten miles or so). Some of the inns took the name of the coach that they serviced. Among them are the **Red Rover** at Northampton (there are others elsewhere), some called the **Greyhound** on the route of the London-Birmingham or the London-Exeter coach, the **Tally Ho** in Eastbourne, the **Flyer** in Chelmsford, the **Gloucester Flying Machine** in Brockworth (Glos), and the **Quicksilver Mail** near Yeovil. The **London** at Weston-super-Mare and the **Royal London** in Sidmouth were named from the coach's destination. The **Upper Bell** near Rochester had a bell which was rung to warn traffic about to go up the narrow hill that the coach was about to come down. And of course there are all the pubs called the **Mail Coach**, the **Stagecoach**, the **Coach and Horses** and the welcome **Halfway House**.

Names on the canal network seem to have been curiously neglected, and this might be an interesting area of research. The town of **Ellesmere Port** grew up where a canal from Ellesmere (Shrops) joins the Mersey, and **Stourport** (H&W) marks the place where the Staffordshire and Worcester Canal meets the Severn. The physical problems associated with canal building are hinted at in **The Tunnel** on the Oxford Canal. There was actually a tunnel until the roof caved in but it is now a cutting. Economic problems are indicated in the history of the **Clarence Harbour** pub in Norwich. This stands on the proposed site for the terminus of a canal from Lowestoft to Norwich, begun under a scheme approved by the Duke of Clarence. The newfangled railway made the canal redundant, and it was never completed. The **Shroppie Fly**, a pub on the Shropshire Union Canal near Crewe, refers to the practice of 'flying' – sailing day and night to speed up a perishable cargo.

Most towns have a **Station Road** or a **Station Approach**, even if they no longer have a railway station, and many have a **Railway Arms**, **Railway Tavern** or a **Station Hotel**. Some street, pub and hotel names refer to the old pre-nationalization railway companies. There is a **Great Eastern Street** and a **Great Eastern Hotel** near Liverpool Street and a **Great Western Street** and **Great Western Hotel** near Paddington, the London termini of the two companies. The **Great Western Industrial Park** beside the tracks in Southall was named many years after the official demise of God's Wonderful Railway.

A pub in Battersea has one of the longest names, the **London, Chatham and Dover Railway Tavern**, while the **Amalgamation** in Strood, Kent recalls the fate of this company. It joined with the South Eastern company to become the South Eastern and Chatham Railway. At least two names commemorate railways that no longer exist: the **Light Railway** at Hulme End near Buxton (the line ran from Leek to Hulme End, and was closed in 1934) and the **Atmospheric Railway** near Exeter, which recalls Brunel's unsuccessful attempt to use atmospheric pressure to move trains. The **Ghost Train** in Purton, Wiltshire and the **Silent Whistle** near Gloucester both refer to lines killed off by Lord Beeching in the 1960s.

Station names, particularly on suburban railways, are an interesting study. The railways both served and made the suburbs. They made it possible for people to commute to work in town from the surrounding 'countryside', creating a demand for housing, which landowners and developers were only too happy to supply.

There was a certain amount of haggling between developers and the railway companies about the siting and naming of stations. The developer would want the station well placed for his proposed residential estate and with an inviting name, whereas the railway company wanted the station at an operationally convenient place and with a name that indicated where it was. Sometimes a mutually agreed solution was possible: **Queensbury** on the London Underground, named in 1934, sounds distinguished and lies next to **Kingsbury**, a genuine Anglo-Saxon manor. The number of south London stations with 'Wimbledon' in their names (**Wimbledon** itself, **Wimbledon Chase** and **Park**, **South** and **West Wimbledon**, not all of which were actually in the borough), reflect the developers' desire to be associated with what had become a fashionable suburb.

Many stations, and associated districts, con-

tain the word **Park**. This conjures up a very pleasant image, and some were indeed built on the parkland of country houses, but developers were sometimes unwilling to distinguish between 'parkland' and a scrubby bit of unproductive farmland. Eventually 'park' became almost a cliché and went out of favour. '**Parkway**' on a station name is a recent innovation, a grand term for a large car-park.

The new neighbours

The flow of immigrants to Britain has never stopped. Craftsmen, businessmen and workers have filled economic gaps, refugees have fled from racial or religious persecution, and many have simply sought to make a better life for themselves than was possible in their own country. Typically the first generation sticks together, living in a small area, perhaps only a few streets. The locals often refer to such an area by adding **Little** to the name of the country where the immigrants came from. Usually such names are unofficial and are lost as later generations spread out into the surrounding community.

Putting a place on the map

Most towns have local names which do not appear on maps or in gazetteers. **Gipsy Corner** in West London (where gipsies camped in the 18th and 19th centuries) and **Staples Corner** on London's North Circular Road (named after Staples furniture factory) are regularly mentioned on traffic reports, but seldom appear on maps. Southall has a series of alleyways, called the **Beak Alleys**, which give a shortcut from neighbouring streets to the Beaconsfield Arms pub. The residents know them, but people living only a few hundred yards away may never have heard of them. Occasionally a local name may make it on to the map, sometimes after many years. The **Iron Bridge** which takes the railway over the Uxbridge Road in west London and the **Three Bridges** nearby, where the Grand Union Canal crossed the railway and both were crossed by Windmill Lane, were both unsung local landmarks. Both have now had small industrial estates named after them, and appear in the latest *London A–Z*.

Such local landmarks may no longer exist. A bus driver in the East End of London may still put you off at **Gardner's Corner** although Gardner's department store burned down in 1971. Many people remember the Firestone Company's tyre factory in west London, if only because of the outcry when it was bulldozed just before a preservation order could be placed on its art deco frontage. A few people still call that stretch of the A4 **Firestone Hill**. In time even the local people will forget the reason for such a name, and it will probably be replaced by another. If it is not on the map the name will be lost, unless someone records it, with its location and origin, for the interest of future local historians.

The usual form of 'little' in medieval and Tudor times was *petty* (French *petit*), and London once had a *Petty Wales*, *Petty Burgundy*, *Petty Calais*, and two streets called **Petty France**, only one of which survives. Most of these represented the London homes of foreign merchants in the wool trade. In this century an area around Clerkenwell became known as *Little Italy*, from Italian immigrants who began to settle here in the 1890s. **Little London** (in Chichester and elsewhere) does not refer to an enclave of stray Londoners, but was once a common ironic term for a small and decrepit area.

Jews were encouraged to settle here by William the Conqueror, who valued their financial skills. The site of the London ghetto is marked by **Jewry Street**, **Old Jewry** and by a Christian church, **St Lawrence Jewry**, by the Guildhall. **Jury Street**, Warwick has a similar name, while York has **Jewbury** and **Jubbergate**. This street marks two sets of incomers. Before the Jews settled here it was called *Bretgate*, from the Britons who came across with the Norwegians from Cumbria. It was recorded as *Jubretegate* in 1356. After the Jews were expelled by Edward I in 1290 their role was taken over by wool merchants from Lombardy in northern Italy. **Lombard Street** in the City of London is still the main banking area. The Lombard's symbol was three balls, which became the sign of pawnbrokers. **Lombard Lane** off Fleet Street was once a slum, and the name referred to the place where the residents usually kept their belongings.

Many of our European neighbours have settled here over the centuries. **Flimby** in Cumbria was *Flemingby* in 1194, and **Flemington**, Pembroke may be from the Flemings who travelled there with the Normans. Two pubs called the **Glass House** and the

Glasscutter in Bristol are from Flemish glassworkers who settled here in the 16th century.

French merchants lived in **Frenchgate** in Richmond, Yorkshire, **French Gate** in Doncaster and **French Row** in St. Albans. **Cheval Place** in South Kensington is from French *cheval* 'horse' as there was stabling here in the 19th century, and the area had a large French population. A pub called the *York Minster* in Soho became the London centre for the Free French in World War II, and was renamed the **French House**.

In the 15th century a number of German wool merchants traded in Bradford. The area where they stayed includes **Mannheim Street** and **Heidelberg Street**. The name **Hammstrasse** (Hamm Street) in Shipley, however, reflects the fact that Shipley and Hamm are twin towns. This is also the significance of **Bonn Square** in Oxford. Twinning arrangements are a common source of overseas town names in modern street names, and it is always worth considering this possibility if the street, or the name, is post-war.

The first Chinese immigrants were seamen working for the East India Company who began to settle in Limehouse in the late 18th century. **Ming Street**, **Canton Street**, **Pekin Street** and **Nankin Street** mark the area. Nowadays most towns have a few Chinese, and London and Manchester each have a thriving **Chinatown** – an unofficial name but one which exists in cities all over the English-speaking world.

The form of most of these names indicates that they were given not by the incomers themselves but by the locals looking on, and defining the area as separate from them. Many such names were unofficial, never appeared on maps, and died out as the new community integrated or moved on. Occasionally a distinguished person would be commemorated as a prominent member of such a community.

Adler Street in London's East End is named after Herman Adler, a former Chief Rabbi. However, this is a rare example as there appear to be very few names left from ethnic communities.

In our own time cities and towns are changing at a tremendous rate, as factories and docks close and whole areas are redeveloped. There has probably not been so much scope for new names since the industrial revolution.

Slowly the Asian and Afro-Caribbean communities, who began coming here in the 1950s, are making their mark. Southall has **Dokal Industrial Estate** named after a prominent Asian businessman, and an old people's home called **Ashiana** (an Asian name meaning 'happy atmosphere'). Acton in West London has **Antilles House**, named after a group of islands in the Caribbean. Bradford has **Bundria Court**, a residential development by a Sikh firm, named after a member of the family.

These are names given by the communities themselves, in ways and for reasons that the Celts, Romans, Anglo-Saxons, Scandinavians, Normans, 18th-century aristocrats and Victorian developers would understand. Though the names may look slightly odd surrounded by English words they are now part of our tradition and culture; the latest layer in the archaeology of British place names.

A temple in Southall. Immigrants of the 20th century are now making their contribution to British place names. It will not be too long before a name containing the word 'temple' will refer to a place of worship such as the one shown here, rather than the Knights Templars. (JOHN COLE/IMPACT)

Historians making history

Abingdon, once the county town of Berkshire but now in Oxfordshire, is an ancient town with a strong sense of its history, and it has several streets named after historians who have worked locally. The most famous is Elias Ashmole, the 17th-century antiquarian and founder of the Ashmolean Museum in Oxford. He recorded the monuments in Abingdon's two main churches, St. Nicholas' and St. Helen's, and **Ashmole Road** is named after him. Others are the local historians Gabrielle Lambrick (**Lambrick Way**), James Townsend (**Townsend**), Agnes Baker (**Baker Road**) and Arthur Preston (**Preston Road**), who was also a local councillor and benefactor of the town. **Stenton Close** commemorates Sir Frank Merry Stenton, a distinguished medievalist and a founder member of the English Place-Name Society.

Where do you go from here – a guide to further information

Nobody can know everything about all the place names in the British Isles – there are just too many of them – so it is best to be limited to an area or category of place names. An enthusiast may choose to study towns and villages in their immediate area or the streets in their town. They may decide to study Celtic or Scandinavian names, to relate place names to changes in the language or the landscape, or to study names with some religious or mythical significance. There are any number of ways of approaching place-name study. Whatever the choice, the amateur researcher may pick up a lot of other information along the way by straying from their chosen path from time to time.

There are several books on place names and place-name dictionaries, and we have listed the most useful ones in the Guide to Further Reading, along with other books that are useful. Some books assume a certain amount of knowledge about linguistics and earlier languages, but with perseverance a great deal can still be learnt.

When researching a particular area maps and a gazetteer are essential. Familiarity with the local history is also a help; the more local background knowledge you have the less likely you are to misinterpret the names. Local public reference libraries will probably have some old maps and some books on local history; some have a large local history collection and an enthusiastic librarian. The library can also give information about evening classes or other courses on local history, some of which now touch on place names.

Councils are now encouraged to make local archives available to the public and they are far more accessible than they were. The library can give the address of the county archives office. The local council will have information about modern names of streets and buildings, as they are responsible for them. It may be difficult at first finding the right department in the town hall, but staff are often fellow place-names enthusiasts and will help with further information.

The addresses of local history societies can be found at the reference libraries. The societies will be able to suggest other reliable sources of local information, and indicate whether any similar research has been done. There is little money to be gained from publishing books on place names, but a book on local names may achieve small but steady sales, especially in a touristy area. Some towns have an oral history unit which records the recollections of elderly residents – especially valuable for folk names which don't appear on maps.

There are two national societies which deal with place-name study:

The English Place-Name Society
University of Nottingham,
Nottingham NG7 2RD

The Society for Name Studies in Britain and
   Ireland
c/o 22 Peel Park Avenue,
Clitheroe,
Lancs.
BB7 1ET

These are prestigious academic organizations which attract the leading scholars in the field. Those serious about studying place names should consider joining them. Both organizations publish journals containing articles on the latest research, book reviews, and general information, and a few large public libraries take these. Subjects can range from the precise meaning of an obscure Celtic word occurring in a single name to the names given to oil rigs in the North Sea. The Society for Name Studies is also interested in the study of personal names.

Further reading

This book is only an introduction to place names, and much more can be found out with further research. The following is a guide to some further reading. Many of the books listed will be difficult to obtain but should be available through the county library service.

General
Cameron, Kenneth *English Place Names*, Batsford 1988 (now out of print)
Gelling, Margaret *Sign-Posts to the Past: place-names and the history of England*, 2nd ed. Chichester, Phillimore 1988
Gelling, Margaret *Place-Names in the Landscape*, Dent 1984
Mawer, A. and F.M. Stenton *Introduction to the Survey of English Place-Names*, Cambridge University Press 1924
Reany, P.H. *The Origin of English Place Names*, Routledge and Kegan Paul 1960
English Place-Name Society (EPNS) County Volumes, Cambridge University Press
Campbell-Kease, John *A Companion to Local History Research*, Black/Sherborne, Alpha Books 1989
The Victoria County Histories
Spittal, Jeffrey and John Field (Eds.) *A Reader's Guide to the Place-Names of the United Kingdom*, Stamford 1990 (Bibliography)

Dictionaries
Dunkling, Leslie and G.A. Wright *Dictionary of Pub Names*, Routledge, Kegan & Paul 1987
Ekwall, Eilert *Concise Oxford Dictionary of English Place-Names* (1960)
Mills, A.D. *A Dictionary of English Place-Names*, Oxford University Press 1991
Field, John *Place Names of Great Britain and Ireland*, David and Charles 1980
Nicolaisen, W.F.H. and Margaret Gelling and Melville Richards *The Names of Towns and Cities in Britain*, Batsford 1970
Room, Adrian *Bloomsbury Dictionary of Place-Names in the British Isles*, Bloomsbury 1988
Oxford English Dictionary, Oxford University Press

General History
Pelican History of England series, Pelican
Oxford History of England series, Oxford University Press
Claiborne, Robert *The Life and Times of the English Language*, Bloomsbury 1990
McCrum, Robert, William Cran and Robert MacNeil *The Story of English*, Faber and Faber and BBC Publications 1992

The following is a list of reading relevant to the chapters in the book.
Chapter 1
Cunliffe, Barry *Greeks, Romans and Barbarians*, Routledge Chapman and Hall 1988
Jackson, Kenneth *Language and History in Early Britain*, Edinburgh University Press 1953
Renfrew, C. *Archaeology and Language*, Cambridge University Press 1987
Rivet, A.L.F. and Colin Smith *The Place-Names of Roman Britain*, Batsford 1972
Salway, Peter *Roman Britain*, Clarendon Press 1981

Chapter 2
Bede *A History of the English Church and People*, translated by Leo Sherley-Price, Penguin Classic series
The Anglo-Saxon Chronicles, translated by G.N. Garmonsway, Everyman 1953
Alfred the Great, translated by Simon Keynes and Michael Lapidge, Penguin Classic series 1983
Mitchell, Bruce and F.C. Robinson *A Guide to Old English*, Blackwell 1986
Wilson, David *The Anglo-Saxons*, Pelican 1971
The Phillimore *Domesday Book* series

Chapter 3
Graham-Campbell, James *The Viking World*, Frances Lincoln Publishers 1980
Richards, Julian *The Viking Age in England*, Hippocrene Books 1991

Chapter 4
Brooke, Christopher *From Alfred to Henry III 871–1272*, Cardinal 1974
Platt, Colin *Medieval England*, Routledge and Kegan Paul 1978 and *The English Medieval Town*, Secker and Warburg 1976

Chapter 5
Kirk, W. 'Prehistoric Scotland' in *Scotland – A New Study*, edited by M. Clapperton, David and Charles 1983
Holmes, Julyan *1000 Cornish Place-Names Explained*, Truran Publications 1983

Johnston, James B. *Place-Names of Scotland*, John Murray (revised) 1934

Kneen, J.J. *The Place Names of the Isle of Man*, Douglas 1925

Nicolaisen, W.F.H. *Scottish Place-Names*, Batsford 1986

Pierce, G. 'Place Names' in *Settlement and Society in Wales*, edited by Huw Owen, Cardiff 1989

Place Names on Maps of Scotland and Wales Ordnance Survey booklet

O'Connell, James *The Meaning of Irish Place Names*, Blackstaff Press 1979

Padel, O.J. *Popular Dictionary of Cornish Place-Names*, A. Hodge 1988

Room, Adrian *A Dictionary of Irish Place-Names*, Appletree Press 1986

Chapter 6

Bebbington, Gillian *Street Names of London*, Batsford 1972

Field, J. *English Field-Names: a dictionary*, David and Charles 1972

Miles, Joyce *House Names around the World*, David and Charles 1972

Room, Adrian *Concise Dictionary of Modern Place-Names in Great Britain and Ireland*, Oxford University Press 1983 and *The Street Names of England*, Paul Watkins 1992

Maps

Old and current Ordnance Survey maps

Ordnance Survey historical maps: *Roman Britain, Britain in the Dark Ages, Britain before the Norman Conquest*

Original Ordnance Survey maps (from the 19th century)

Illustrated Atlas of Victorian and Edwardian Britain, Ordnance Survey

Hill, David *Atlas of Anglo-Saxon England*, Blackwell 1981

Speed, John *The Counties of Britain: A Tudor Atlas*, Pavilion Books 1988

Index

We have included in the index a number of place-name elements with an indication of their possible meaning. This can be used to get a rough idea of the possible meaning of place names not mentioned in the book. However, please remember that this is only a rough indication and many other derivations are possible, particularly from personal names which are not covered. The following abbreviations have been used: C = Common Celtic or found in two or more Celtic languages, 'e' shows that the word is used as a place name element, E = English of any period, G = Gaelic and Irish, L = Latin, ME = Middle English, OE = Old English, OF = Old French, ON = Old Norse, W = Welsh, and 'see text' indicates that the meaning of the element is too complicated to condense.